# JEWISH HISTORY ATLAS

ALSO BY MARTIN GILBERT

British History Atlas
American History Atlas
Recent History Atlas: 1870 to the Present Day
The Roots of Appeasement
The European Powers
The Appeasers (*with Richard Gott*)
Winston Churchill (Clarendon Biographies)

*Editions of documents*

Britain and Germany Between the Wars
Plough My Own Furrow: the Life of Lord Allen of Hurtwood
Servant of India: Diaries of the Viceroy's Private Secretary 1905–1910
Churchill (*Spectrum Books*)
Lloyd George (*Spectrum Books*)

# JEWISH HISTORY ATLAS

## Martin Gilbert
*Fellow of Merton College, Oxford*

Cartography by ARTHUR BANKS

Weidenfeld and Nicolson
London

ISBN 0 297 76343 1 cased

ISBN 0 297 76344 X paperback

PRINTED BY Unwin Brothers Limited
THE GRESHAM PRESS OLD WOKING SURREY ENGLAND

*Produced by offset lithography*

# Preface

This atlas traces the world-wide Jewish migrations from ancient Mesopotamia to modern Israel. It seeks to follow the diverse—and sometimes obscure—path of a far-ranging people, and to map their strange experiences in good times and bad.

My original concern was to avoid undue emphasis upon the many horrific aspects of Jewish history. I wished to portray with equal force the construction, achievements and normalities of Jewish life through almost four thousand years. In part I believe that I have succeeded; for there are many maps of traders, philosophers, financiers, settlers and sages. But as my research into Jewish history progressed, I was surprised, depressed, and to some extent overwhelmed by the perpetual and irrational violence which pursued the Jews in every century and to almost every corner of the globe. If, therefore, persecution, expulsion, torture, humiliation, and mass murder haunt these pages, it is because they also haunt the Jewish story.

But not all terrors are unmitigated; and I have felt a great relief in being able also to map the other side of the coin—the Jewish revolts against Roman, Chinese and Persian oppression—the often repeated pattern of mutual self-help and communal charity, the self-defence leagues organized against the Russian and Ukrainian pogroms, the brave if hopeless risings in ghetto and concentration camp during the Nazi era, and the stubborn resistance to Arab pressures by modern Israel.

If this Atlas can help to answer even a small portion of the questions which Jews so often ask about themselves, or can tell Christians something more about the varied experiences of their neighbours, it will have served a purpose. In particular, I hope that the maps succeed in portraying the complex comings and goings of many different sorts of Jews, and the extraordinary diversity of the Jewish saga.

The Index which follows the maps is intended as an introductory guide to the Atlas. I have selected for it certain themes, countries, and cities which play an important part in Jewish history. The Atlas looks at the role of the Jews in their different national settings, and shows their reaction to persecution, whether by dispersal, acceptance or defence. Both in resisting the continual pressure of hostile societies and in braving the dangers of flight and exile, the Jewish people have shown high courage and a keen capacity to rise again; "trampled into the dust" as Cardinal Manning described it, "and yet never combining with the dust into which it is trampled."

For those who wish to follow up some of the themes covered by the maps, I have provided a short bibliography. In it I have included a few general books, together with a number of specialist works in which I found information for remote or neglected topics.

Many of my maps are intended to make certain obscure episodes in Jewish history better known, if only in outline. There are many equally fascinating problems on which no detailed research has yet been done; and the history of the Jews which most people know is primarily the history of those episodes on which books or monographs have been written. There are still many areas of darkness. But as I hope this Atlas shows, those aspects of Jewish history which can be mapped are full of unusual details and dramatic moments, ranging over every continent and every civilization, and adding a unique dimension to the story of mankind.

I should like to thank all those who have offered me advice, or scrutinized the maps at different stages. I am particularly grateful to Mr. Joshua Sherman and Dr. Harry Shukman of St. Antony's College, Oxford, to Miss Joanna Kaye, and to Mr. Jonathan Zamit, each of whom gave me valuable advice and criticism.

In asking for corrections, and suggestions for further maps, I realize that I am risking a spate of correspondence. On a subject so wide, so controversial, and in some areas so uncertain, error is perhaps inevitable, and omission unavoidable. Nevertheless, in the hope of being able to improve on the maps with each edition, and to enlarge on the range of maps, I invite the reader to send on all corrections or suggestions that seem necessary.

MARTIN GILBERT
*Merton College, Oxford*

You may say you have been oppressed
and persecuted – that has been your
power! You have been hammered into
very fine steel, and that is why you
have never been broken.

LLOYD GEORGE IN 1925

# List of Maps

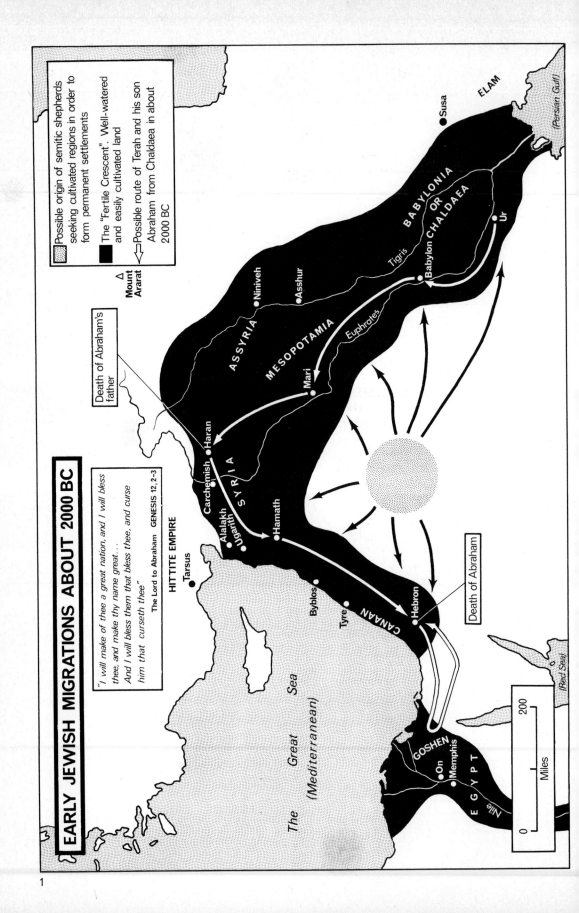

# EARLY JEWISH MIGRATIONS ABOUT 2000 BC

"I will make of thee a great nation, and I will bless thee, and make thy name great ...
And I will bless them that bless thee, and curse him that curseth thee"

The Lord to Abraham GENESIS 12, 2–3

Possible origin of semitic shepherds seeking cultivated regions in order to form permanent settlements

The "Fertile Crescent". Well-watered and easily cultivated land

Possible route of Terah and his son Abraham from Chaldaea in about 2000 BC

△ Mount Ararat

Death of Abraham's father

Death of Abraham

ELAM

Susa

BABYLONIA OR CHALDAEA

(Persian Gulf)

Babylon

Ur

Tigris

ASSYRIA

Niniveh

Asshur

MESOPOTAMIA

Euphrates

Mari

Haran

SYRIA

Carchemish

Alalakh

Ugarith

Hamath

HITTITE EMPIRE

Tarsus

Byblos

Tyre

CANAAN

Hebron

GOSHEN

On

Memphis

E G Y P T

Nile

The Great Sea (Mediterranean)

(Red Sea)

0    200

Miles

1

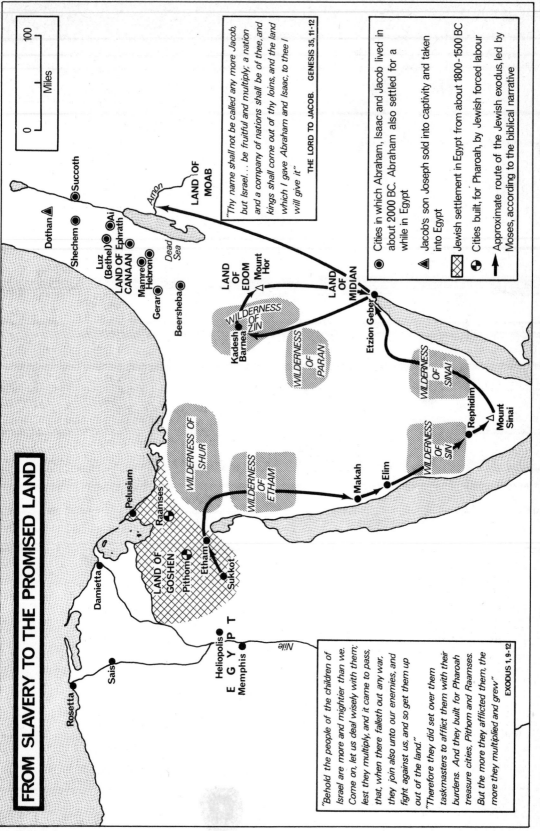

# FROM SLAVERY TO THE PROMISED LAND

"Behold the people of the children of Israel are more and mightier than we. Come on, let us deal wisely with them; lest they multiply, and it come to pass, that, when there falleth out any war, they join also unto our enemies, and fight against us, and so get them up out of the land."

"Therefore they did set over them taskmasters to afflict them with their burdens. And they built for Pharoah treasure cities, Pithom and Raamses. But the more they afflicted them, the more they multiplied and grew"

EXODUS 1, 9-12

"Thy name shall not be called any more Jacob, but Israel... be fruitful and multiply; a nation and a company of nations shall be of thee, and kings shall come out of thy loins, and the land which I gave Abraham and Isaac, to thee I will give it"

THE LORD TO JACOB.    GENESIS 35, 11-12

◉  Cities in which Abraham, Isaac and Jacob lived in about 2000 BC. Abraham also settled for a while in Egypt

▲  Jacob's son Joseph sold into captivity and taken into Egypt

▨  Jewish settlement in Egypt from about 1800-1500 BC

◑  Cities built, for Pharoah, by Jewish forced labour

↑  Approximate route of the Jewish exodus, led by Moses, according to the biblical narrative

2

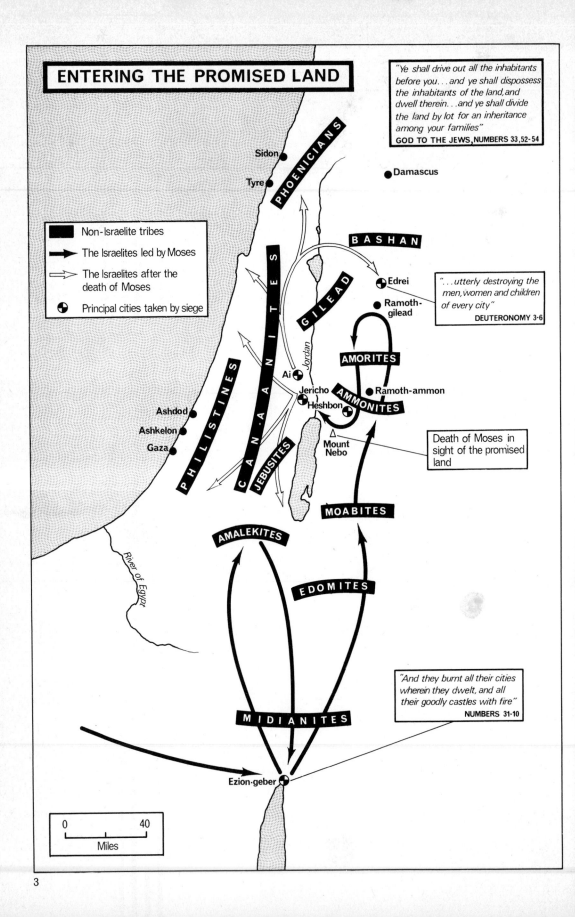

# ENTERING THE PROMISED LAND

"Ye shall drive out all the inhabitants before you...and ye shall dispossess the inhabitants of the land, and dwell therein...and ye shall divide the land by lot for an inheritance among your families"
**GOD TO THE JEWS, NUMBERS 33,52-54**

Sidon

Tyre

PHOENICIANS

Damascus

BASHAN

GILEAD

Edrei

Ramoth-gilead

"...utterly destroying the men, women and children of every city"
**DEUTERONOMY 3-6**

Non-Israelite tribes

The Israelites led by Moses

The Israelites after the death of Moses

Principal cities taken by siege

AMORITES

CANAANITES

Jordan

Ai

Jericho

Heshbon

Ramoth-ammon

AMMONITES

Death of Moses in sight of the promised land

Mount Nebo

PHILISTINES

Ashdod

Ashkelon

Gaza

JEBUSITES

MOABITES

River of Egypt

AMALEKITES

EDOMITES

"And they burnt all their cities wherein they dwelt, and all their goodly castles with fire"
**NUMBERS 31-10**

MIDIANITES

Ezion-geber

0        40
Miles

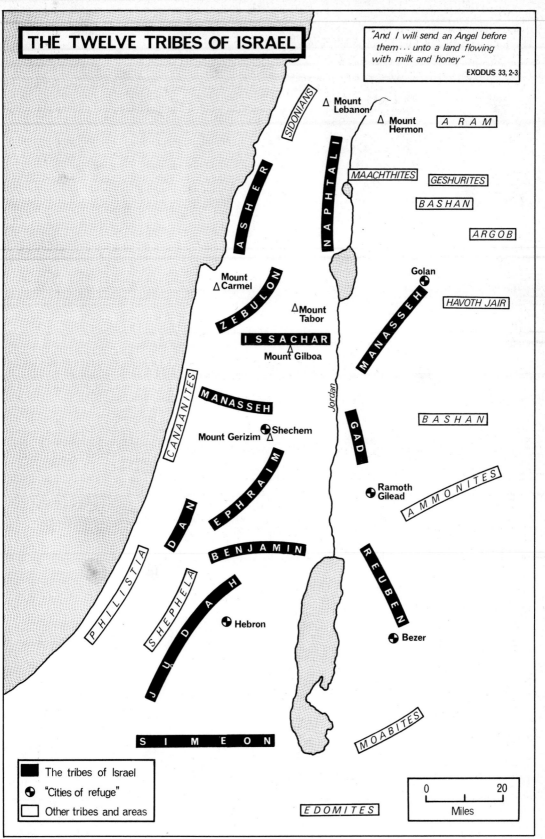

# THE TWELVE TRIBES OF ISRAEL

"And I will send an Angel before them... unto a land flowing with milk and honey"

EXODUS 33, 2-3

△ Mount Lebanon

△ Mount Hermon

*ARAM*

SIDONIANS

ASHER

NAPHTALI

*MAACHTHITES*

*GESHURITES*

*BASHAN*

*ARGOB*

Golan ✪

△ Mount Carmel

ZEBULON

△ Mount Tabor

MANASSEH

*HAVOTH JAIR*

ISSACHAR

△ Mount Gilboa

CANAANITES

MANASSEH

Mount Gerizim △ Shechem ✪

*Jordan*

GAD

*BASHAN*

EPHRAIM

DAN

Ramoth ✪ Gilead

*AMMONITES*

BENJAMIN

PHILISTIA

SHEPHELA

JUDAH

✪ Hebron

REUBEN

✪ Bezer

SIMEON

*MOABITES*

■ The tribes of Israel

✪ "Cities of refuge"

□ Other tribes and areas

| 0 | | 20 |
|---|---|---|

Miles

*EDOMITES*

4

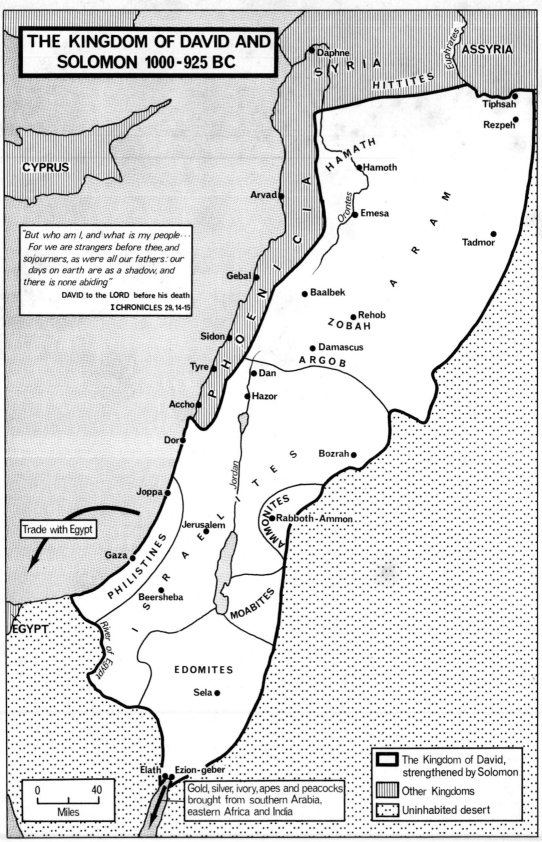

# THE KINGDOM OF DAVID AND SOLOMON 1000-925 BC

ASSYRIA

Daphne

SYRIA

HITTITES

Euphrates

Tiphsah

Rezpeh

HAMATH

Hamoth

Arvad

A R A M

Orontes

Emesa

Tadmor

CYPRUS

*"But who am I, and what is my people··· For we are strangers before thee, and sojourners, as were all our fathers: our days on earth are as a shadow, and there is none abiding"*

DAVID to the LORD before his death
I CHRONICLES 29, 14-15

Gebal

Baalbek

Rehob

ZOBAH

Sidon

Damascus

ARGOB

Tyre

Dan

Hazor

Accho

Bozrah

Dor

Joppa

AMMONITES

Rabboth-Ammon

Trade with Egypt

Jerusalem

PHILISTINES

Gaza

ISRAEL

Jordan

MOABITES

Beersheba

EGYPT

River of Egypt

EDOMITES

Sela

| | The Kingdom of David, strengthened by Solomon |
| | Other Kingdoms |
| | Uninhabited desert |

0    40
Miles

Elath  Ezion-geber

Gold, silver, ivory, apes and peacocks brought from southern Arabia, eastern Africa and India

5

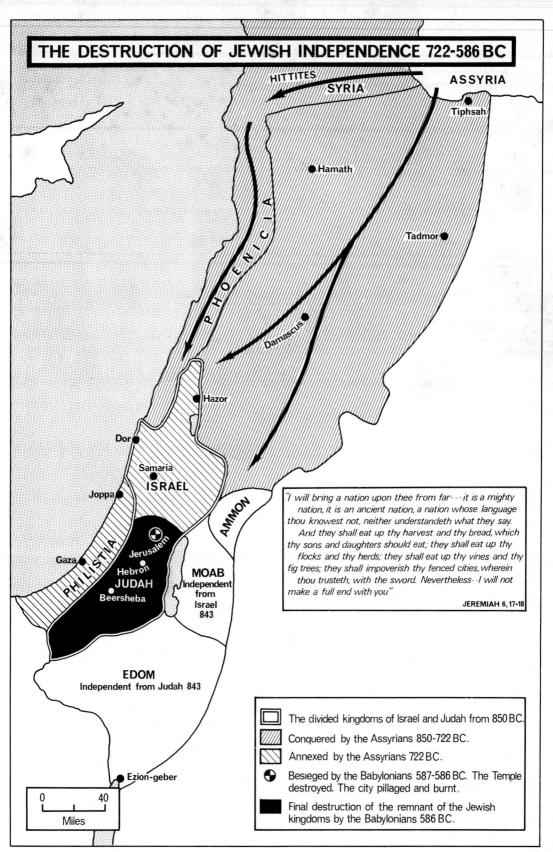

# THE DESTRUCTION OF JEWISH INDEPENDENCE 722-586 BC

HITTITES
SYRIA
ASSYRIA
Tiphsah

Hamath

P
H
O
E
N
I
C
I
A

Tadmor

Damascus

Hazor

Dor

Samaria
ISRAEL

Joppa

AMMON

PHILISTIA

Gaza

Jerusalem
Hebron
JUDAH
Beersheba

MOAB
Independent
from
Israel
843

EDOM
Independent from Judah 843

Ezion-geber

"I will bring a nation upon thee from far···it is a mighty
nation, it is an ancient nation, a nation whose language
thou knowest not, neither understandeth what they say.
And they shall eat up thy harvest and thy bread, which
thy sons and daughters should eat; they shall eat up thy
flocks and thy herds; they shall eat up thy vines and thy
fig trees; they shall impoverish thy fenced cities, wherein
thou trusteth, with the sword. Nevertheless···I will not
make a full end with you"

JEREMIAH 6, 17-18

| | |
|---|---|
| ☐ | The divided kingdoms of Israel and Judah from 850 BC. |
| ▨ | Conquered by the Assyrians 850-722 BC. |
| ▨ | Annexed by the Assyrians 722 BC. |
| ◉ | Besieged by the Babylonians 587-586 BC. The Temple destroyed. The city pillaged and burnt. |
| ■ | Final destruction of the remnant of the Jewish kingdoms by the Babylonians 586 BC. |

0        40
Miles

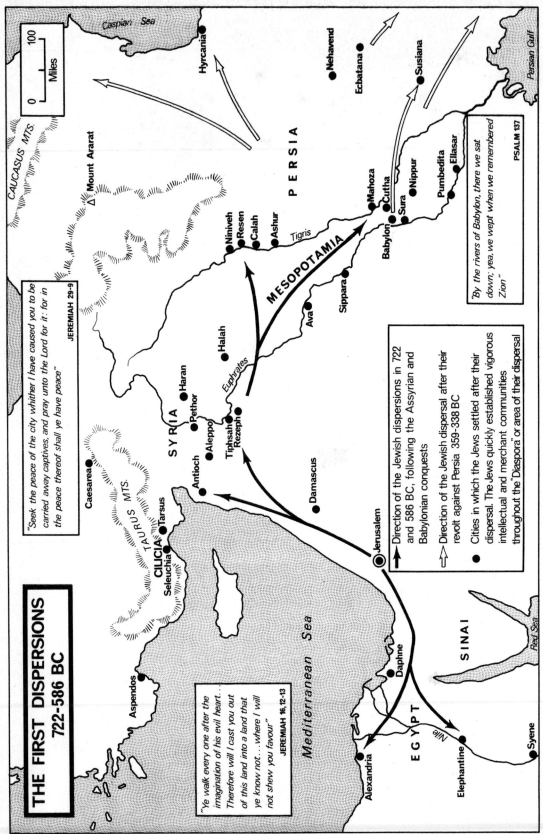

# THE FIRST DISPERSIONS
# 722-586 BC

Caspian Sea

100

0    Miles

CAUCASUS MTS.

Hyrcania

Nehavend

Ecbatana

Susiana

P E R S I A

Persian Gulf

Δ Mount Ararat

Mahoza

Cutha

Nineveh
Resen
Calah
Ashur

Babylon

Sura

Nippur

Pumbedita

Ellasar

Tigris

MESOPOTAMIA

PSALM 137

"Seek the peace of the city whither I have caused you to be carried away captives, and pray unto the Lord for it: for in the peace thereof shall ye have peace"

JEREMIAH 29-9

Sippara

Ava

Halah

Euphrates

Haran

Pethor

Aleppo

Tiphsah
Rezeph

S Y R I A

Damascus

"By the rivers of Babylon, there we sat down; yea, we wept when we remembered Zion"

Caesarea

Antioch

T A U R U S   MTS.

Tarsus

CILICIA

Seleuchia

Jerusalem

Direction of the Jewish dispersions in 722 and 586 BC, following the Assyrian and Babylonian conquests

Direction of the Jewish dispersal after their revolt against Persia 359-338 BC

Cities in which the Jews settled after their dispersal. The Jews quickly established vigorous intellectual and merchant communities throughout the Diaspora or area of their dispersal

Aspendos

"Ye walk every one after the imagination of his evil heart... Therefore will I cast you out of this land into a land that ye know not...where I will not shew you favour"

JEREMIAH 16,12-13

Mediterranean Sea

Daphne

E G Y P T

Nile

S I N A I

Red Sea

Alexandria

Elephantine

Syene

7

# THE IMPERIAL POWERS 586–165 BC

## THE PERSIAN EMPIRE 550–333 BC

Jerusalem

0 300
Miles

## THE BABYLONIAN EMPIRE 586–550 BC

"The virgin of Israel is fallen,
She shall no more rise;
She is cast down upon the ground,
There is none to raise her up."
**AMOS 5–2**

Jerusalem

## THE PTOLEMAIC EMPIRE 270 BC

Jerusalem

"Our inheritance is turned to strangers,
Our houses to aliens.
We are orphans and fatherless,
Our mothers are as widows.
Our necks are under persecution,
We labour, and have no rest."
**LAMENTATIONS 5, 2–5**

## THE EMPIRE OF ALEXANDER THE GREAT 323 BC

Jerusalem

■ Empires controlling Jerusalem after the Assyrian conquest. The Jews gradually settled throughout the territory of the imperial powers.

8

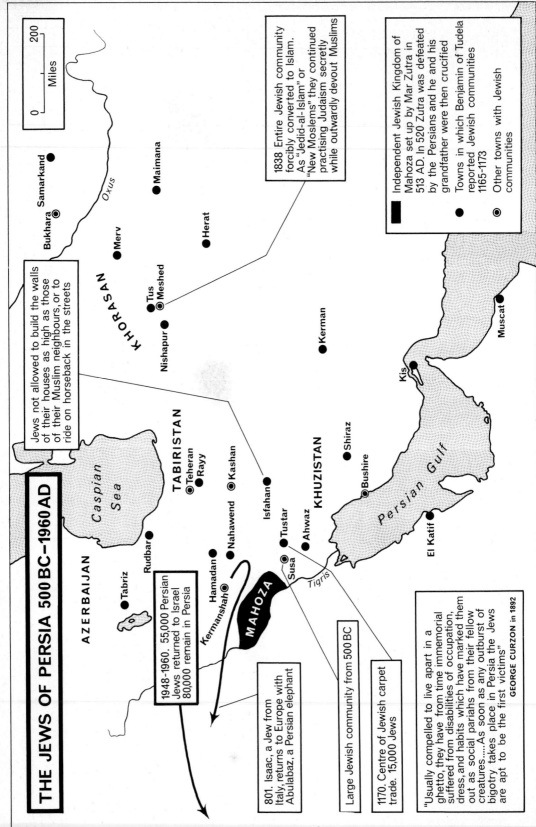

# THE JEWS OF PERSIA 500 BC–1960 AD

0 — 200 Miles

1838 Entire Jewish community forcibly converted to Islam. As "Jedid-al-Islam" or "New Moslems" they continued practising Judaism secretly while outwardly devout Muslims

■ Independent Jewish Kingdom of Mahoza set up by Mar Zutra in 513 AD. In 520 Zutra was defeated by the Persians and he and his grandfather were then crucified

● Towns in which Benjamin of Tudela reported Jewish communities 1165-1173

◉ Other towns with Jewish communities

Jews not allowed to build the walls of their houses as high as those of their Muslim neighbours, or to ride on horseback in the streets

KHORASAN

Oxus

Samarkand
Bukhara
Maimana
Merv
Herat
Tus
Meshed
Nishapur
Kerman
Kis
Muscat

Caspian Sea

AZERBAIJAN

TABIRISTAN
Teheran
Rayy
Kashan

Tabriz
Rudbar
Hamadan
Kermanshah
Nahawend
Isfahan
Susa
Tustar
Ahwaz

MAHOZA

Tigris

KHUZISTAN
Shiraz
Bushire
El Katif

Persian Gulf

1948-1960. 55,000 Persian Jews returned to Israel 80,000 remain in Persia

801. Isaac, a Jew from Italy, returns to Europe with Abulabaz, a Persian elephant

Large Jewish community from 500 BC

1170. Centre of Jewish carpet trade. 15,000 Jews

"Usually compelled to live apart in a ghetto, they have from time immemorial suffered from disabilities of occupation, dress, and habits which have marked them out as social pariahs from their fellow creatures.....As soon as any outburst of bigotry takes place in Persia the Jews are apt to be the first victims"
GEORGE CURZON in 1892

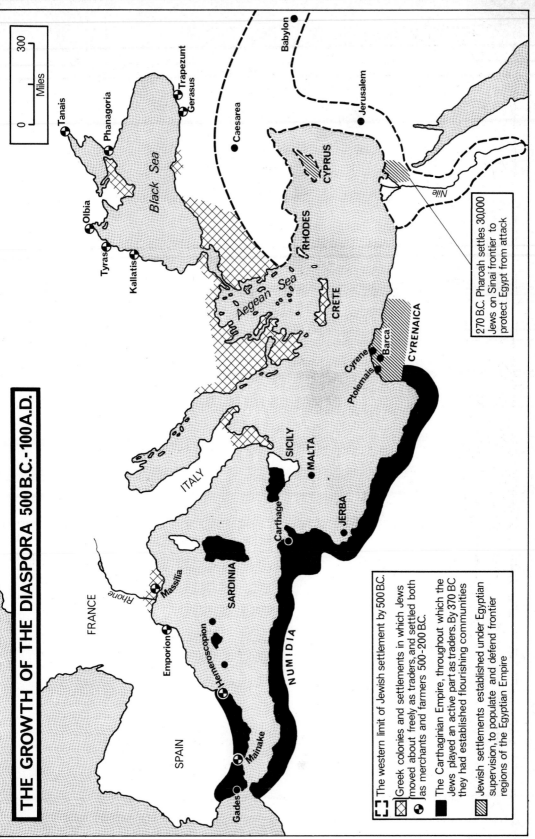

# THE GROWTH OF THE DIASPORA 500 B.C.-100 A.D.

0    300
Miles

270 B.C. Pharoah settles 30,000 Jews on Sinai frontier to protect Egypt from attack

Babylon

Tanais
Phanagoria
Trapezunt
Gerasus
Olbia
Tyras
Kallatis

*Black Sea*

Caesarea

*Aegean Sea*

CYPRUS

Jerusalem

RHODES

CRETE

*Nile*

CYRENAICA
Barca
Cyrene
Ptolemais

ITALY

SICILY
MALTA

JERBA

Carthage

SARDINIA

NUMIDIA

FRANCE
*Rhone*
Massilia

Emporion
Hemeroscopion

SPAIN
Mainake
Gades

The western limit of Jewish settlement by 500 B.C.

Greek colonies and settlements in which Jews moved about freely as traders, and settled both as merchants and farmers 500-200 B.C.

The Carthaginian Empire, throughout which the Jews played an active part as traders. By 370 BC they had established flourishing communities

Jewish settlements established under Egyptian supervision, to populate and defend frontier regions of the Egyptian Empire

10

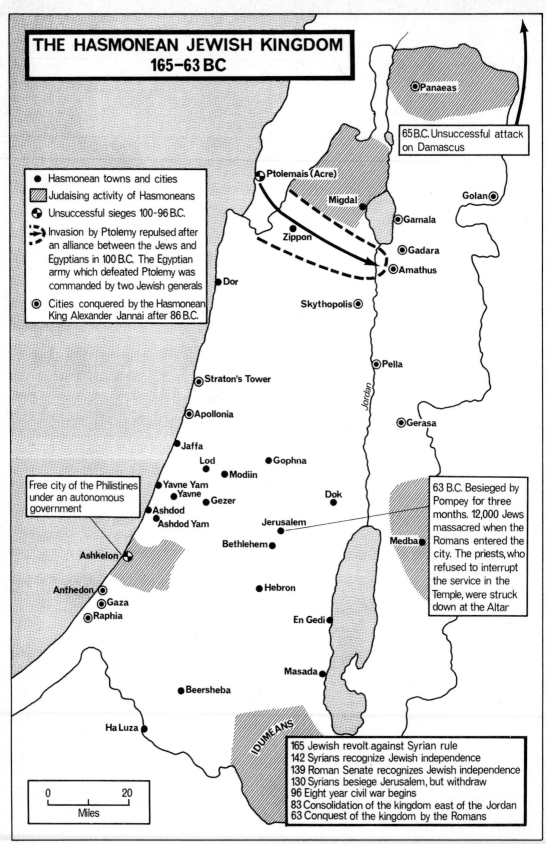

# THE HASMONEAN JEWISH KINGDOM
## 165–63 BC

65 B.C. Unsuccessful attack on Damascus

- ● Hasmonean towns and cities
- ▨ Judaising activity of Hasmoneans
- ⊕ Unsuccessful sieges 100-96 B.C.
- ⇢ Invasion by Ptolemy repulsed after an alliance between the Jews and Egyptians in 100 B.C. The Egyptian army which defeated Ptolemy was commanded by two Jewish generals
- ◉ Cities conquered by the Hasmonean King Alexander Jannai after 86 B.C.

Panaeas

Ptolemais (Acre)

Migdal

Golan

Gamala

Zippon

Gadara

Amathus

Dor

Skythopolis

Pella

Jordan

Straton's Tower

Apollonia

Gerasa

Jaffa

Lod

Gophna

Modiin

Free city of the Philistines under an autonomous government

Yavne Yam
Yavne
Gezer

Dok

Ashdod
Ashdod Yam

Jerusalem

63 B.C. Besieged by Pompey for three months. 12,000 Jews massacred when the Romans entered the city. The priests, who refused to interrupt the service in the Temple, were struck down at the Altar

Bethlehem

Medba

Ashkelon

Anthedon

Gaza

Hebron

Raphia

En Gedi

Masada

Beersheba

Ha Luza

IDUMEANS

165 Jewish revolt against Syrian rule
142 Syrians recognize Jewish independence
139 Roman Senate recognizes Jewish independence
130 Syrians besiege Jerusalem, but withdraw
96 Eight year civil war begins
83 Consolidation of the kingdom east of the Jordan
63 Conquest of the kingdom by the Romans

0    20
Miles

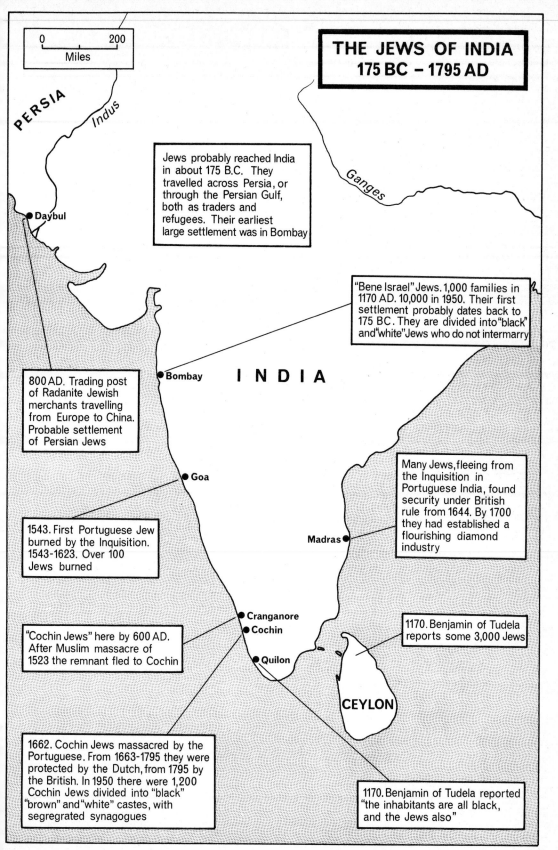

THE JEWS OF INDIA
175 BC – 1795 AD

0    200
Miles

PERSIA

Indus

Ganges

Jews probably reached India in about 175 B.C. They travelled across Persia, or through the Persian Gulf, both as traders and refugees. Their earliest large settlement was in Bombay

● Daybul

"Bene Israel" Jews. 1,000 families in 1170 AD. 10,000 in 1950. Their first settlement probably dates back to 175 BC. They are divided into "black" and "white" Jews who do not intermarry

800 AD. Trading post of Radanite Jewish merchants travelling from Europe to China. Probable settlement of Persian Jews

● Bombay

I N D I A

● Goa

1543. First Portuguese Jew burned by the Inquisition. 1543-1623. Over 100 Jews burned

Many Jews, fleeing from the Inquisition in Portuguese India, found security under British rule from 1644. By 1700 they had established a flourishing diamond industry

Madras ●

● Cranganore
● Cochin

1170. Benjamin of Tudela reports some 3,000 Jews

"Cochin Jews" here by 600 AD. After Muslim massacre of 1523 the remnant fled to Cochin

● Quilon

CEYLON

1662. Cochin Jews massacred by the Portuguese. From 1663-1795 they were protected by the Dutch, from 1795 by the British. In 1950 there were 1,200 Cochin Jews divided into "black" "brown" and "white" castes, with segregated synagogues

1170. Benjamin of Tudela reported "the inhabitants are all black, and the Jews also"

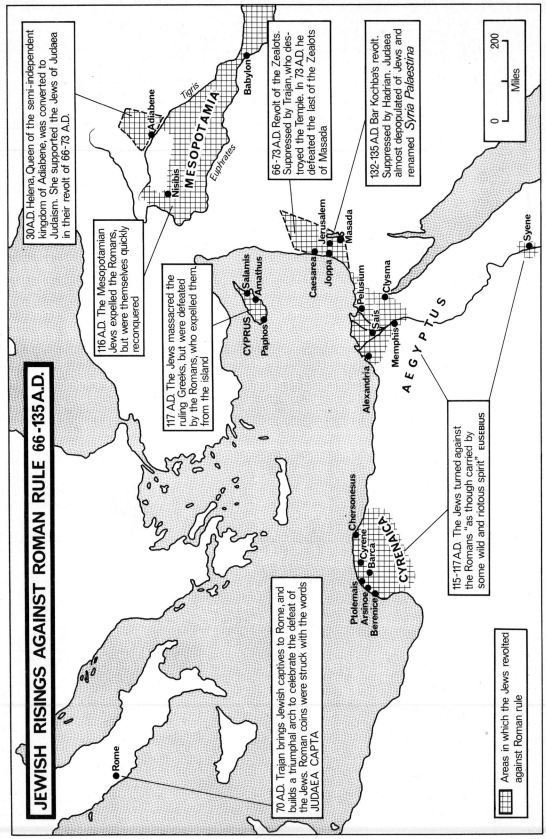

# JEWISH RISINGS AGAINST ROMAN RULE 66-135 A.D.

30A.D. Helena, Queen of the semi-independent kingdom of Adiabene, was converted to Judaism. She supported the Jews of Judaea in their revolt of 66-73 A.D.

116 A.D. The Mesopotamian Jews expelled the Romans, but were themselves quickly reconquered

117 A.D. The Jews massacred the ruling Greeks, but were defeated by the Romans, who expelled them from the island

66-73A.D. Revolt of the Zealots. Suppressed by Trajan, who destroyed the Temple. In 73 A.D. he defeated the last of the Zealots of Masada

132-135 A.D. Bar Kochba's revolt. Suppressed by Hadrian. Judaea almost depopulated of Jews and renamed *Syria Palaestina*

115-117A.D. The Jews turned against the Romans "as though carried by some wild and riotous spirit" EUSEBIUS

70 A.D. Trajan brings Jewish captives to Rome, and builds a triumphal arch to celebrate the defeat of the Jews. Roman coins were struck with the words JUDAEA CAPTA

Areas in which the Jews revolted against Roman rule

MESOPOTAMIA

*Tigris*

*Euphrates*

Babylon

Adiabene

Nisibis

Jerusalem

Masada

Caesarea

Joppa

Pelusium

Sais

Clysma

Memphis

Alexandria

A E G Y P T U S

Syene

CYPRUS

Salamis

Amathus

Paphos

Chersonesus

Cyrene

Barca

CYRENAICA

Ptolemais

Arsinoe

Berenice

Rome

0        200

Miles

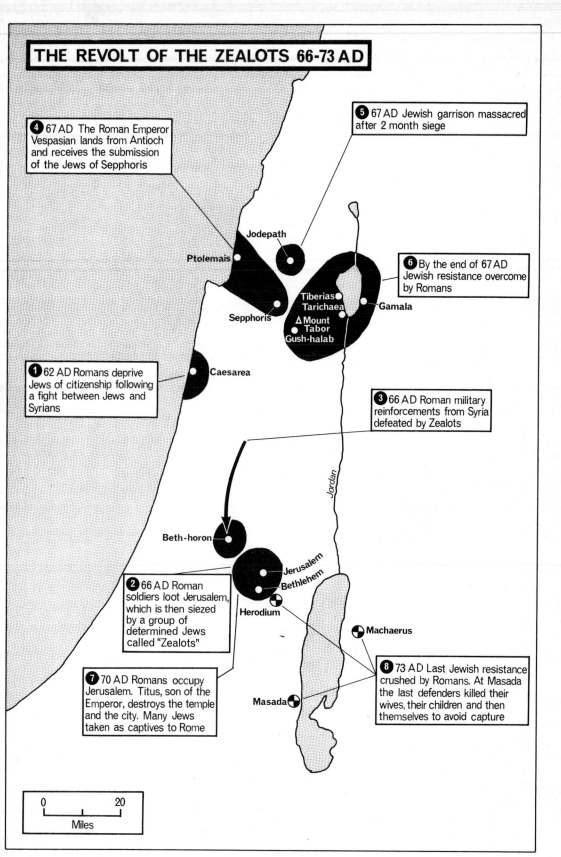

# THE REVOLT OF THE ZEALOTS 66-73 AD

**5** 67 AD Jewish garrison massacred after 2 month siege

**4** 67 AD The Roman Emperor Vespasian lands from Antioch and receives the submission of the Jews of Sepphoris

**6** By the end of 67 AD Jewish resistance overcome by Romans

**1** 62 AD Romans deprive Jews of citizenship following a fight between Jews and Syrians

**3** 66 AD Roman military reinforcements from Syria defeated by Zealots

**2** 66 AD Roman soldiers loot Jerusalem, which is then siezed by a group of determined Jews called "Zealots"

**7** 70 AD Romans occupy Jerusalem. Titus, son of the Emperor, destroys the temple and the city. Many Jews taken as captives to Rome

**8** 73 AD Last Jewish resistance crushed by Romans. At Masada the last defenders killed their wives, their children and then themselves to avoid capture

Jodepath

Ptolemais

Tiberias
Tarichaea
△ Mount
Tabor
Gush-halab

Gamala

Sepphoris

Caesarea

Jordan

Beth-horon

Jerusalem
Bethlehem

Herodium

Machaerus

Masada

0        20
Miles

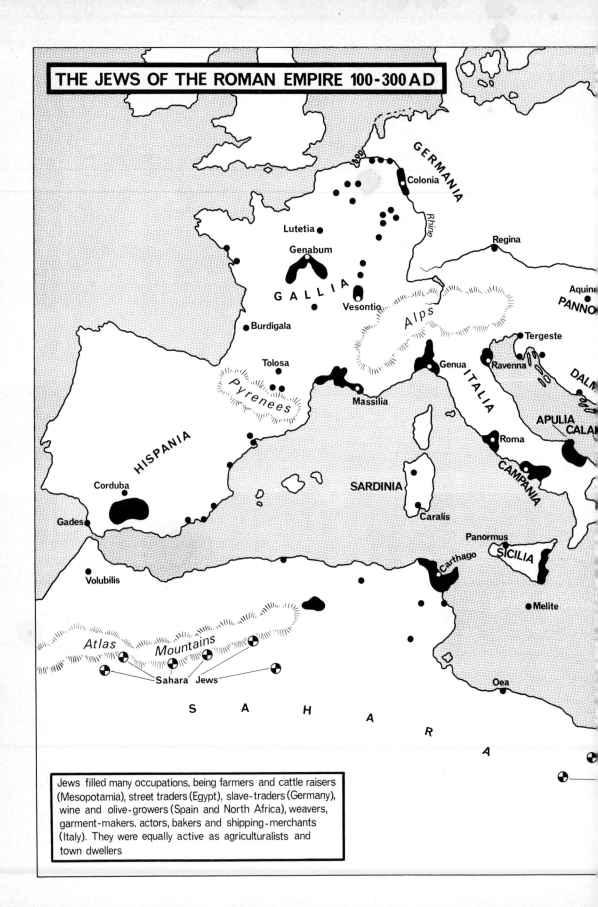

# THE JEWS OF THE ROMAN EMPIRE 100-300 AD

GERMANIA

Colonia

Rhine

Regina

Aquinc

PANNO

Lutetia

Genabum

Vesontio

GALLIA

Alps

Tergeste

Ravenna

DALM

Genua

ITALIA

Burdigala

Tolosa

Pyrenees

Massilia

APULIA

CALA

Roma

CAMPANIA

HISPANIA

SARDINIA

Corduba

Caralis

Gades

Panormus

Carthago

SICILIA

Volubilis

Melite

Atlas

Mountains

Sahara Jews

Oea

S  A  H  A  R  A

Jews filled many occupations, being farmers and cattle raisers
(Mesopotamia), street traders (Egypt), slave-traders (Germany),
wine and olive-growers (Spain and North Africa), weavers,
garment-makers, actors, bakers and shipping-merchants
(Italy). They were equally active as agriculturalists and
town dwellers

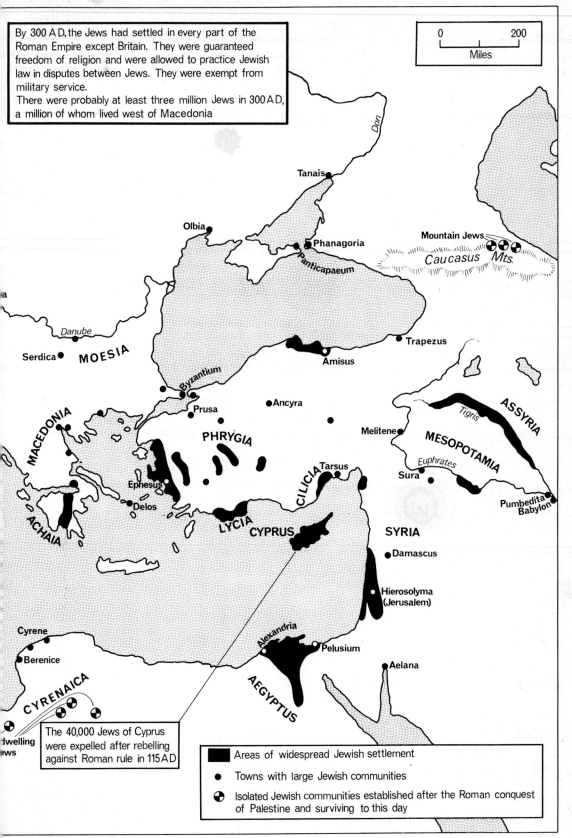

By 300 A D, the Jews had settled in every part of the Roman Empire except Britain. They were guaranteed freedom of religion and were allowed to practice Jewish law in disputes between Jews. They were exempt from military service.
There were probably at least three million Jews in 300 A D, a million of whom lived west of Macedonia

0        200
Miles

Don

Tanais

Olbia

Phanagoria

Panticapaeum

Mountain Jews

Caucasus Mts.

Danube

Serdica ● MOESIA

Trapezus

Byzantium

Amisus

Prusa

Ancyra

ASSYRIA

Tigris

Melitene ●

MESOPOTAMIA

PHRYGIA

Ephesus

Tarsus

Euphrates

Delos

Sura

CILICIA

LYCIA

CYPRUS

Pumbedita
Babylon

MACEDONIA

ACHAIA

SYRIA

Damascus ●

Hierosolyma
(Jerusalem)

Cyrene

Alexandria

Pelusium

Berenice

Aelana

CYRENAICA

AEGYPTUS

The 40,000 Jews of Cyprus were expelled after rebelling against Roman rule in 115 A D

dwelling
ws

■ Areas of widespread Jewish settlement

● Towns with large Jewish communities

✪ Isolated Jewish communities established after the Roman conquest of Palestine and surviving to this day

15

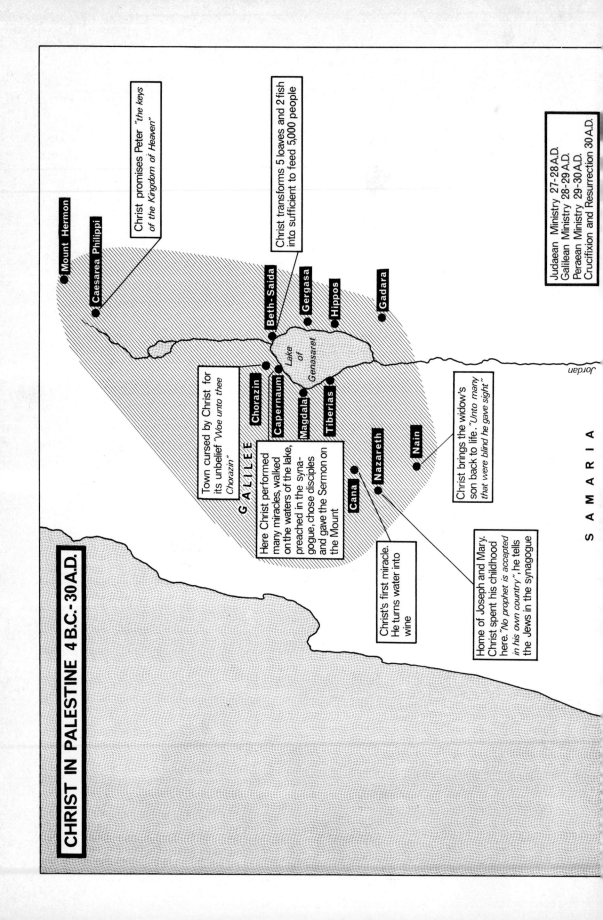

# CHRIST IN PALESTINE 4 B.C.-30 A.D.

Mount Hermon

Caesarea Philippi

Christ promises Peter "the keys of the Kingdom of Heaven"

Christ transforms 5 loaves and 2 fish into sufficient to feed 5,000 people

Beth-Saida

Gergasa

Hippos

Gadara

Town cursed by Christ for its unbelief "Woe unto thee Chorazin"

Chorazin

Capernaum

Magdala

Tiberias

Lake of Genesaret

GALILEE

Here Christ performed many miracles, walked on the waters of the lake, preached in the synagogue, chose disciples and gave the Sermon on the Mount

Nazareth

Nain

Cana

Christ brings the widow's son back to life. "Unto many that were blind he gave sight"

Christ's first miracle. He turns water into wine

Home of Joseph and Mary. Christ spent his childhood here. "No prophet is accepted in his own country", he tells the Jews in the synagogue

Jordan

SAMARIA

Judaean Ministry 27-28 A.D.
Galilean Ministry 28-29 A.D.
Peraean Ministry 29-30 A.D.
Crucifixion and Resurrection 30 A.D.

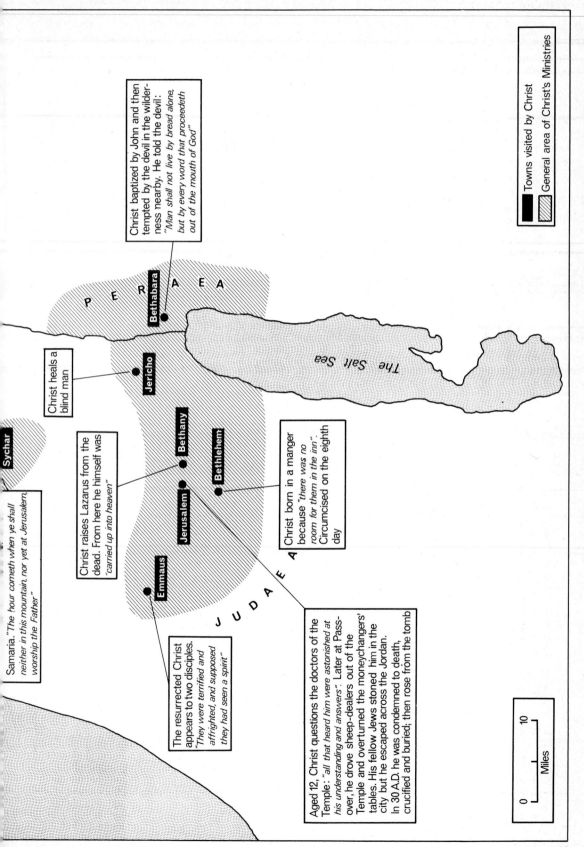

Christ baptized by John and then tempted by the devil in the wilderness nearby. He told the devil: *"Man shall not live by bread alone, but by every word that proceedeth out of the mouth of God"*

Christ heals a blind man

Samaria. *"The 'hour cometh when ye shall neither in this mountain, nor yet at Jerusalem, worship the Father"*

Christ raises Lazarus from the dead. From here he himself was *"carried up into heaven"*

Christ born in a manger because *"there was no room for them in the inn".* Circumcised on the eighth day

The resurrected Christ appears to two disciples. *"They were terrified and affrighted, and supposed they had seen a spirit"*

Aged 12, Christ questions the doctors of the Temple: *"all that heard him were astonished at his understanding and answers".* Later at Passover, he drove sheep-dealers out of the Temple and overturned the moneychangers' tables. His fellow Jews stoned him in the city but he escaped across the Jordan. In 30 A.D. he was condemned to death, crucified and buried; then rose from the tomb

**PERAEA**

**JUDAEA**

**Bethabara**

**Jericho**

**Sychar**

**Bethany**

**Jerusalem**

**Bethlehem**

**Emmaus**

*The Salt Sea*

■ Towns visited by Christ

▨ General area of Christ's Ministries

0        10
Miles

16

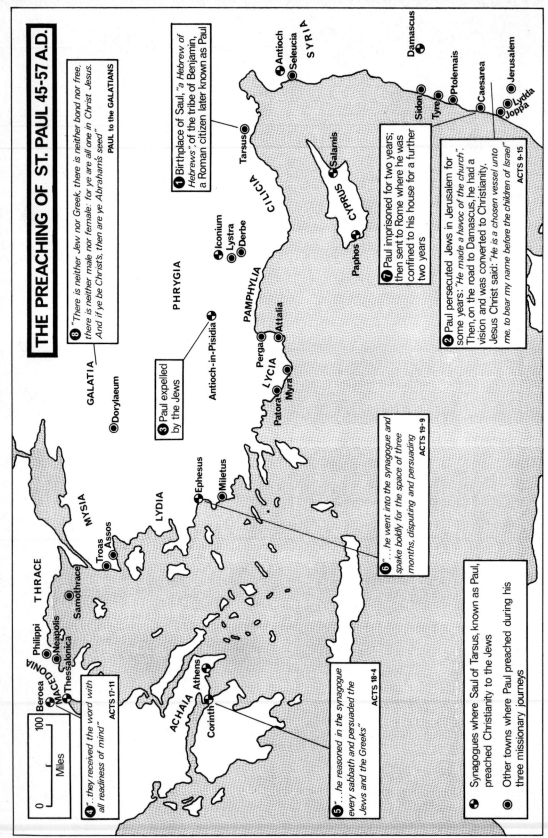

# THE PREACHING OF ST. PAUL 45-57 A.D.

**8** *"There is neither Jew nor Greek, there is neither bond nor free, there is neither male nor female: for ye are all one in Christ Jesus. And if ye be Christ's, then are ye Abraham's seed"*
**PAUL to the GALATIANS**

**1** Birthplace of Saul, *"a Hebrew of Hebrews"*, of the tribe of Benjamin, a Roman citizen later known as Paul

**7** Paul imprisoned for two years; then sent to Rome where he was confined to his house for a further two years

**2** Paul persecuted Jews in Jerusalem for some years: *"He made a havoc of the church"*. Then, on the road to Damascus, he had a vision and was converted to Christianity. Jesus Christ said: *"He is a chosen vessel unto me, to bear my name before the children of Israel"*
**ACTS 9-15**

**3** Paul expelled by the Jews

**6** *"...he went into the synagogue and spake boldly for the space of three months, disputing and persuading"*
**ACTS 19-9**

**4** *"...they received the word with all readiness of mind"*
**ACTS 17-11**

**5** *"...he reasoned in the synagogue every sabbath and persuaded the Jews and the Greeks"*
**ACTS 18-4**

⊕ Synagogues where Saul of Tarsus, known as Paul, preached Christianity to the Jews

◉ Other towns where Paul preached during his three missionary journeys

Antioch
Seleucia
SYRIA
Damascus
Sidon
Tyre
Ptolemais
Caesarea
Jerusalem
Lydda
Joppa
Tarsus
CILICIA
CYPRUS
Salamis
Paphos
Iconium
Lystra
Derbe
PHRYGIA
GALATIA
Dorylaeum
Antioch-in-Pisidia
PAMPHYLIA
Perga
Attalia
LYCIA
Myra
Patara
Ephesus
Miletus
MYSIA
LYDIA
Troas
Assos
Samothrace
THRACE
Philippi
Neapolis
MACEDONIA
Thessalonica
Beroea
Athens
ACHAIA
Corinth

0    100
Miles

17

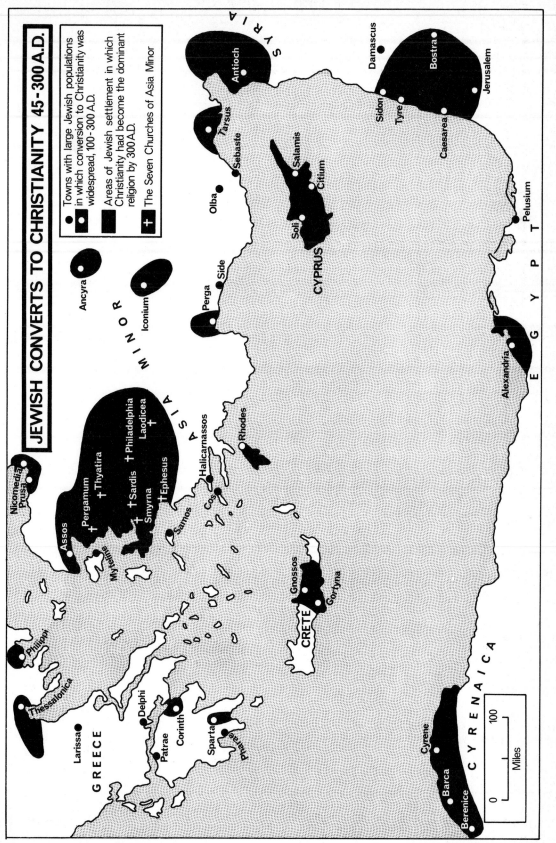

# JEWISH CONVERTS TO CHRISTIANITY 45-300 A.D.

● Towns with large Jewish populations in which conversion to Christianity was widespread, 100-300 A.D.

◐ Areas of Jewish settlement in which Christianity had become the dominant religion by 300 A.D.

✝ The Seven Churches of Asia Minor

**SYRIA**

Antioch
Tarsus
Sebaste
Olba
Damascus
Bostra
Jerusalem
Sidon
Tyre
Caesarea
Pelusium

**ASIA MINOR**

Ancyra
Iconium
Perga
Side
Salamis
Citium
Soli

**CYPRUS**

**EGYPT**

Alexandria

Nicomedia
Prusa
Assos
Pergamum ✝
Thyatira ✝
Myteline
Sardis ✝
Smyrna ✝
Philadelphia ✝
Laodicea ✝
Ephesus ✝
Samos
Halicarnassos
Cos
Rhodes

**GREECE**

Larissa
Thessalonica
Delphi
Patrae
Corinth
Sparta
Philippi

Gnossos
Gortyna

**CRETE**

**CYRENAICA**

Cyrene
Barca
Berenice

0    100
Miles

18

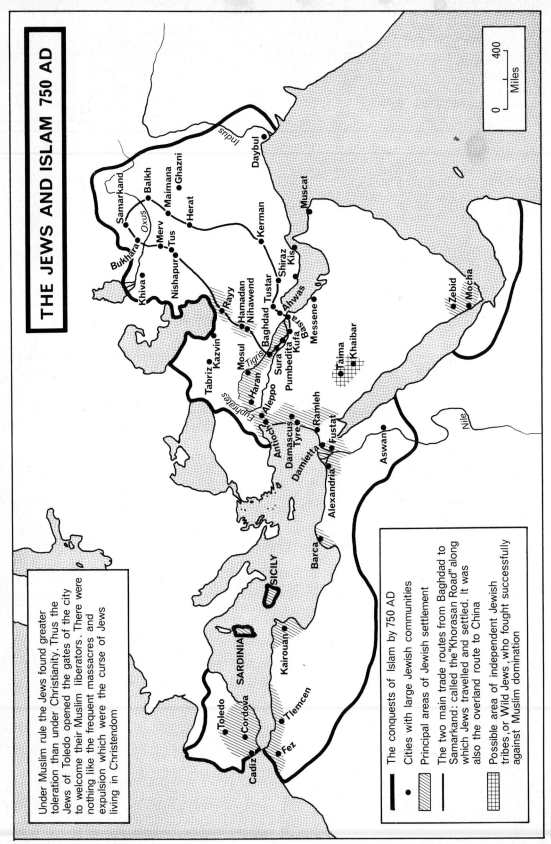

# THE JEWS AND ISLAM 750 AD

Under Muslim rule the Jews found greater toleration than under Christianity. Thus the Jews of Toledo opened the gates of the city to welcome their Muslim liberators. There were nothing like the frequent massacres and expulsion which were the curse of Jews living in Christendom

Indus

Daybul
Balkh
Samarkand
Ghazni
Maimana
Oxus
Herat
Merv
Bukhara
Tus
Nishapur
Kerman
Khiva
Muscat
Rayy
Hamadan
Shiraz
Nihawend
Kis
Baghdad Tustar
Zebid
Tabriz
Ahwas
Mocha
Kazvin
Basra
Mosul
Kufa
Messene
Tigris
Sura
Taima
Harran
Pumbedita
Khaibar
Aleppo
Euphrates
Antioch
Ramleh
Damascus
Tyre
Fustat
Damietta
Aswan
Alexandria
Nile

SICILY
Barca
SARDINIA
Kairouan
Toledo
Tlemcen
Cordova
Cadiz
Fez

0 — 400
Miles

— The conquests of Islam by 750 AD

• Cities with large Jewish communities

▨ Principal areas of Jewish settlement

— The two main trade routes from Baghdad to Samarkand: called the "Khorasan Road" along which Jews travelled and settled. It was also the overland route to China

▦ Possible area of independent Jewish tribes, or Wild Jews, who fought successfully against Muslim domination

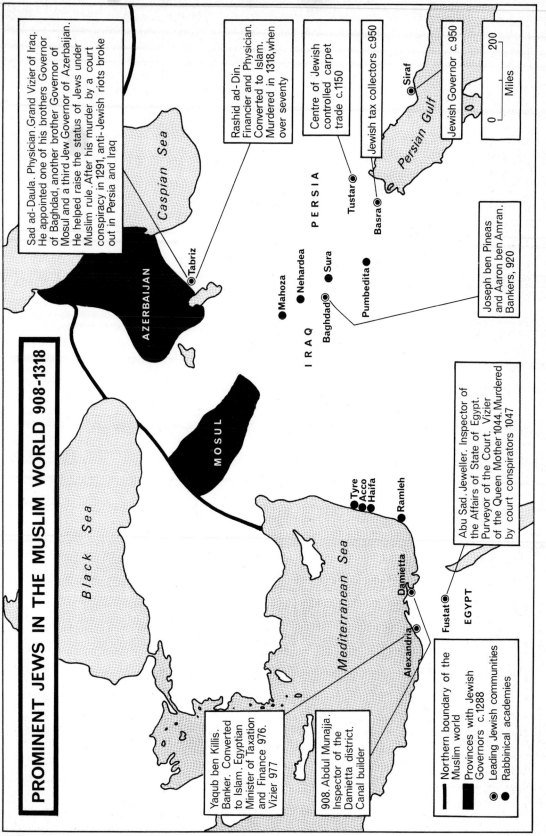

# PROMINENT JEWS IN THE MUSLIM WORLD 908-1318

Sad ad-Daula. Physician. Grand Vizier of Iraq. He appointed one of his brothers Governor of Baghdad, another brother Governor of Mosul and a third Jew Governor of Azerbaijan. He helped raise the status of Jews under Muslim rule. After his murder by a court conspiracy in 1291, anti-Jewish riots broke out in Persia and Iraq

Rashid ad-Din. Financier and Physician. Converted to Islam. Murdered in 1318, when over seventy

Centre of Jewish controlled carpet trade c.1150

Jewish tax collectors c.950

Jewish Governor c.950

Joseph ben Pineas and Aaron ben Amran. Bankers, 920

Abu Sad. Jeweller. Inspector of the Affairs of State of Egypt. Purveyor of the Court. Vizier of the Queen Mother 1044. Murdered by court conspirators 1047

Yaqub ben Killis. Banker. Converted to Islam. Egyptian Minister of Taxation and Finance 976. Vizier 977

908. Abdul Munajja. Inspector of the Damietta district. Canal builder

*Caspian Sea*

*Black Sea*

*Mediterranean Sea*

*Persian Gulf*

AZERBAIJAN

MOSUL

PERSIA

IRAQ

EGYPT

● Tabriz

● Mahoza

● Nehardea

● Sura

● Baghdad

● Pumbedita

◉ Tustar

● Basra

◉ Siraf

● Tyre
● Acco
● Haifa

● Ramleh

◉ Damietta

◉ Alexandria

◉ Fustat

0    200
Miles

— Northern boundary of the Muslim world

■ Provinces with Jewish Governors c.1288

◉ Leading Jewish communities

● Rabbinical academies

20

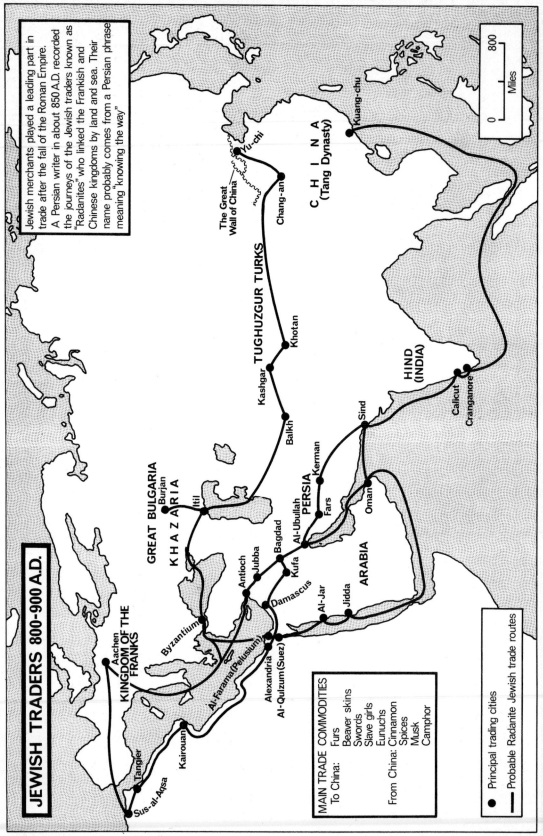

# JEWISH TRADERS 800-900 A.D.

Jewish merchants played a leading part in trade after the fall of the Roman Empire. A Persian writer in about 850 A.D. recorded the journeys of the Jewish traders known as "Radanites" who linked the Frankish and Chinese kingdoms by land and sea. Their name probably comes from a Persian phrase meaning "knowing the way"

MAIN TRADE COMMODITIES
To China: Furs
Beaver skins
Swords
Slave girls
Eunuchs
From China: Cinnamon
Spices
Musk
Camphor

• Principal trading cities

— Probable Radanite Jewish trade routes

0   800
Miles

CHINA (Tang Dynasty)

The Great Wall of China

Kuang-chu

Yu-chi

Chang-an

TUGHUZGUR TURKS

Khotan

Kashgar

Balkh

HIND (INDIA)

Sind

Calicut
Cranganore

Kerman

PERSIA

Fars

Oman

GREAT BULGARIA

Burjan

KHAZARIA

Itil

Al-Ubullah

Bagdad

Kufa

ARABIA

Jubba

Antioch

Damascus

Al-Jar

Jidda

Byzantium

Al-Farama(Pelusium)

Alexandria

Al-Quizum(Suez)

KINGDOM OF THE FRANKS

Aachen

Kairouan

Tangier

Sus-al-Aqsa

21

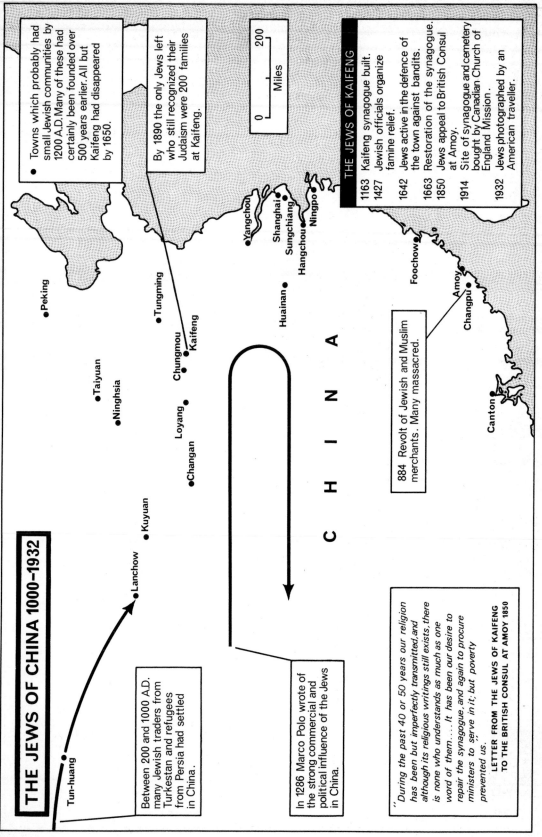

# THE JEWS OF CHINA 1000–1932

- Towns which probably had small Jewish communities by 1200 A.D. Many of these had certainly been founded over 500 years earlier. All but Kaifeng had disappeared by 1650.

By 1890 the only Jews left who still recognized their Judaism were 200 families at Kaifeng.

### THE JEWS OF KAIFENG

| | |
|---|---|
| 1163 | Kaifeng synagogue built. |
| 1427 | Jewish officials organize famine relief. |
| 1642 | Jews active in the defence of the town against bandits. |
| 1663 | Restoration of the synagogue. |
| 1850 | Jews appeal to British Consul at Amoy. |
| 1914 | Site of synagogue and cemetery bought by Canadian Church of England Mission. |
| 1932 | Jews photographed by an American traveller. |

Between 200 and 1000 A.D. many Jewish traders from Turkestan and refugees from Persia had settled in China.

In 1286 Marco Polo wrote of the strong commercial and political influence of the Jews in China.

884 Revolt of Jewish and Muslim merchants. Many massacred.

''During the past 40 or 50 years our religion has been but imperfectly transmitted, and although its religious writings still exists, there is none who understands as much as one word of them.... It has been our desire to repair the synagogue, and again to procure ministers to serve in it; but poverty prevented us.''

**LETTER FROM THE JEWS OF KAIFENG TO THE BRITISH CONSUL AT AMOY 1850**

C H I N A

0   200
Miles

Tun-huang
Lanchow • Kuyuan
Peking
Taiyuan
• Ninghsia
Tungming
Loyang • Chungmou
• Changan     Kaifeng
Huainan •
Yangchou
Shanghai
Sungchiang
Hangchou
Ningpo
Foochow
Amoy
Changpu
Canton

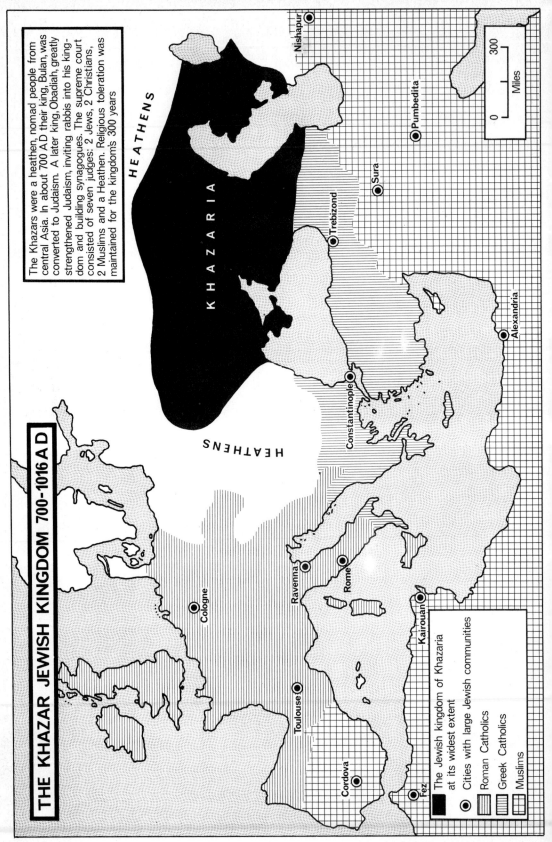

# THE KHAZAR JEWISH KINGDOM 700-1016 AD

The Khazars were a heathen, nomad people from central Asia. In about 700 AD their king, Bulan, was converted to Judaism. A later king, Obadiah, greatly strengthened Judaism, inviting rabbis into his kingdom and building synagogues. The supreme court consisted of seven judges: 2 Jews, 2 Christians, 2 Muslims and a Heathen. Religious toleration was maintained for the kingdom's 300 years

HEATHENS

KHAZARIA

HEATHENS

Nishapur

Pumbedita

Sura

Trebizond

Constantinople

Alexandria

Cologne

Ravenna

Rome

Kairouan

Toulouse

Cordova

Fez

0   300

Miles

The Jewish kingdom of Khazaria at its widest extent

◉ Cities with large Jewish communities

Roman Catholics

Greek Catholics

Muslims

23

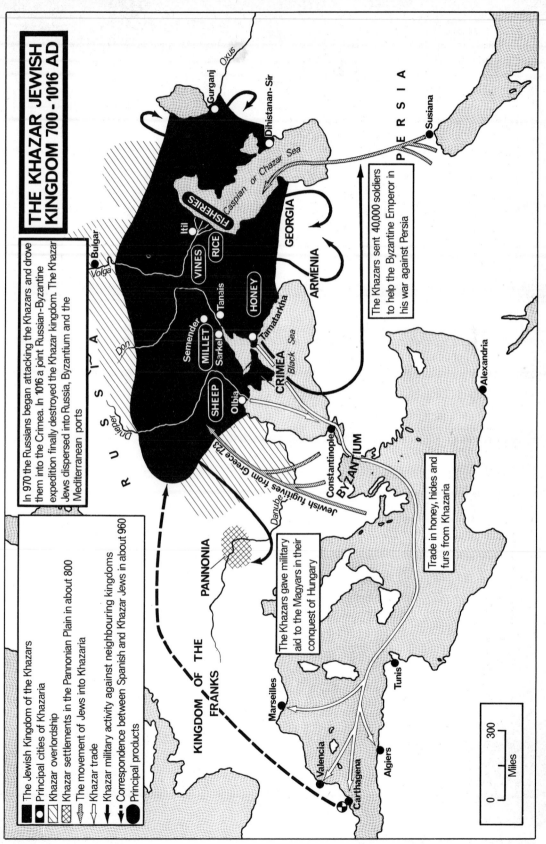

## THE KHAZAR JEWISH KINGDOM 700 - 1016 AD

In 970 the Russians began attacking the Khazars and drove them into the Crimea. In 1016 a joint Russian-Byzantine expedition finally destroyed the Khazar kingdom. The Khazar Jews dispersed into Russia, Byzantium and the Mediterranean ports

The Khazars sent 40,000 soldiers to help the Byzantine Emperor in his war against Persia

Trade in honey, hides and furs from Khazaria

The Khazars gave military aid to the Magyars in their conquest of Hungary

■ The Jewish Kingdom of the Khazars
○ Principal cities of Khazaria
▨ Khazar overlordship
▨ Khazar settlements in the Pannonian Plain in about 800
⇨ The movement of Jews into Khazaria
↗ Khazar trade
▬ Khazar military activity against neighbouring kingdoms
┅ Correspondence between Spanish and Khazar Jews in about 960
● Principal products

PERSIA
Susiana

GEORGIA
ARMENIA

Oxus
Gurganj
Dihistanan - Sir
Caspian or Chazar Sea
FISHERIES
Itil
VINES
RICE
Bulgar
Volga
HONEY
Tanais
Semender
MILLET
Sarkel
Tamatarkha
Black Sea
CRIMEA
SHEEP
Olbia
Don
Dnieper
R U S S I A

Jewish fugitives from Greece 723

Danube
PANNONIA
KINGDOM OF THE FRANKS

Constantinople
BYZANTIUM

Alexandria
Tunis
Marseilles
Valencia
Algiers
Carthagena

0    300
Miles

24

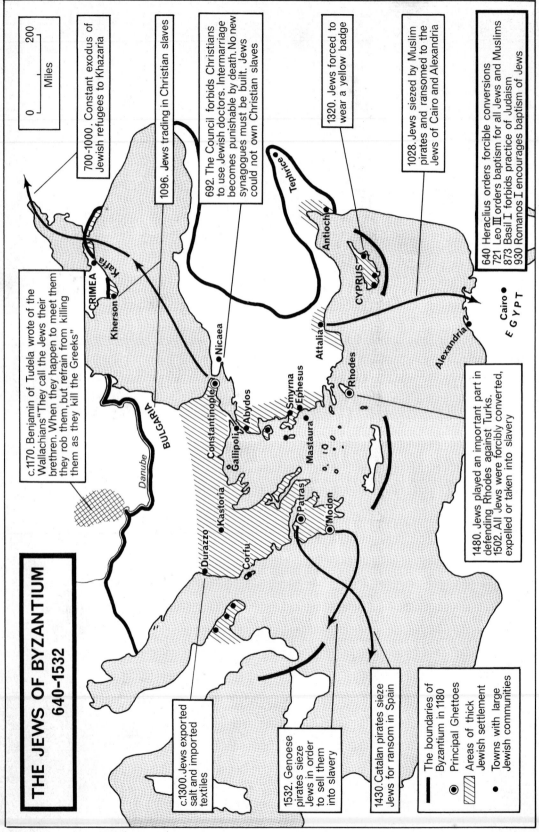

# THE JEWS OF BYZANTIUM 640-1532

700-1000. Constant exodus of Jewish refugees to Khazaria

1096. Jews trading in Christian slaves

692. The Council forbids Christians to use Jewish doctors. Intermarriage becomes punishable by death. No new synagogues must be built. Jews could not own Christian slaves

1320. Jews forced to wear a yellow badge

1028. Jews siezed by Muslim pirates and ransomed to the Jews of Cairo and Alexandria

640 Heraclius orders forcible conversions
721 Leo III orders baptism for all Jews and Muslims
873 Basil II forbids practice of Judaism
930 Romanos I encourages baptism of Jews

c.1170. Benjamin of Tudela wrote of the Wallachians "They call the Jews their brethren. When they happen to meet them they rob them, but refrain from killing them as they kill the Greeks"

c.1300. Jews exported salt and imported textiles

1532. Genoese pirates sieze Jews in order to sell them into slavery

1430. Catalan pirates sieze Jews for ransom in Spain

1480. Jews played an important part in defending Rhodes against Turks.
1502. All Jews were forcibly converted, expelled or taken into slavery

Tephrice

Antioch

CYPRUS

Cairo
EGYPT

Alexandria

Attalia

Rhodes

Kherson

CRIMEA

Kaffa

Nicaea

Constantinople

Abydos

Gallipoli

Smyrna
Ephesus

Mastaura

BULGARIA

Danube

Durazzo

Corfu

Kastoria

Patras

Modon

—— The boundaries of Byzantium in 1180
⊙ Principal Ghettoes
▨ Areas of thick Jewish settlement
• Towns with large Jewish communities

0   200
Miles

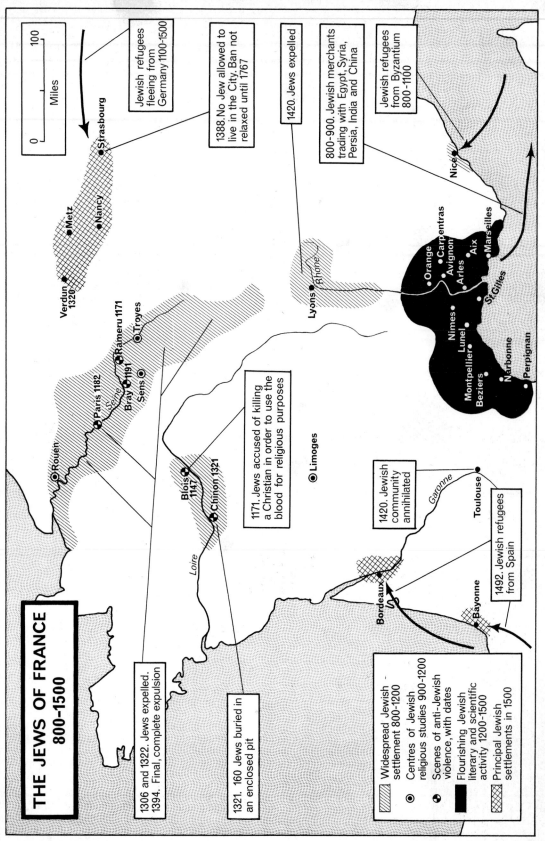

# THE JEWS OF FRANCE 800-1500

Miles
0        100

Jewish refugees fleeing from Germany 1100-1500

1388. No Jew allowed to live in the City. Ban not relaxed until 1767

1420. Jews expelled

800-900. Jewish merchants trading with Egypt, Syria, Persia, India and China

Jewish refugees from Byzantium 800-1100

Strasbourg

Metz
Nancy

Verdun 1320

Troyes
Rameru 1171
Bray 1191
Sens

Paris 1182

Rouen

Lyons
Rhône
Seine

Orange
Carpentras
Avignon
Arles
Aix
Marseilles
Nîmes
Lunel
Montpellier
Béziers
Narbonne
Perpignan
St Gilles

Nice

1171. Jews accused of killing a Christian in order to use the blood for religious purposes

Limoges

Blois 1147
Chinon 1321

Loire

1420. Jewish community annihilated

Garonne
Toulouse

Bordeaux

Bayonne

1492. Jewish refugees from Spain

1306 and 1322. Jews expelled. 1394. Final, complete expulsion

1321. 160 Jews buried in an enclosed pit

Widespread Jewish settlement 800-1200

Centres of Jewish religious studies 900-1200

Scenes of anti-Jewish violence, with dates

Flourishing Jewish literary and scientific activity 1200-1500

Principal Jewish settlements in 1500

26

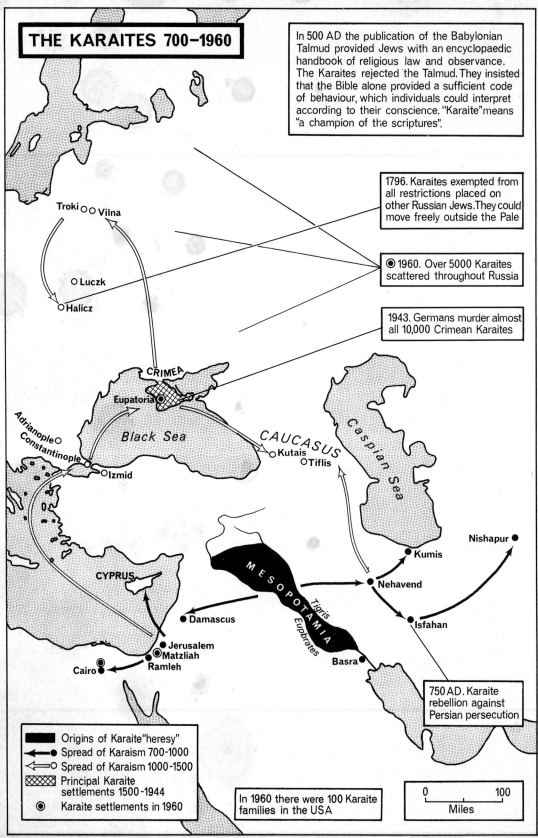

# THE KARAITES 700–1960

In 500 AD the publication of the Babylonian Talmud provided Jews with an encyclopaedic handbook of religious law and observance. The Karaites rejected the Talmud. They insisted that the Bible alone provided a sufficient code of behaviour, which individuals could interpret according to their conscience. "Karaite" means "a champion of the scriptures".

1796. Karaites exempted from all restrictions placed on other Russian Jews. They could move freely outside the Pale

◉ 1960. Over 5000 Karaites scattered throughout Russia

1943. Germans murder almost all 10,000 Crimean Karaites

Troki ○○ Vilna

○ Luczk

○ Halicz

CRIMEA

Eupatoria ○

Black Sea

CAUCASUS

Caspian Sea

Adrianople ○
Constantinople ○
○ Izmid

○ Kutais
○ Tiflis

CYPRUS

Nishapur ●

● Kumis

M E S O P O T A M I A

Tigris

Euphrates

● Nehavend

● Damascus

● Isfahan

● Jerusalem
◉ Matzliah
Ramleh

Cairo ◉

Basra ●

750 AD. Karaite rebellion against Persian persecution

**Legend:**
- ▬ Origins of Karaite "heresy"
- ◄━● Spread of Karaism 700-1000
- ◁═○ Spread of Karaism 1000-1500
- ▨ Principal Karaite settlements 1500-1944
- ◉ Karaite settlements in 1960

In 1960 there were 100 Karaite families in the USA

0 ——— 100
Miles

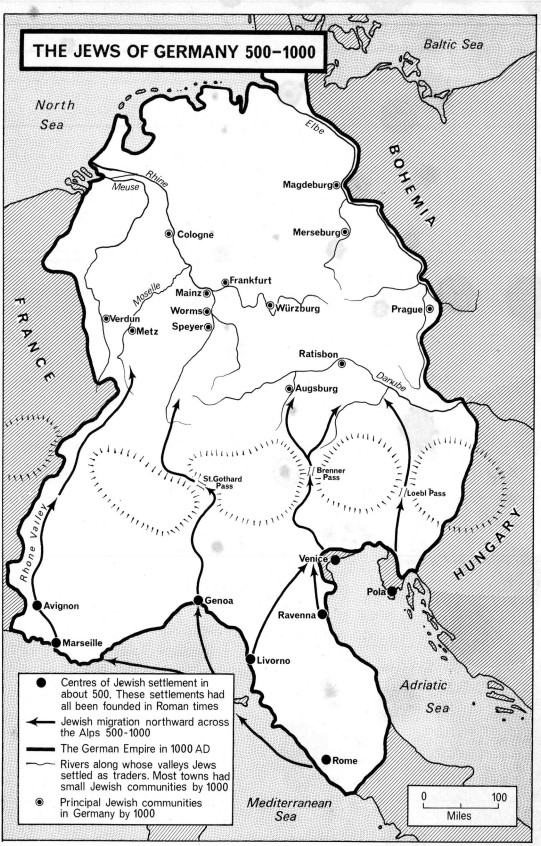

# THE JEWS OF GERMANY 500–1000

North Sea

Baltic Sea

BOHEMIA

*Elbe*

●◎ **Magdeburg**

●◎ **Cologne**

●◎ **Merseburg**

*Rhine*

*Meuse*

●**Frankfurt**

**Mainz**◎●

●**Würzburg**

*Moselle*

**Worms**◎●

**Prague**◎●

●**Verdun**

**Speyer**◎●

◎**Metz**

**Ratisbon**◎

*Danube*

◎**Augsburg**

F R A N C E

St.Gothard Pass

Brenner Pass

Loebl Pass

*Rhone Valley*

H U N G A R Y

**Venice**●

**Pola**●

●**Avignon**

●**Genoa**

**Ravenna**●

●**Marseille**

●**Livorno**

*Adriatic Sea*

● Centres of Jewish settlement in about 500. These settlements had all been founded in Roman times

← Jewish migration northward across the Alps 500–1000

━━ The German Empire in 1000 AD

〜 Rivers along whose valleys Jews settled as traders. Most towns had small Jewish communities by 1000

◎ Principal Jewish communities in Germany by 1000

●**Rome**

*Mediterranean Sea*

0      100
Miles

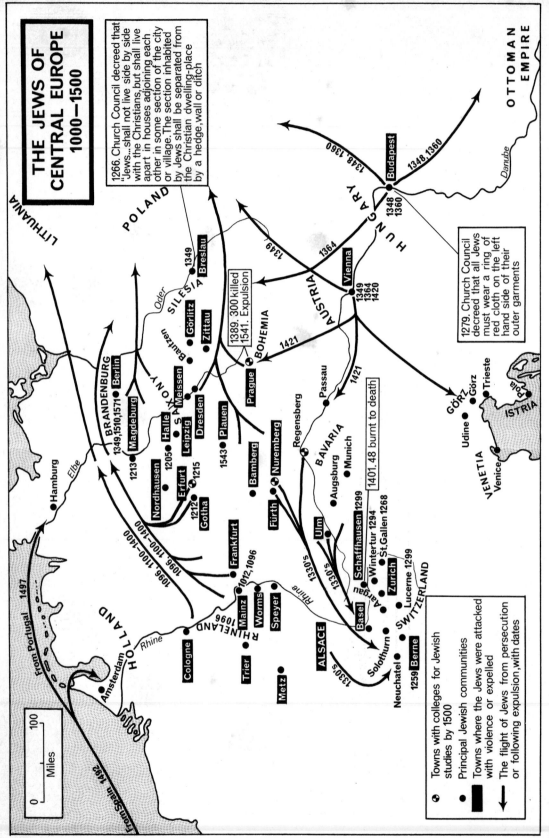

# THE JEWS OF CENTRAL EUROPE 1000–1500

1266. Church Council decreed that "Jews...shall not live side by side with the Christians, but shall live apart in houses adjoining each other in some section of the city or village. The section inhabited by Jews shall be separated from the Christian dwelling-place by a hedge, wall or ditch

1279. Church Council decreed that all Jews must wear a ring of red cloth on the left hand side of their outer garments

OTTOMAN EMPIRE

LITHUANIA

POLAND

HUNGARY

Danube

Budapest

1348,1360

1348 1360

1349

Breslau 1349

Görlitz

Zittau

SILESIA

Oder

Bautzen

Vienna

AUSTRIA

1349
1364
1420

1364

1421

BOHEMIA

1389. 300 killed
1541. Expulsion

Prague

BRANDENBURG

Berlin

Magdeburg

1349,1510,1571

1213

Meissen

SAXONY

Halle

Leipzig

Dresden

Plauen

1205

1543

Bamberg

Passau

Regensberg

Nuremberg

1421

GÖRZ

Görz

Trieste

Pola

ISTRIA

Udine

VENETIA

Venice

Hamburg

Elbe

Nordhausen

Erfurt

1212

Gotha

1215

Fürth

BAVARIA

Munich

Augsburg

1401. 48 burnt to death

Schaffhausen 1299

Wintertur 1294

St.Gallen 1268

Zürich

Aargau

Lucerne 1299

SWITZERLAND

1096, 1100–1400

1096, 1100–1400

Frankfurt

1012, 1096

Mainz

Worms

Speyer

RHINELAND

Rhine

Cologne

HOLLAND

Amsterdam

Rhine

1330's

1330's

Ulm

1330's

Basel

Solothurn

Berne 1259

Neuchatel

ALSACE

1330's

Trier

Metz

From Portugal 1497

From Spain 1492

Miles

0       100

## Legend

- **Towns with colleges for Jewish studies by 1500**
- **Principal Jewish communities**
- **Towns where the Jews were attacked with violence or expelled**
- **The flight of Jews from persecution or following expulsion, with dates**

29

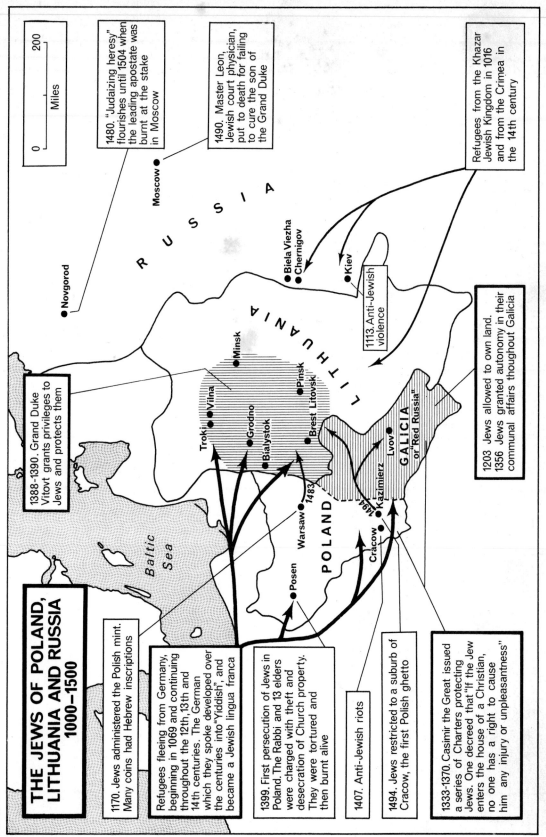

# THE JEWS OF POLAND, LITHUANIA AND RUSSIA 1000-1500

0 — 200
Miles

**1480.** "Judaizing heresy" flourishes until 1504 when the leading apostate was burnt at the stake in Moscow

**1490.** Master Leon, Jewish court physician, put to death for failing to cure the son of the Grand Duke

Refugees from the Khazar Jewish Kingdom in 1016 and from the Crimea in the 14th century

R  U  S  S  I  A

● Moscow

● Novgorod

● Biela Viezha
● Chernigov

● Kiev

**1113.** Anti-Jewish violence

L  I  T  H  U  A  N  I  A

● Minsk

Troki ● ● Vilna

● Grodno

● Bialystok

● Pinsk
● Brest Litovski

**1388-1390.** Grand Duke Vitovt grants privileges to Jews and protects them

GALICIA or "Red Russia"

● Lvov

Kazimierz ●

**1203** Jews allowed to own land.
**1356** Jews granted autonomy in their communal affairs thoughout Galicia

Baltic Sea

● Posen

Warsaw ● 1483

P O L A N D

Cracow ● 1494

**1170.** Jews administered the Polish mint. Many coins had Hebrew inscriptions

Refugees fleeing from Germany, beginning in 1069 and continuing throughout the 12th,13th and 14th centuries. The German which they spoke developed over the centuries into "Yiddish", and became a Jewish lingua franca

**1399.** First persecution of Jews in Poland. The Rabbi and 13 elders were charged with theft and desecration of Church property. They were tortured and then burnt alive

**1407.** Anti-Jewish riots

**1494.** Jews restricted to a suburb of Cracow, the first Polish ghetto

**1333-1370.** Casimir the Great issued a series of Charters protecting Jews. One decreed that "If the Jew enters the house of a Christian, no one has a right to cause him any injury or unpleasantness"

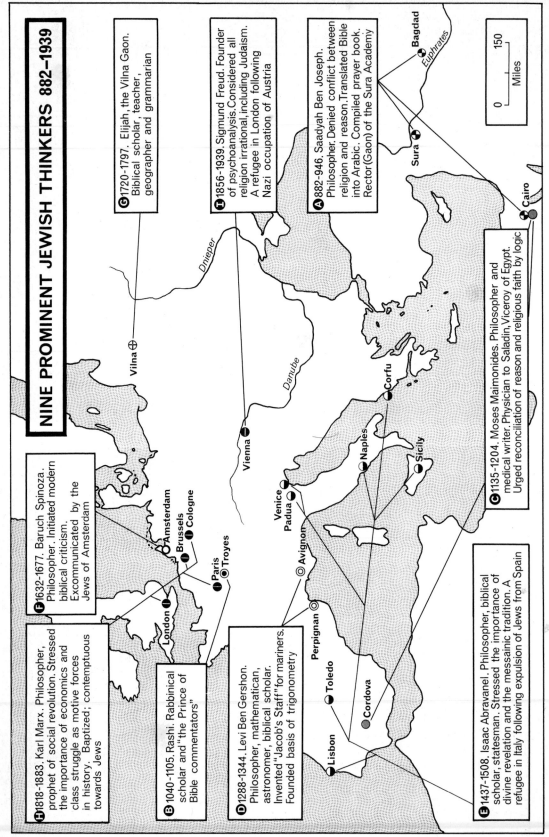

# NINE PROMINENT JEWISH THINKERS 882–1939

**G** 1720-1797. Elijah, the Vilna Gaon. Biblical scholar, teacher, geographer and grammarian

**I** 1856-1939. Sigmund Freud. Founder of psychoanalysis. Considered all religion irrational, including Judaism. A refugee in London following Nazi occupation of Austria

**A** 882-946. Saadyah Ben Joseph. Philosopher. Denied conflict between religion and reason. Translated Bible into Arabic. Compiled prayer book. Rector (Gaon) of the Sura Academy

**C** 1135-1204. Moses Maimonides. Philosopher and medical writer. Physician to Saladin, Viceroy of Egypt. Urged reconciliation of reason and religious faith by logic

**F** 1632-1677. Baruch Spinoza. Philosopher. Initiated modern biblical criticism. Excommunicated by the Jews of Amsterdam

**H** 1818-1883. Karl Marx. Philosopher, prophet of social revolution. Stressed the importance of economics and class struggle as motive forces in history. Baptized; contemptuous towards Jews

**B** 1040-1105. Rashi. Rabbinical scholar and "the Prince of Bible commentators"

**D** 1288-1344. Levi Ben Gershon. Philosopher, mathematican, astronomer, biblical scholar. Invented "Jacob's Staff" for mariners. Founded basis of trigonometry

**E** 1437-1508. Isaac Abravanel. Philosopher, biblical scholar, statesman. Stressed the importance of divine revelation and the messainic tradition. A refugee in Italy following expulsion of Jews from Spain

Bagdad
Euphrates

0    150
Miles

Sura

Cairo

Dnieper

Vilna

Danube

Vienna

Corfu

Naples

Sicily

Amsterdam
Brussels
Cologne

Venice
Padua

Paris
Troyes

London

Avignon

Perpignan

Toledo

Cordova

Lisbon

31

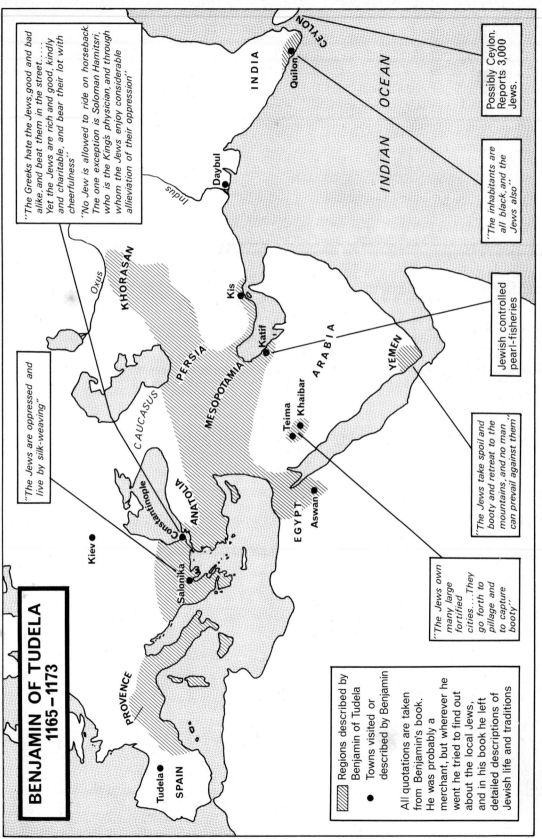

# BENJAMIN OF TUDELA
# 1165–1173

"The Greeks hate the Jews, good and bad alike, and beat them in the street..... Yet the Jews are rich and good, kindly and charitable, and bear their lot with cheerfulness"

"No Jew is allowed to ride on horseback. The one exception is Soloman Hamitsri, who is the King's physician, and through whom the Jews enjoy considerable allieviation of their oppression"

"The inhabitants are all black, and the Jews also"

Possibly Ceylon. Reports 3,000 Jews.

"The Jews are oppressed and live by silk-weaving"

Jewish controlled pearl-fisheries

"The Jews take spoil and booty and retreat to the mountains, and no man can prevail against them"

"The Jews own many large fortified cities....They go forth to pillage and to capture booty"

INDIA

CEYLON

Quilon

Daybul

Indus

INDIAN OCEAN

KHORASAN

Oxus

Kis

Katif

ARABIA

YEMEN

PERSIA

MESOPOTAMIA

CAUCASUS

Teima Khaibar

Aswan

EGYPT

ANATOLIA

Constantinople

Kiev

Salonika

PROVENCE

Tudela
SPAIN

Regions described by Benjamin of Tudela

● Towns visited or described by Benjamin

All quotations are taken from Benjamin's book. He was probably a merchant, but wherever he went he tried to find out about the local Jews, and in his book he left detailed descriptions of Jewish life and traditions

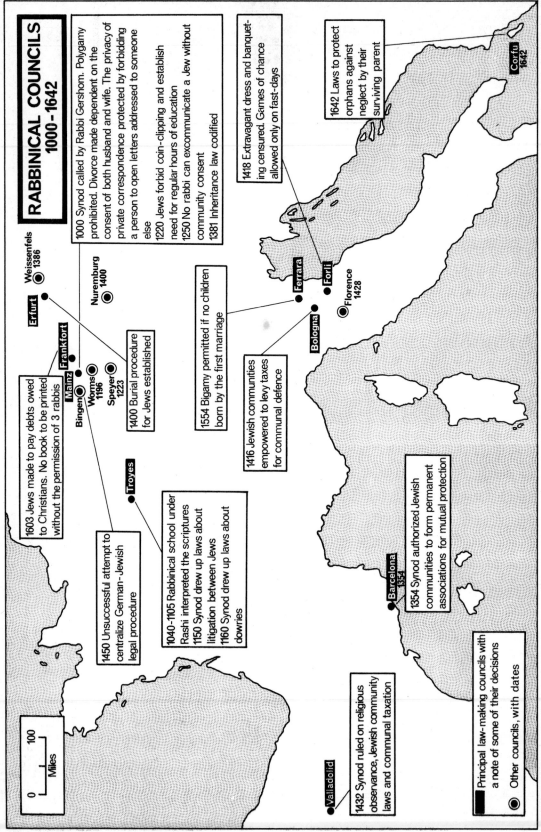

# RABBINICAL COUNCILS 1000-1642

**1000** Synod called by Rabbi Gershom. Polygamy prohibited. Divorce made dependent on the consent of both husband and wife. The privacy of private correspondence protected by forbidding a person to open letters addressed to someone else
**1220** Jews forbid coin-clipping and establish need for regular hours of education
**1250** No rabbi can excommunicate a Jew without community consent
**1381** Inheritance law codified

**1603** Jews made to pay debts owed to Christians. No book to be printed without the permission of 3 rabbis

**1450** Unsuccessful attempt to centralize German-Jewish legal procedure

**1400** Burial procedure for Jews established

**1040-1105** Rabbinical school under Rashi interpreted the scriptures
**1150** Synod drew up laws about litigation between Jews
**1160** Synod drew up laws about dowries

**1554** Bigamy permitted if no children born by the first marriage

**1418** Extravagant dress and banqueting censured. Games of chance allowed only on fast-days

**1642** Laws to protect orphans against neglect by their surviving parent

**1416** Jewish communities empowered to levy taxes for communal defence

**1354** Synod authorized Jewish communities to form permanent associations for mutual protection

**1432** Synod ruled on religious observance, Jewish community laws and communal taxation

Weissenfels ● 1386
Erfurt ●
Nuremburg ◉ 1400
Frankfort ◉
Mainz ◉
Bingen ●
Worms ◉ 1196
Speyer ◉ 1223
Troyes ●
Ferrara ●
Forli ●
Bologna ●
Florence ● 1428
Corfu 1642
Barcelona ●
Valladolid ●

■ Principal law-making councils with a note of some of their decisions
◉ Other councils, with dates

0    100
Miles

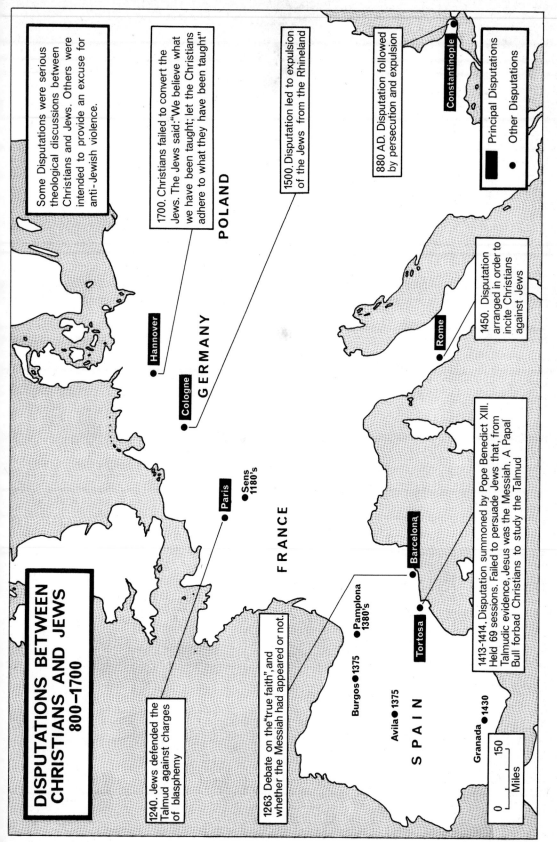

# DISPUTATIONS BETWEEN CHRISTIANS AND JEWS 800–1700

Some Disputations were serious theological discussions between Christians and Jews. Others were intended to provide an excuse for anti-Jewish violence.

1700. Christians failed to convert the Jews. The Jews said:"We believe what we have been taught; let the Christians adhere to what they have been taught"

1500. Disputation led to expulsion of the Jews from the Rhineland

880 AD. Disputation followed by persecution and expulsion

1450. Disputation arranged in order to incite Christians against Jews

1240. Jews defended the Talmud against charges of blasphemy

1263 Debate on the"true faith", and whether the Messiah had appeared or not.

1413-1414. Disputation summoned by Pope Benedict XIII. Held 69 sessions. Failed to persuade Jews that, from Talmudic evidence, Jesus was the Messiah. A Papal Bull forbad Christians to study the Talmud

**Key:**
- ▬ Principal Disputations
- ● Other Disputations

POLAND

GERMANY
- ● Hannover
- ▮ Cologne

FRANCE
- ▮ Paris
- ● Sens 1180's

● Rome

▮ Constantinople

SPAIN
- Burgos ● 1375
- ● Pamplona 1380's
- Avila ● 1375
- ▮ Tortosa
- ▮ Barcelona
- Granada ● 1430

Miles
0    150

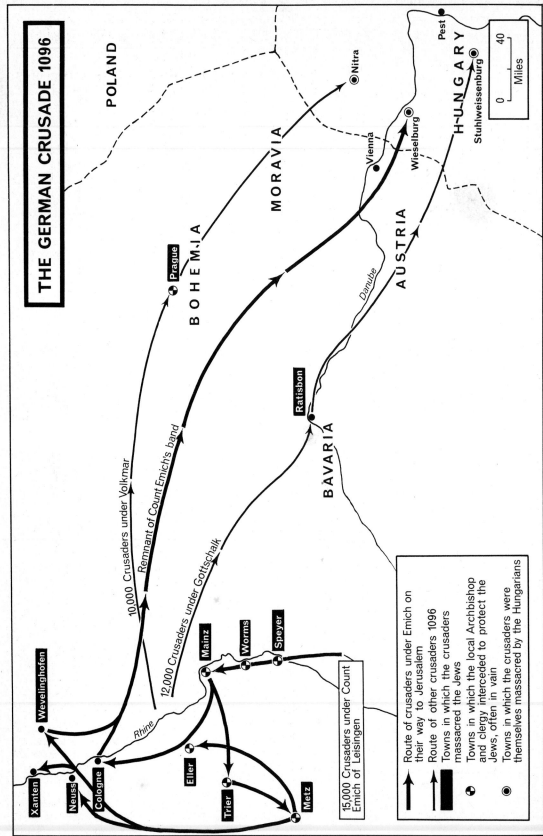

# THE GERMAN CRUSADE 1096

POLAND

Nitra

Vienna

Wieselburg

Pest

HUNGARY

Stuhlweissenburg

0        40
Miles

MORAVIA

Prague

BOHEMIA

AUSTRIA

Danube

Ratisbon

BAVARIA

10,000 Crusaders under Volkmar

Remnant of Count Emich's band

12,000 Crusaders under Gottschalk

Rhine

Wevelinghofen

Mainz

Worms

Speyer

Xanten

Neuss

Cologne

Eller

Trier

Metz

15,000 Crusaders under Count
Emich of Leisingen

Route of crusaders under Emich on
their way to Jerusalem

Route of other crusaders 1096

Towns in which the crusaders
massacred the Jews

Towns in which the local Archbishop
and clergy interceded to protect the
Jews, often in vain

Towns in which the crusaders were
themselves massacred by the Hungarians

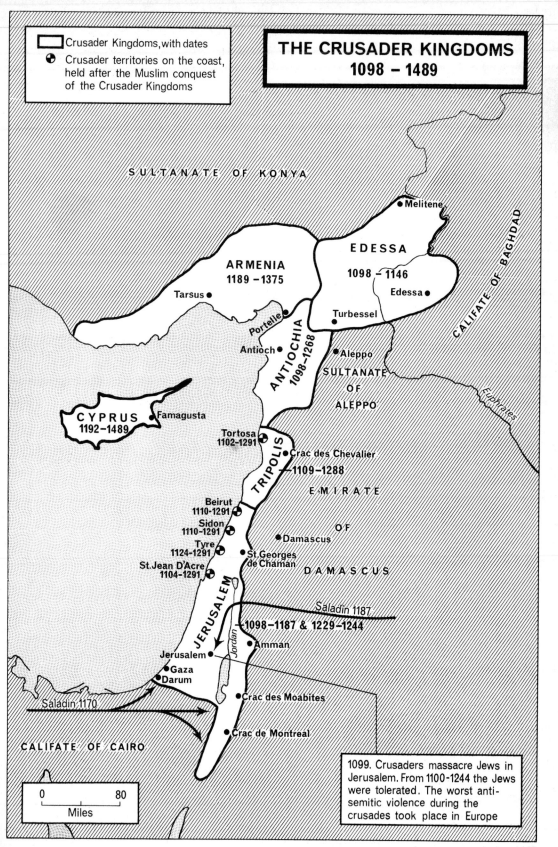

# THE CRUSADER KINGDOMS
## 1098 – 1489

Crusader Kingdoms, with dates

Crusader territories on the coast, held after the Muslim conquest of the Crusader Kingdoms

SULTANATE OF KONYA

● Melitene

EDESSA
1098 – 1146

ARMENIA
1189 – 1375

Tarsus ●

Edessa ●

Portelle

Turbessel ●

ANTIOCHIA
1098 – 1268

Antioch ●

● Aleppo

SULTANATE
OF
ALEPPO

CALIFATE OF BAGHDAD

Euphrates

CYPRUS
1192 – 1489

● Famagusta

Tortosa
1102 – 1291

● Crac des Chevalier
1109 – 1288

TRIPOLIS

EMIRATE

Beirut
1110 – 1291

OF

Sidon
1110 – 1291

● Damascus

Tyre
1124 – 1291

St. Georges
de Chaman

St. Jean D'Acre
1104 – 1291

DAMASCUS

JERUSALEM

Jordan

Saladin 1187

1098 – 1187 & 1229 – 1244

● Amman

Jerusalem ●

● Gaza
Darum

Saladin 1170

● Crac des Moabites

CALIFATE OF CAIRO

● Crac de Montreal

0        80
Miles

1099. Crusaders massacre Jews in Jerusalem. From 1100-1244 the Jews were tolerated. The worst anti-semitic violence during the crusades took place in Europe

36

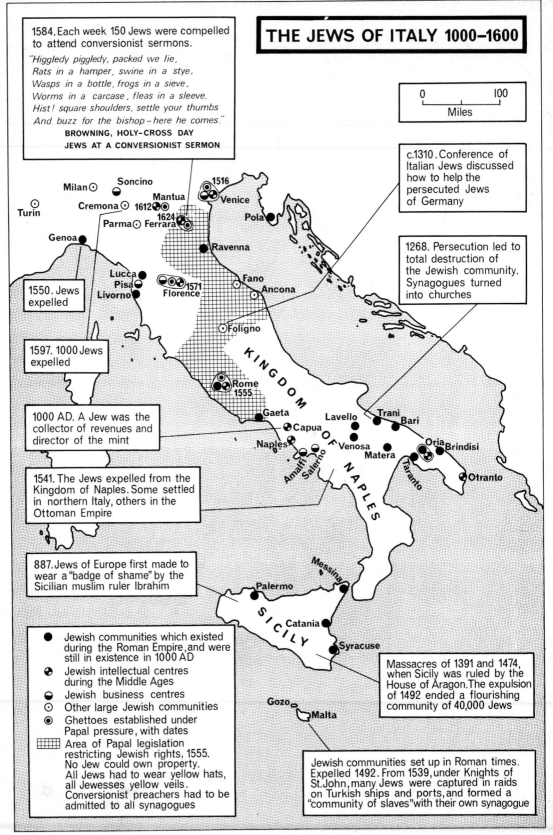

# THE JEWS OF ITALY 1000–1600

**1584.** Each week 150 Jews were compelled to attend conversionist sermons.

*"Higgledy piggledy, packed we lie,*
*Rats in a hamper, swine in a stye,*
*Wasps in a bottle, frogs in a sieve,*
*Worms in a carcase, fleas in a sleeve.*
*Hist! square shoulders, settle your thumbs*
*And buzz for the bishop – here he comes."*
**BROWNING, HOLY-CROSS DAY**
**JEWS AT A CONVERSIONIST SERMON**

0 — 100
Miles

**c.1310.** Conference of Italian Jews discussed how to help the persecuted Jews of Germany

**1268.** Persecution led to total destruction of the Jewish community. Synagogues turned into churches

**1550.** Jews expelled

**1597.** 1000 Jews expelled

**1000 AD.** A Jew was the collector of revenues and director of the mint

**1541.** The Jews expelled from the Kingdom of Naples. Some settled in northern Italy, others in the Ottoman Empire

**887.** Jews of Europe first made to wear a "badge of shame" by the Sicilian muslim ruler Ibrahim

**Massacres of 1391 and 1474,** when Sicily was ruled by the House of Aragon. The expulsion of 1492 ended a flourishing community of 40,000 Jews

Jewish communities set up in Roman times. Expelled 1492. From 1539, under Knights of St. John, many Jews were captured in raids on Turkish ships and ports, and formed a "community of slaves" with their own synagogue

Milan · Soncino · Mantua · 1612 · Cremona · 1624 · Parma · Ferrara · Turin · Genoa · 1516 · Venice · Pola · Ravenna · Lucca · Pisa · Livorno · 1571 · Florence · Fano · Ancona · Foligno · KINGDOM · Rome 1555 · Gaeta · Capua · Lavello · Trani · Bari · Naples · Venosa · Oria · Brindisi · Amalfi · Salerno · Matera · Taranto · Otranto · OF NAPLES · Messina · Palermo · Catania · Syracuse · SICILY · Gozo · Malta

● Jewish communities which existed during the Roman Empire, and were still in existence in 1000 AD

◕ Jewish intellectual centres during the Middle Ages

◒ Jewish business centres

⊙ Other large Jewish communities

◉ Ghettoes established under Papal pressure, with dates

▦ Area of Papal legislation restricting Jewish rights, 1555. No Jew could own property. All Jews had to wear yellow hats, all Jewesses yellow veils. Conversionist preachers had to be admitted to all synagogues

# THE JEWS OF ENGLAND
## 1066–1290

- ◉ Towns with Archae, or official registers of Jewish financial transactions
- ● Other towns with Jewish communities, often of only three or four families
- ◑ Towns from which the Jews were expelled before 1290

"All Jews, wherever in the realm they are, must be under the King's protection.... nor can any of them put himself under the protection of any powerful person without the King's licence, because the Jews themselves and all their chattels are the Kings.... If anyone detain them or their money the King may claim them, if he so desire, as his own". **TWELFTH CENTURY LAW**

1190. Violent attack on Jews by crusaders. The Jews killed themselves rather than surrender

1255. Ritual murder charge. 18 Jews executed

1281. Synod forbids Jews to hold public office

The first Jews came to England from Rouen with William the Conqueror. They were mostly moneylenders, dealing both with the King and his barons. After 1189, under the impetus of the crusades, they were much persecuted, fined, assaulted, and expelled from particular towns. In 1290 all 5000 were expelled, and crossed to France and Flanders, having had all their property confiscated.

Newcastle

Lancaster
York
Beverley
Doncaster
Grimsby

Beaumaris
Newborough
Flint
Carnarvon
Rhuddlan
Conway
Criccieth
Bala
Harlech

Lincoln

Derby
Nottingham
King's Lynn
Stamford
Norwich
Leicester
Thetford
Bungay
Coventry
Eye
Huntingdon
Warwick
Northampton
Bury St. Edmunds
Worcester
Cambridge
Newport
Bedford
Ipswich
Hereford
Sudbury
Dunstable
Hitchin
Colchester
Gloucester
Oxford
Hertford
Cricklade
Wallingford
Berkhampsted
Marlborough
Wycombe
London
Bristol
Reading
Faversham
Devizes
Windsor
Rochester
Newbury
Canterbury
Guildford
Wells
Wilton
Winchester
Rye
Romsey
Arundel
Winchelsea
Southampton
Dorchester
Bosham
Chichester
Exeter

0    50
Miles

38

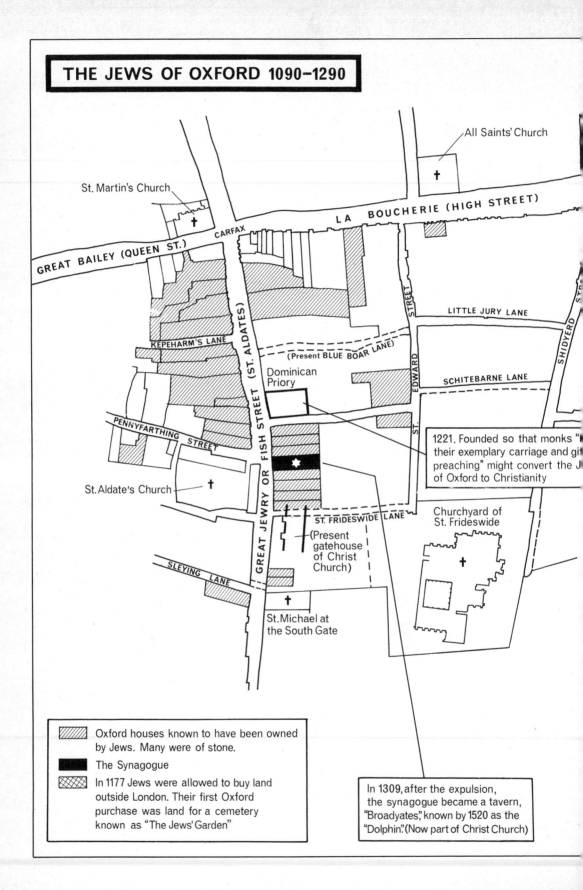

# THE JEWS OF OXFORD 1090–1290

All Saints' Church

St. Martin's Church

LA BOUCHERIE (HIGH STREET)

GREAT BAILEY (QUEEN ST.)

CARFAX

LITTLE JURY LANE

KEPEHARM'S LANE

(Present BLUE BOAR LANE)

SCHITEBARNE LANE

PENNYFARTHING STREET

Dominican Priory

1221. Founded so that monks "… their exemplary carriage and gi[ft] preaching" might convert the J[ews] of Oxford to Christianity

St. Aldate's Church

GREAT JEWRY OR FISH STREET (ST. ALDATES)

ST. FRIDESWIDE LANE

Churchyard of St. Frideswide

(Present gatehouse of Christ Church)

SLEYING LANE

St. Michael at the South Gate

SHIDYERD

ST. EDWARD STREET

Oxford houses known to have been owned by Jews. Many were of stone.

The Synagogue

In 1177 Jews were allowed to buy land outside London. Their first Oxford purchase was land for a cemetery known as "The Jews' Garden"

In 1309, after the expulsion, the synagogue became a tavern, "Broadyates," known by 1520 as the "Dolphin". (Now part of Christ Church)

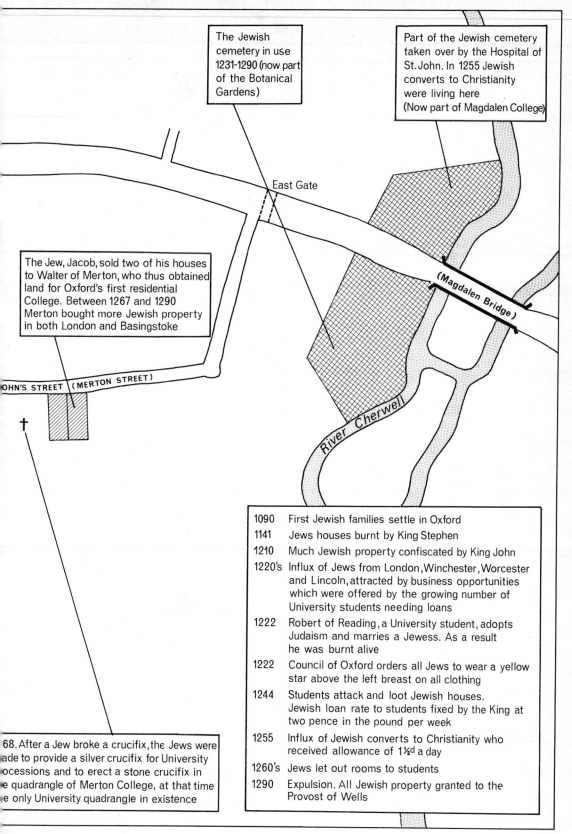

The Jewish cemetery in use 1231-1290 (now part of the Botanical Gardens)

Part of the Jewish cemetery taken over by the Hospital of St. John. In 1255 Jewish converts to Christianity were living here (Now part of Magdalen College)

East Gate

The Jew, Jacob, sold two of his houses to Walter of Merton, who thus obtained land for Oxford's first residential College. Between 1267 and 1290 Merton bought more Jewish property in both London and Basingstoke

(Magdalen Bridge)

OHN'S STREET (MERTON STREET)

River Cherwell

†

68. After a Jew broke a crucifix, the Jews were ade to provide a silver crucifix for University ocessions and to erect a stone crucifix in e quadrangle of Merton College, at that time e only University quadrangle in existence

| | |
|---|---|
| 1090 | First Jewish families settle in Oxford |
| 1141 | Jews houses burnt by King Stephen |
| 1210 | Much Jewish property confiscated by King John |
| 1220's | Influx of Jews from London, Winchester, Worcester and Lincoln, attracted by business opportunities which were offered by the growing number of University students needing loans |
| 1222 | Robert of Reading, a University student, adopts Judaism and marries a Jewess. As a result he was burnt alive |
| 1222 | Council of Oxford orders all Jews to wear a yellow star above the left breast on all clothing |
| 1244 | Students attack and loot Jewish houses. Jewish loan rate to students fixed by the King at two pence in the pound per week |
| 1255 | Influx of Jewish converts to Christianity who received allowance of 1½d a day |
| 1260's | Jews let out rooms to students |
| 1290 | Expulsion. All Jewish property granted to the Provost of Wells |

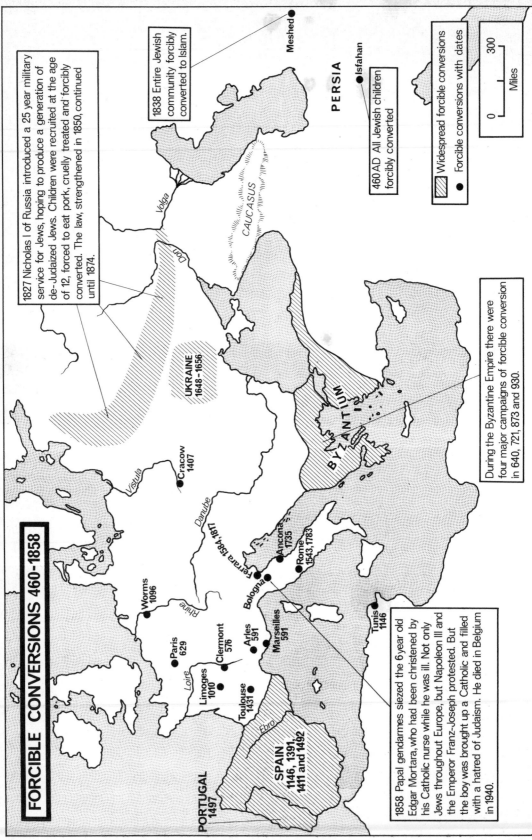

# FORCIBLE CONVERSIONS 460-1858

1827 Nicholas I of Russia introduced a 25 year military service for Jews, hoping to produce a generation of de-Judaized Jews. Children were recruited at the age of 12, forced to eat pork, cruelly treated and forcibly converted. The law, strengthened in 1850, continued until 1874.

1838 Entire Jewish community forcibly converted to Islam.

460 AD All Jewish children forcibly converted

Widespread forcible conversions

● Forcible conversions with dates

0    300
Miles

During the Byzantine Empire there were four major campaigns of forcible conversion in 640, 721, 873 and 930.

1858 Papal gendarmes siezed the 6 year old Edgar Mortara, who had been christened by his Catholic nurse while he was ill. Not only Jews throughout Europe, but Napoleon III and the Emperor Franz-Joseph protested. But the boy was brought up a Catholic and filled with a hatred of Judaism. He died in Belgium in 1940.

PERSIA

BYZANTIUM

CAUCASUS

UKRAINE
1648-1656

SPAIN
1146, 1391,
1411 and 1492

PORTUGAL
1497

Volga

Don

Vistula

Danube

Rhine

Loire

Ebro

● Meshed

● Isfahan

● Cracow
1407

● Worms
1096

● Paris
629

● Clermont
576

● Arles
591

● Marseilles
591

● Limoges
1010

● Toulouse
1431

Ferrara 1584, 1817

● Bologna

● Ancona
1735

● Rome
1543, 1783

● Tunis
1146

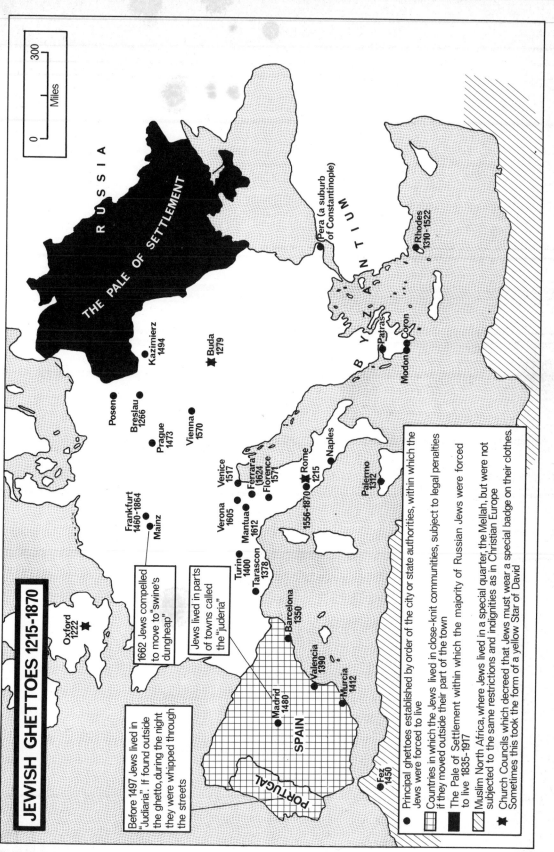

# JEWISH GHETTOES 1215-1870

Miles
0 — 300

RUSSIA

THE PALE OF SETTLEMENT

B Y Z A N T I U M

Pera (a suburb of Constantinople)

Rhodes
1310-1522

Patras

Modon Coron

Kazimierz
1494

Buda
1279

Posen

Breslau
1266

Prague
1473

Vienna
1570

Venice
1517

Ferrara
1624

Florence
1571

Rome
1215

Naples

Palermo
1312

1556-1870

Verona
1605

Mantua
1612

Frankfurt
1460-1864

Mainz

Turin
1400

Tarascon
1378

Barcelona
1350

Valencia
1390

Murcia
1412

Madrid
1480

SPAIN

PORTUGAL

Fez
1450

Oxford
1222

Before 1497 Jews lived in "Judiaria". If found outside the ghetto, during the night they were whipped through the streets

1662 Jews compelled to move to "swine's dungheap"

Jews lived in parts of towns called the "judería"

● Principal ghettoes established by order of the city or state authorities, within which the Jews were forced to live

▦ Countries in which the Jews lived in close-knit communities, subject to legal penalties if they moved outside their part of the town

■ The Pale of Settlement within which the majority of Russian Jews were forced to live 1835-1917

▨ Muslim North Africa, where Jews lived in a special quarter, the Mellah, but were not subjected to the same restrictions and indignities as in Christian Europe

★ Church Councils which decreed that Jews must wear a special badge on their clothes. Sometimes this took the form of a yellow Star of David

41

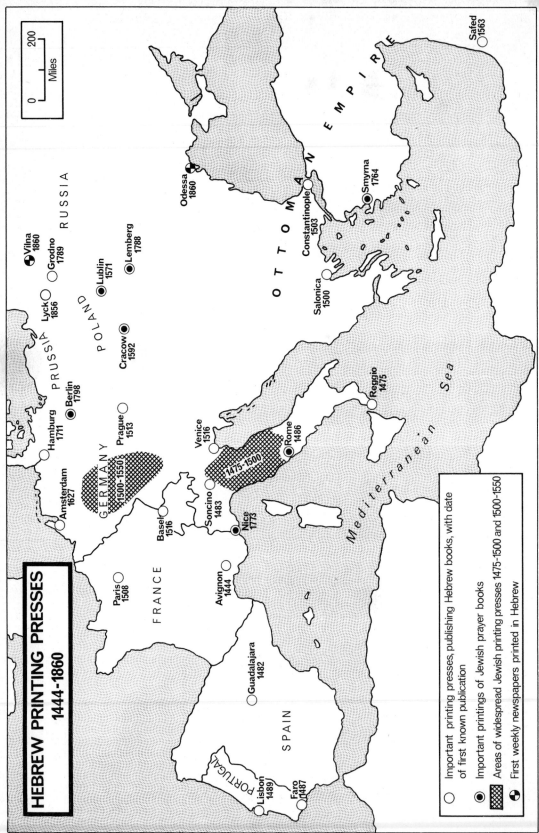

# HEBREW PRINTING PRESSES
## 1444-1860

Miles
0 — 200

**RUSSIA**

Safed
1563

Smyrna
1764

Odessa
1860

Vilna
1860

Grodno
1789

Lublin
1571

Lemberg
1788

Constantinople
1503

Lyck
1856

Cracow
1592

Salonica
1500

**PRUSSIA**

**POLAND**

Berlin
1798

Hamburg
1711

Prague
1513

Reggio
1475

**GERMANY**

1500-1550

Amsterdam
1627

Venice
1516

Rome
1486

1475-1500

Basel
1516

Soncino
1483

Nice
1773

**OTTOMAN EMPIRE**

**FRANCE**

Paris
1508

Avignon
1444

*Mediterranean Sea*

Guadalajara
1482

**SPAIN**

**PORTUGAL**

Lisbon
1489

Faro
1487

○ Important printing presses, publishing Hebrew books, with date
of first known publication

◉ Important printings of Jewish prayer books

▨ Areas of widespread Jewish printing presses 1475-1500 and 1500-1550

◕ First weekly newspapers printed in Hebrew

42

# THE JEWS OF SPAIN AND PORTUGAL 1000–1497

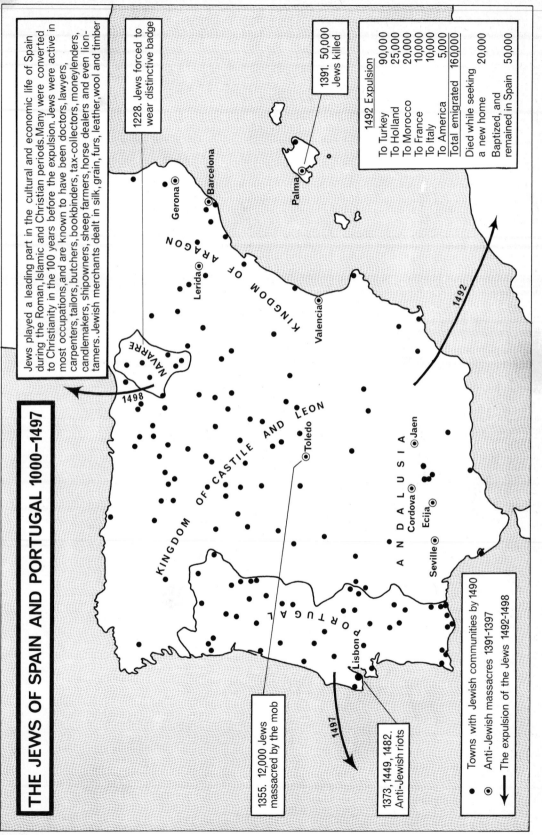

Jews played a leading part in the cultural and economic life of Spain during the Roman, Islamic and Christian periods. Many were converted to Christianity in the 100 years before the expulsion. Jews were active in most occupations, and are known to have been doctors, lawyers, carpenters, tailors, butchers, bookbinders, tax-collectors, moneylenders, candlemakers, shipowners, sheep farmers, horse dealers and even lion-tamers. Jewish merchants dealt in silk, grain, furs, leather, wool and timber

1228. Jews forced to wear distinctive badge

1391. 50,000 Jews killed

| 1492 Expulsion | |
|---|---|
| To Turkey | 90,000 |
| To Holland | 25,000 |
| To Morocco | 20,000 |
| To France | 10,000 |
| To Italy | 10,000 |
| To America | 5,000 |
| Total emigrated | 160,000 |
| Died while seeking a new home | 20,000 |
| Baptized, and remained in Spain | 50,000 |

Gerona

Barcelona

Palma

KINGDOM OF ARAGON

Lerida

Valencia

NAVARRE

1498

1492

KINGDOM OF CASTILE AND LEON

Toledo

Jaen

ANDALUSIA

Cordova

Ecija

Seville

PORTUGAL

Lisbon

1497

1355. 12,000 Jews massacred by the mob

1373, 1449, 1482. Anti-Jewish riots

- • Towns with Jewish communities by 1490
- ◉ Anti-Jewish massacres 1391-1397
- ⟶ The expulsion of the Jews 1492-1498

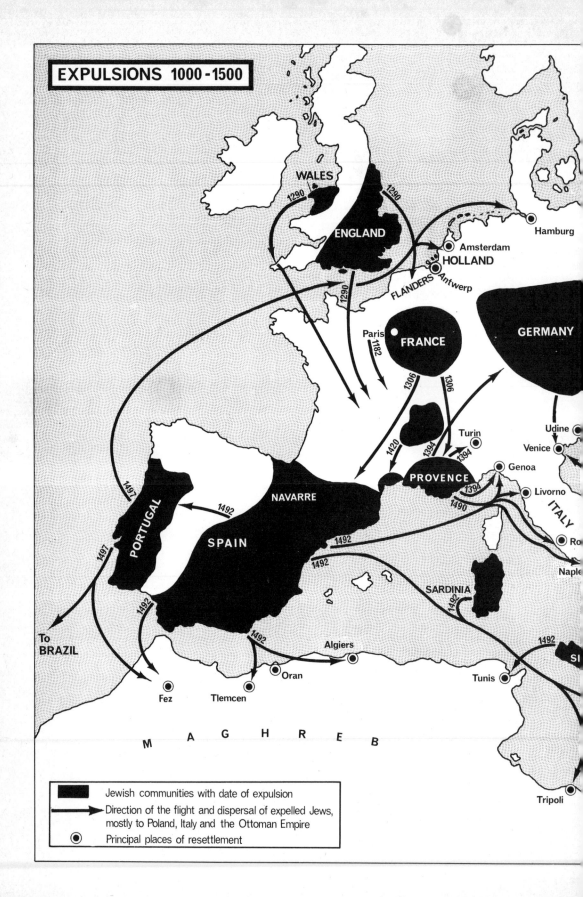

# EXPULSIONS 1000-1500

WALES

ENGLAND
1290
1290

Hamburg

Amsterdam
HOLLAND
Antwerp
FLANDERS

GERMANY

Paris
1182
FRANCE
1306
1306

Udine

Turin
Venice

1420
1394
1394
PROVENCE
Genoa
Livorno

1497

1492
NAVARRE

PORTUGAL
SPAIN
1497
1492
1492
1492

ITALY

Ro

Naple

1490
1394

SARDINIA

To
BRAZIL
1492

1492
Algiers

1492
1492
SI

Oran
Tunis

Fez
Tlemcen

M   A   G   H   R   E   B

Tripoli

| | Jewish communities with date of expulsion |
| --- | --- |
| → | Direction of the flight and dispersal of expelled Jews, mostly to Poland, Italy and the Ottoman Empire |
| ⊙ | Principal places of resettlement |

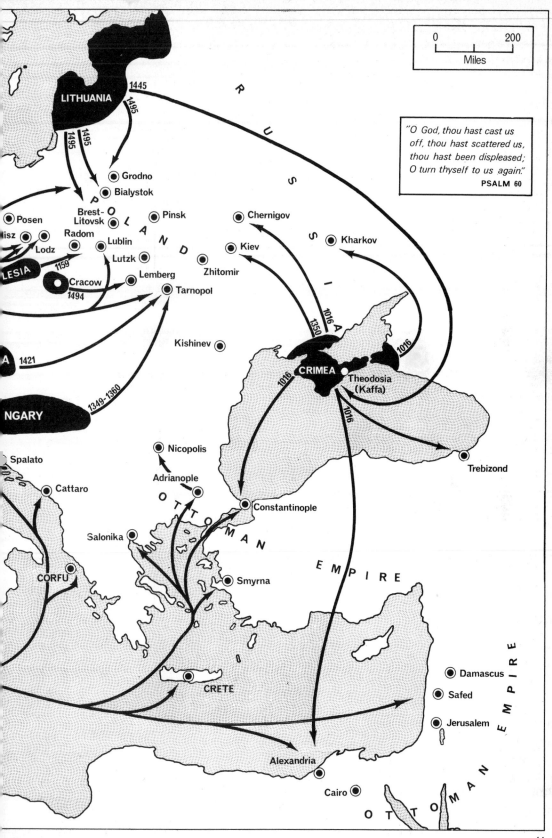

LITHUANIA
1445
1495
1495
1495

R
U
S
S
I
A

Grodno
Bialystok
Brest-Litovsk
Pinsk
Chernigov
Kharkov
Posen
nisz
Lodz
Radom
Lublin
Kiev
Zhitomir
LESIA
1159
Lutzk
Cracow
1494
Lemberg
Tarnopol
1016
1350
Kishinev
A
1421
1349-1360
NGARY

"O God, thou hast cast us
off, thou hast scattered us,
thou hast been displeased;
O turn thyself to us again."
**PSALM 60**

1016

CRIMEA
Theodosia
(Kaffa)
1016
Trebizond

1016

Nicopolis
Adrianople
Spalato
Cattaro
O
T
T
O
M
A
N
E
M
P
I
R
E
Constantinople
Salonika
CORFU
Smyrna

CRETE

Damascus
Safed
Jerusalem

O
T
T
O
M
A
N
E
M
P
I
R
E

Alexandria
Cairo

O T T O M A N   E M P I R E

0        200
Miles

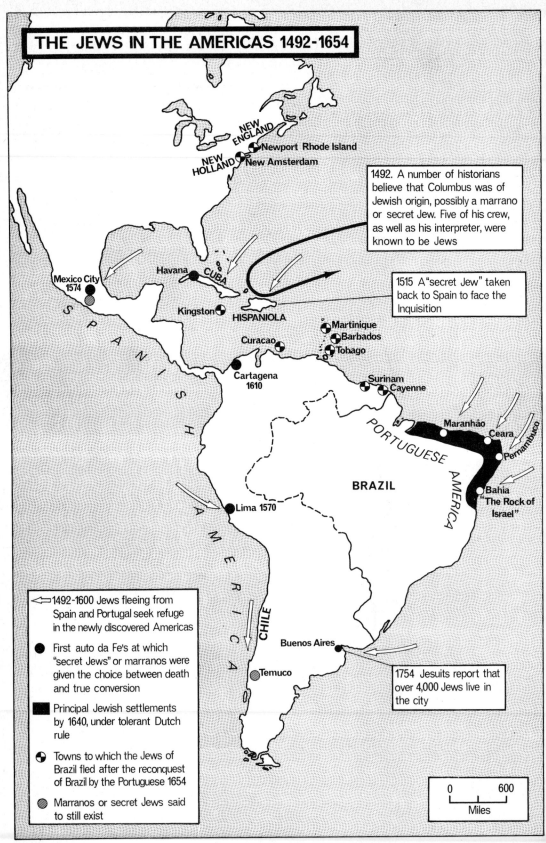

# THE JEWS IN THE AMERICAS 1492-1654

**NEW ENGLAND**

**NEW HOLLAND**

Newport Rhode Island

New Amsterdam

1492. A number of historians believe that Columbus was of Jewish origin, possibly a marrano or secret Jew. Five of his crew, as well as his interpreter, were known to be Jews

Havana **CUBA**

Mexico City 1574

1515 A "secret Jew" taken back to Spain to face the Inquisition

Kingston **HISPANIOLA**

**S P A N I S H   A M E R I C A**

Martinique

Barbados

Curacao

Tobago

Cartagena 1610

Surinam

Cayenne

Maranhâo   Ceara

**PORTUGUESE AMERICA**

Pernambuco

**BRAZIL**

Bahia "The Rock of Israel"

Lima 1570

**CHILE**

Buenos Aires

1754 Jesuits report that over 4,000 Jews live in the city

Temuco

←⊂ 1492-1600 Jews fleeing from Spain and Portugal seek refuge in the newly discovered Americas

● First auto da Fe's at which "secret Jews" or marranos were given the choice between death and true conversion

■ Principal Jewish settlements by 1640, under tolerant Dutch rule

◓ Towns to which the Jews of Brazil fled after the reconquest of Brazil by the Portuguese 1654

◑ Marranos or secret Jews said to still exist

0        600
Miles

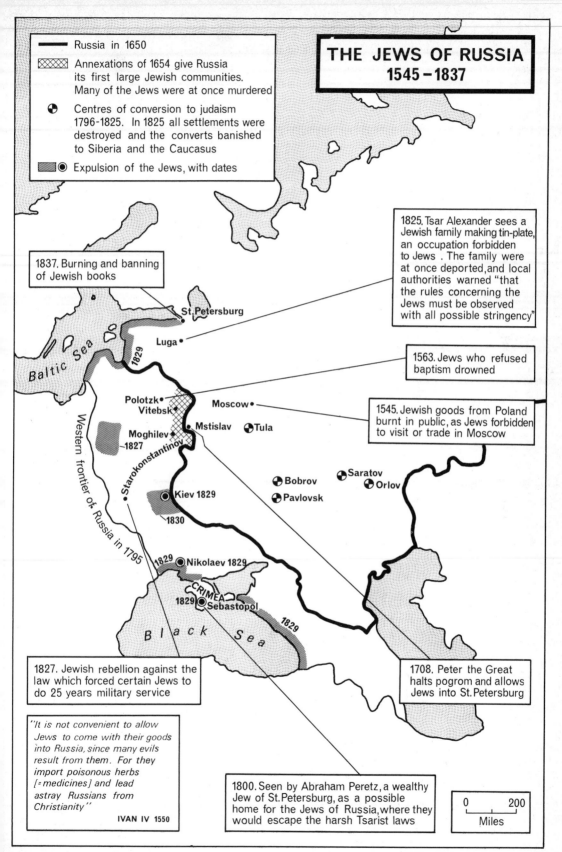

# THE JEWS OF RUSSIA
# 1545 – 1837

**Legend:**

— Russia in 1650

▨ Annexations of 1654 give Russia its first large Jewish communities. Many of the Jews were at once murdered

◑ Centres of conversion to judaism 1796-1825. In 1825 all settlements were destroyed and the converts banished to Siberia and the Caucasus

◉ Expulsion of the Jews, with dates

1837. Burning and banning of Jewish books

1825. Tsar Alexander sees a Jewish family making tin-plate, an occupation forbidden to Jews . The family were at once deported, and local authorities warned "that the rules concerning the Jews must be observed with all possible stringency"

1563. Jews who refused baptism drowned

1545. Jewish goods from Poland burnt in public, as Jews forbidden to visit or trade in Moscow

Baltic Sea

St. Petersburg

Luga

1829

Western frontier of Russia in 1795

Polotzk
Vitebsk

Moscow

Moghilev
—1827

Mstislav    Tula

Starokonstantinov

Bobrov    Saratov
Pavlovsk    Orlov

Kiev 1829

1830

1829  Nikolaev 1829

CRIMEA

1829  Sebastopol    1829

Black Sea

1827. Jewish rebellion against the law which forced certain Jews to do 25 years military service

1708. Peter the Great halts pogrom and allows Jews into St. Petersburg

"It is not convenient to allow Jews to come with their goods into Russia, since many evils result from them. For they import poisonous herbs [=medicines] and lead astray Russians from Christianity"

**IVAN IV 1550**

1800. Seen by Abraham Peretz, a wealthy Jew of St. Petersburg, as a possible home for the Jews of Russia, where they would escape the harsh Tsarist laws

0    200
Miles

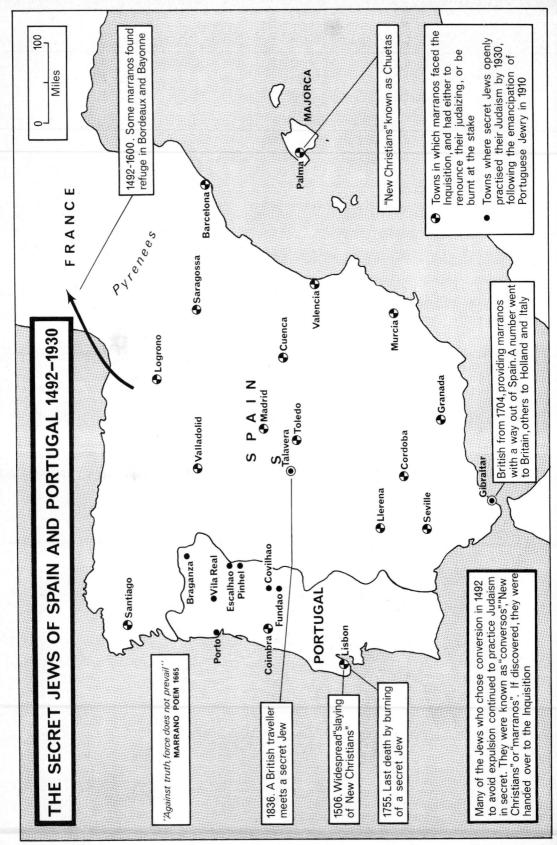

# THE SECRET JEWS OF SPAIN AND PORTUGAL 1492–1930

*"Against truth, force does not prevail"* MARRANO POEM 1665

1836. A British traveller meets a secret Jew

1506. Widespread "slaying of New Christians"

1755. Last death by burning of a secret Jew

Many of the Jews who chose conversion in 1492 to avoid expulsion continued to practice Judaism in secret. They were known as "conversos" "New Christians" or "marranos". If discovered, they were handed over to the Inquisition

1492-1600. Some marranos found refuge in Bordeaux and Bayonne

"New Christians" known as Chuetas

● ⊕ Towns in which marranos faced the Inquisition, and had either to renounce their judaizing, or be burnt at the stake

● Towns where secret Jews openly practised their Judaism by 1930, following the emancipation of Portuguese Jewry in 1910

British from 1704, providing marranos with a way out of Spain. A number went to Britain, others to Holland and Italy

FRANCE

Pyrenees

SPAIN

PORTUGAL

MAJORCA

⊕ Palma

⊕ Barcelona

⊕ Saragossa

⊕ Logrono

⊕ Valladolid

⊕ Madrid
Ⓢ Talavera
⊕ Toledo

⊕ Cuenca

⊕ Valencia

⊕ Murcia

⊕ Granada

⊕ Cordoba

⊕ Llerena

⊕ Seville

⊕ Gibraltar

⊕ Santiago

● Braganza
● Vila Real
● Escalhao  ● Pinhel
⊕ Coimbra  ● Fundao
● Covilhao

● Porto

⊕ Lisbon

0    100
Miles

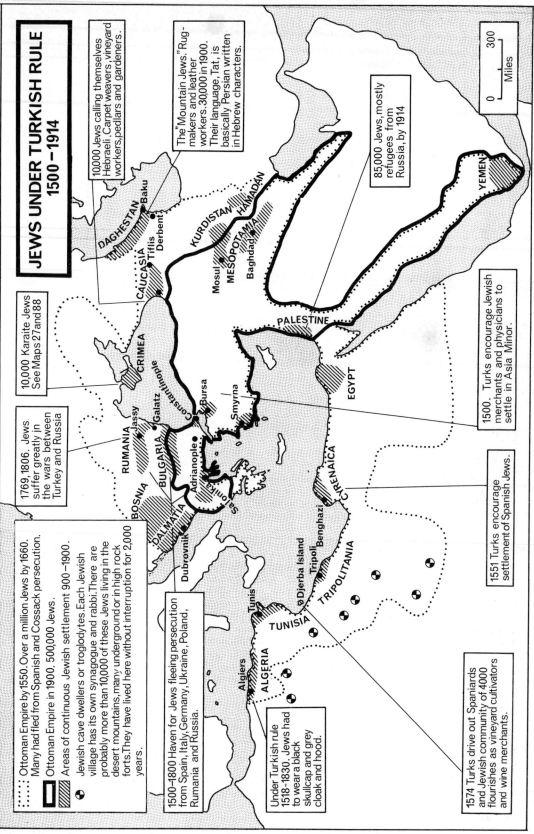

# JEWS UNDER TURKISH RULE
## 1500–1914

10000 Jews calling themselves Hebraeli. Carpet weavers, vineyard workers, pedlars and gardeners.

The "Mountain Jews." Rug-makers and leather workers. 30,000 in 1900. Their language, Tat, is basically Persian written in Hebrew characters.

85,000 Jews, mostly refugees from Russia, by 1914

10,000 Karaite Jews See Maps 27 and 88

1769, 1806. Jews suffer greatly in the wars between Turkey and Russia

1500. Turks encourage Jewish merchants and physicians to settle in Asia Minor.

1551 Turks encourage settlement of Spanish Jews.

Ottoman Empire by 1550. Over a million Jews by 1660. Many had fled from Spanish and Cossack persecution.

Ottoman Empire in 1900. 500,000 Jews.

Areas of continuous Jewish settlement 900–1900.

Jewish cave dwellers or troglodytes. Each Jewish village has its own synagogue and rabbi. There are probably more than 10,000 of these Jews living in the desert mountains, many underground or in high rock forts. They have lived here without interruption for 2,000 years.

1500–1800 Haven for Jews fleeing persecution from Spain, Italy, Germany, Ukraine, Poland, Rumania, and Russia.

Under Turkish rule 1518-1830. Jews had to wear a black skullcap and grey cloak and hood.

1574 Turks drive out Spaniards and Jewish community of 4000 flourishes as vineyard cultivators and wine merchants.

DAGHESTAN
Baku
Derbent
Tiflis
CAUCASIA
KURDISTAN
HAMADAN
MESOPOTAMIA
Mosul
Baghdad
YEMEN
PALESTINE
EGYPT
CRIMEA
Constantinople
Bursa
Smyrna
Jassy
Galatz
RUMANIA
BULGARIA
Adrianople
Salonika
BOSNIA
DALMATIA
Dubrovnik
CYRENAICA
Benghazi
Tripoli
TRIPOLITANIA
Djerba Island
Tunis
TUNISIA
Algiers
ALGERIA

0    300
Miles

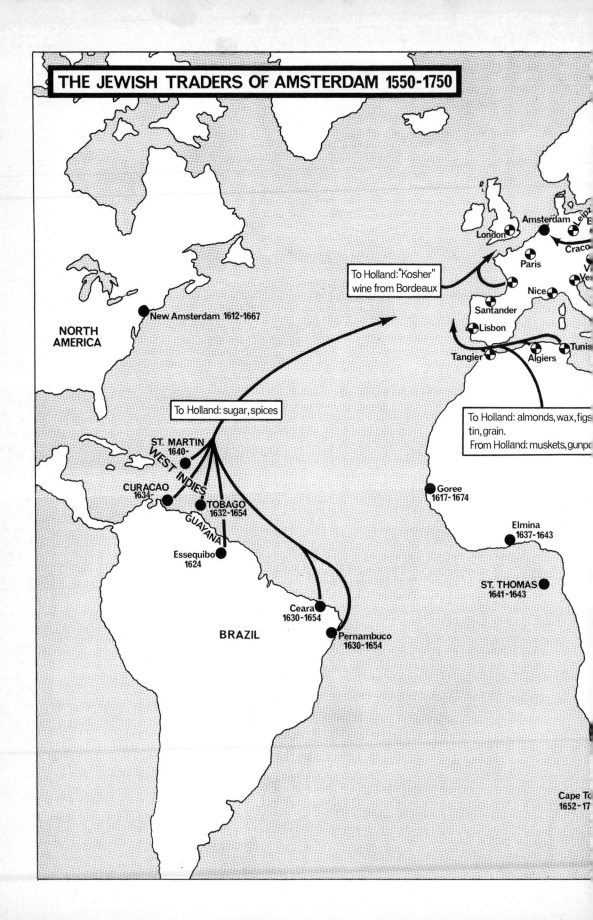

# THE JEWISH TRADERS OF AMSTERDAM 1550-1750

Amsterdam
Leipz
London
Craco
Paris
V
Ve
Nice
Santander
Lisbon
Tangier    Algiers    Tunis

To Holland:"Kosher"
wine from Bordeaux

NORTH
AMERICA

New Amsterdam 1612-1667

To Holland: sugar, spices

To Holland: almonds, wax, figs
tin, grain.
From Holland: muskets, gunpo

ST. MARTIN
1640-
WEST INDIES

CURACAO
1634-

TOBAGO
1632-1654

GUAYANA

Essequibo
1624

Ceara
1630-1654

BRAZIL

Pernambuco
1630-1654

Goree
1617-1674

Elmina
1637-1643

ST. THOMAS
1641-1643

Cape To
1652-17

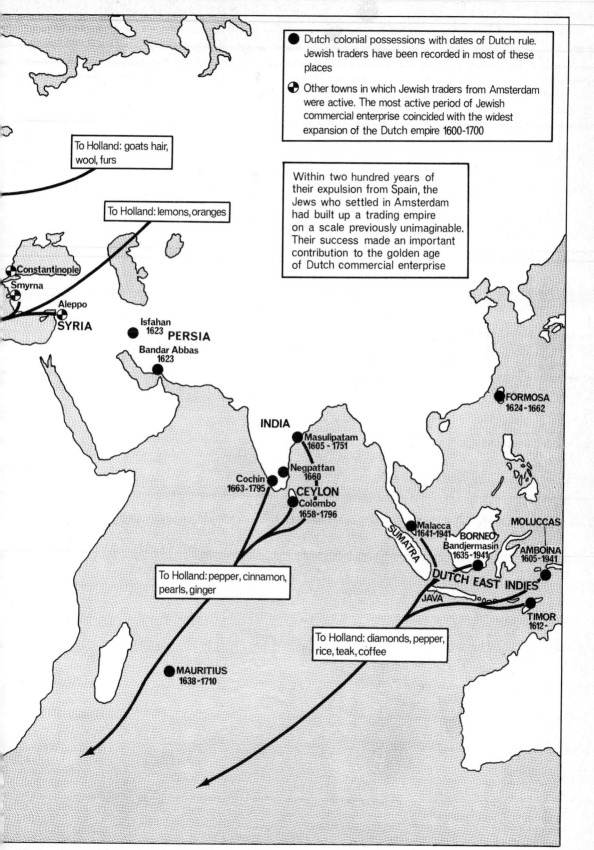

- ● Dutch colonial possessions with dates of Dutch rule. Jewish traders have been recorded in most of these places
- ◑ Other towns in which Jewish traders from Amsterdam were active. The most active period of Jewish commercial enterprise coincided with the widest expansion of the Dutch empire 1600-1700

Within two hundred years of their expulsion from Spain, the Jews who settled in Amsterdam had built up a trading empire on a scale previously unimaginable. Their success made an important contribution to the golden age of Dutch commercial enterprise

To Holland: goats hair, wool, furs

To Holland: lemons, oranges

Constantinople
Smyrna
Aleppo
SYRIA

Isfahan
1623
PERSIA

Bandar Abbas
1623

FORMOSA
1624-1662

INDIA

Masulipatam
1605 - 1751

Negpattan
1660

Cochin
1663-1795

CEYLON

Colombo
1658-1796

MOLUCCAS

Malacca
1641-1941

SUMATRA

BORNEO

Bandjermasin
1635-1941

AMBOINA
1605-1941

To Holland: pepper, cinnamon, pearls, ginger

DUTCH EAST INDIES

JAVA

TIMOR
1612

To Holland: diamonds, pepper, rice, teak, coffee

MAURITIUS
1638-1710

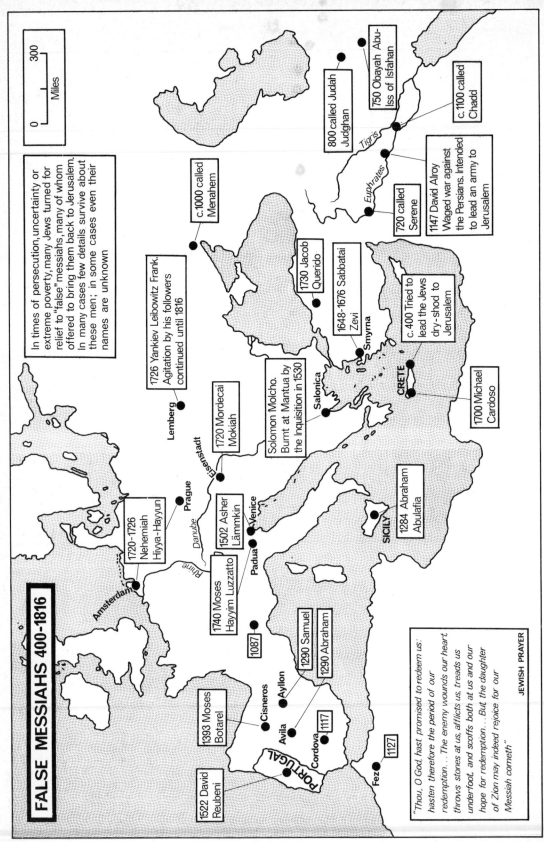

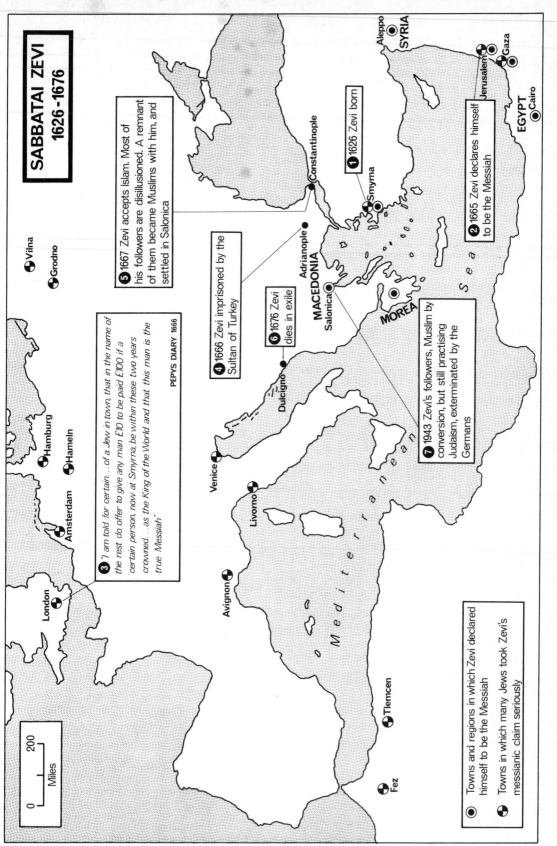

**SABBATAI ZEVI**
**1626 - 1676**

**①** 1626 Zevi born

**②** 1665 Zevi declares himself to be the Messiah

**③** "I am told for certain... of a Jew in town, that in the name of the rest do offer to give any man £10 to be paid £100 if a certain person, now at Smyrna, be within these two years crowned... as the King of the World and that this man is the true Messiah"

PEPYS DIARY 1666

**④** 1666 Zevi imprisoned by the Sultan of Turkey

**⑤** 1667 Zevi accepts Islam. Most of his followers are disillusioned. A remnant of them became Muslims with him, and settled in Salonica

**⑥** 1676 Zevi dies in exile

**⑦** 1943 Zevi's followers, Muslim by conversion, but still practising Judaism, exterminated by the Germans

Vilna
Grodno
Hamburg
Hameln
Amsterdam
London

Fez
Tlemcen
Avignon
Livorno
Venice
Dulcigno
Mediterranean Sea

Salonica
MACEDONIA
MOREA
Adrianople
Constantinople
Smyrna

Aleppo
SYRIA
Gaza
Jerusalem
EGYPT
Cairo

● Towns and regions in which Zevi declared himself to be the Messiah

◑ Towns in which many Jews took Zevi's messianic claim seriously

0   200
Miles

51

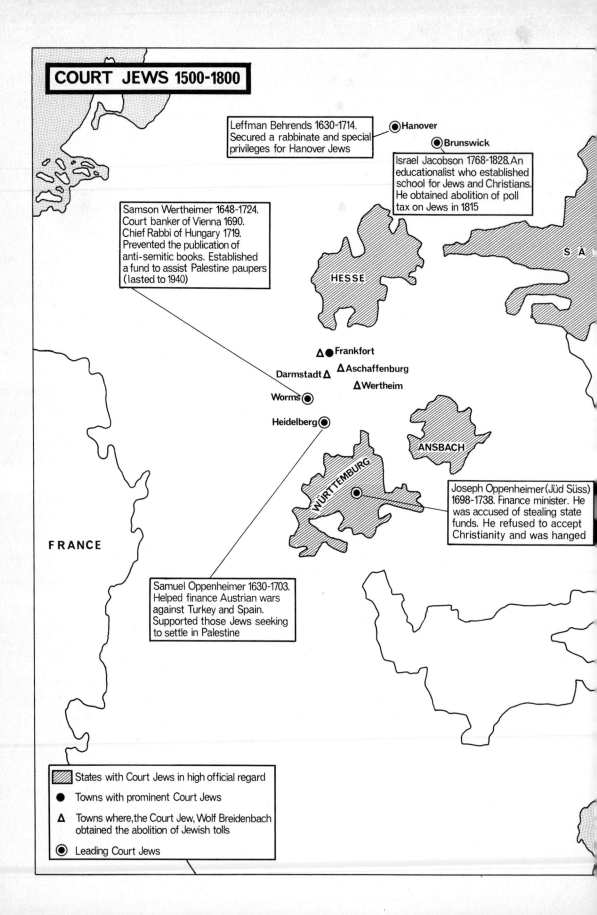

# COURT JEWS 1500-1800

Leffman Behrends 1630-1714. Secured a rabbinate and special privileges for Hanover Jews

● Hanover

● Brunswick

Israel Jacobson 1768-1828. An educationalist who established school for Jews and Christians. He obtained abolition of poll tax on Jews in 1815

Samson Wertheimer 1648-1724. Court banker of Vienna 1690. Chief Rabbi of Hungary 1719. Prevented the publication of anti-semitic books. Established a fund to assist Palestine paupers (lasted to 1940)

HESSE

S A

△ ● Frankfort

△ Aschaffenburg

Darmstadt △

△ Wertheim

Worms ◉

Heidelberg ◉

ANSBACH

WÜRTTEMBURG

Joseph Oppenheimer (Jüd Süss) 1698-1738. Finance minister. He was accused of stealing state funds. He refused to accept Christianity and was hanged

FRANCE

Samuel Oppenheimer 1630-1703. Helped finance Austrian wars against Turkey and Spain. Supported those Jews seeking to settle in Palestine

States with Court Jews in high official regard

● Towns with prominent Court Jews

△ Towns where, the Court Jew, Wolf Breidenbach obtained the abolition of Jewish tolls

◉ Leading Court Jews

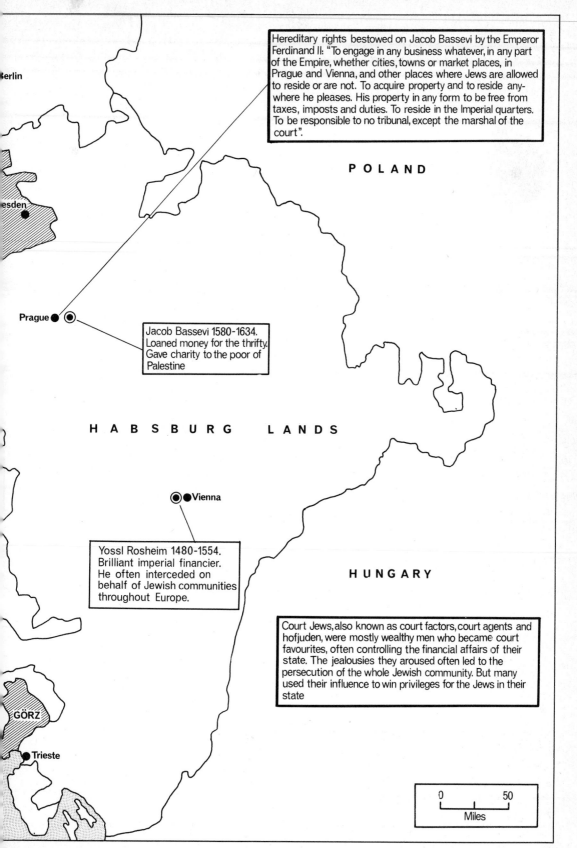

Berlin

Dresden

Prague ●

**POLAND**

Hereditary rights bestowed on Jacob Bassevi by the Emperor Ferdinand II: "To engage in any business whatever, in any part of the Empire, whether cities, towns or market places, in Prague and Vienna, and other places where Jews are allowed to reside or are not. To acquire property and to reside anywhere he pleases. His property in any form to be free from taxes, imposts and duties. To reside in the Imperial quarters. To be responsible to no tribunal, except the marshal of the court".

Jacob Bassevi 1580-1634. Loaned money for the thrifty. Gave charity to the poor of Palestine

**H A B S B U R G     L A N D S**

⊙●Vienna

Yossl Rosheim 1480-1554. Brilliant imperial financier. He often interceded on behalf of Jewish communities throughout Europe.

**HUNGARY**

Court Jews, also known as court factors, court agents and hofjuden, were mostly wealthy men who became court favourites, often controlling the financial affairs of their state. The jealousies they aroused often led to the persecution of the whole Jewish community. But many used their influence to win privileges for the Jews in their state

**GÖRZ**

● Trieste

0          50

Miles

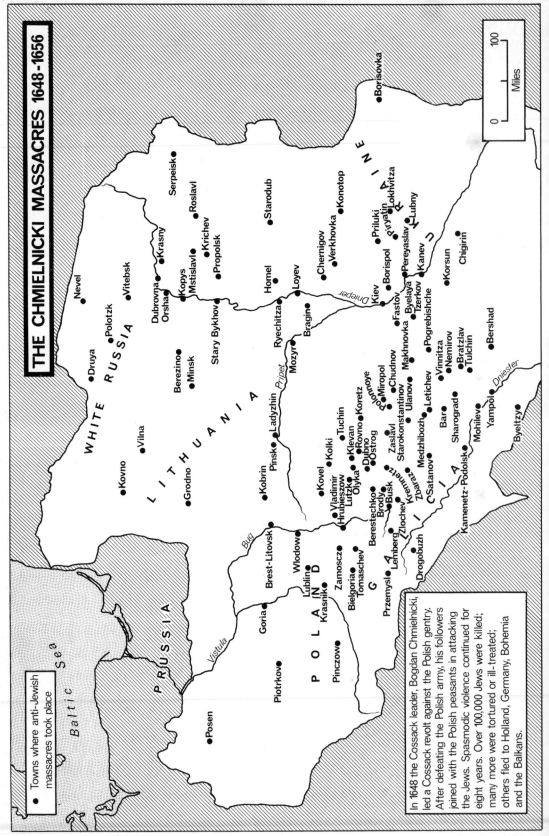

# THE CHMIELNICKI MASSACRES 1648-1656

- Towns where anti-Jewish massacres took place

Baltic Sea

PRUSSIA

WHITE RUSSIA

LITHUANIA

POLAND

UKRAINE

GALICIA

Posen

Piotrkov

Goria

Pinczow

Krasnik
Lublin

Zamoscz

Bielgoria
Tomaschev

Przemysl
Lemberg

Wlodow

Brest-Litovsk

Kovno

Vilna

Grodno

Kobrin

Pinsk
Ladyzhin

Kovel

Kolki

Tuchin

Vladimir
Hrubieszow
Lutzk
Olyka

Drogobuzh

Berestechko
Brody
Busk
Zlochev
Kremenetz
Zbaraz
C Satanov

Rovno
Dubno
Ostrog

Zaslavl
Starokonstantinov

Kamenetz-Podolsk

Klevan
Koretz
Ulanov

Medzhibozh

Polonnoye
Miropol
Chudnov

Letichev

Bar
Sharograd

Vinnitza
Nemirov
Bratzlav
Tulchin

Mohilev

Yampol

Byeltzy

Bershad

Dniester

Nevel

Druya
Polotzk

Vitebsk

Berezino
Minsk

Stary Bykhov

Dubrovna
Orsha

Krasny

Kopys
Mstislavl
Propolsk

Krichev

Roslavl

Serpeisk

Starodub

Homel

Loyev

Bragin

Ryechitza

Mozyr

Pripet

Dnieper

Chernigov
Verkhovka

Kiev
Fastov
Byelaya

Borispol
Tzerkov

Makhnovka
Pogrebishche

Priluki
Pyryatin
Pereyaslav
Kanev

Lokhvitza
Lubny

Konotop

Korsun

Chigirin

Borisovka

Bug

Vistula

In 1648 the Cossack leader, Bogdan Chmielnicki, led a Cossack revolt against the Polish gentry. After defeating the Polish army, his followers joined with the Polish peasants in attacking the Jews. Spasmodic violence continued for eight years. Over 100,000 Jews were killed; many more were tortured or ill-treated; others fled to Holland, Germany, Bohemia and the Balkans.

0        100
Miles

53

# THE MYSTERY OF THE TEN LOST TRIBES OF ISRAEL

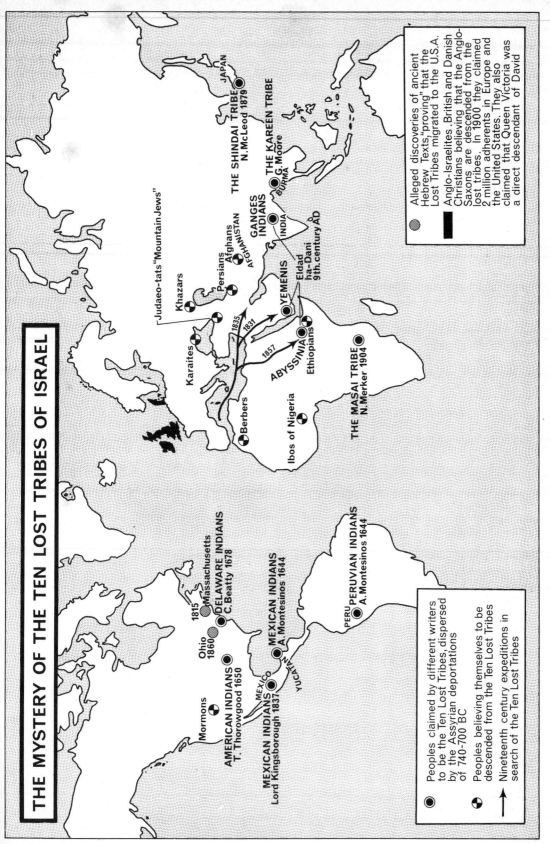

Alleged discoveries of ancient Hebrew Texts,"proving" that the Lost Tribes migrated to the U.S.A.

Anglo-Israelites. British and Danish Christians believing that the Anglo-Saxons are descended from the lost tribes.. In 1900 they claimed 2 million adherents in Europe and the United States. They also claimed that Queen Victoria was a direct descendant of David

THE SHINDAI TRIBE N.McLeod 1879

JAPAN

THE KAREEN TRIBE G.Moore

BURMA

GANGES INDIANS

INDIA

Judaeo-tats"Mountain Jews"

Khazars

Persians

Afghans

AFGHANISTAN

Karaites

YEMENIS

Eldad ha-Dani 9th.century AD

ABYSSINIA

Ethiopians

Berbers

Ibos of Nigeria

THE MASAI TRIBE N.Merker 1904

1835
1831
1857

Mormons

AMERICAN INDIANS T.Thorowgood 1650

Ohio 1860

Massachusetts

DELAWARE INDIANS C.Beatty 1678

1815

PERU

MEXICO

MEXICAN INDIANS Lord Kingsborough 1837

YUCATAN

MEXICAN INDIANS A.Montesinos 1644

PERU

PERUVIAN INDIANS A.Montesinos 1644

Peoples claimed by different writers to be the Ten Lost Tribes, dispersed by the Assyrian deportations of 740-700 BC

Peoples believing themselves to be descended from the Ten Lost Tribes

Nineteenth century expeditions in search of the Ten Lost Tribes

54

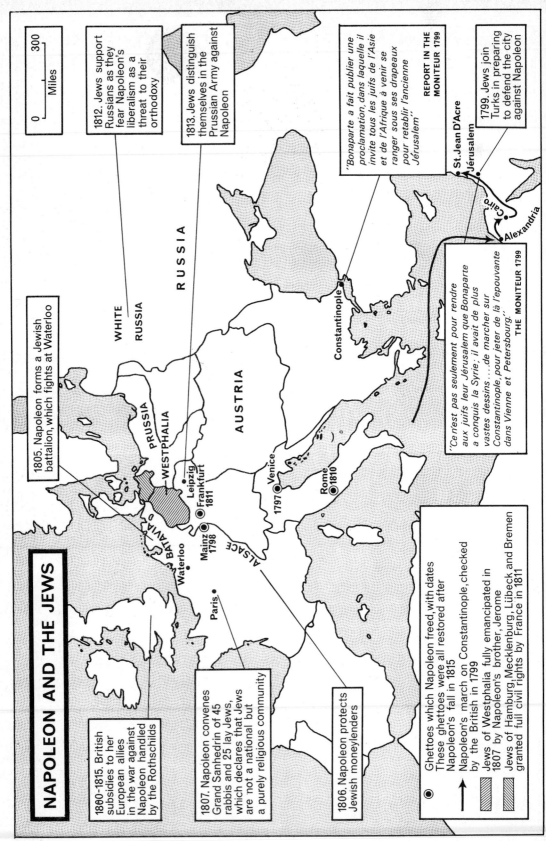

# NAPOLEON AND THE JEWS

1800-1815. British subsidies to her European allies in the war against Napoleon handled by the Rothschilds

1807. Napoleon convenes Grand Sanhedrin of 45 rabbis and 25 lay Jews, which declares that Jews are not a national but a purely religious community

1806. Napoleon protects Jewish moneylenders

1805. Napoleon forms a Jewish battalion, which fights at Waterloo

1812. Jews support Russians as they fear Napoleon's liberalism as a threat to their orthodoxy

1813. Jews distinguish themselves in the Prussian Army against Napoleon

"Bonaparte a fait publier une proclamation, dans laquelle il invite tous les juifs de l'Asie et de l'Afrique à venir se ranger sous ses drapeaux pour retablir l'ancienne Jérusalem"

**REPORT IN THE MONITEUR 1799**

1799. Jews join Turks in preparing to defend the city against Napoleon

"Ce n'est pas seulement pour rendre aux juifs leur Jérusalem que Bonaparte a conquis la Syrie; il avait de plus vastes dessins…de marcher sur Constantinople, pour jeter de là l'epouvante dans Vienne et Petersbourg."

**THE MONITEUR 1799**

RUSSIA

WHITE RUSSIA

PRUSSIA

WESTPHALIA

BATAVIA

Waterloo

Mainz 1798

ALSACE

Paris

AUSTRIA

Leipzig

Frankfurt 1811

Venice 1797

Rome 1810

Constantinople

St.Jean D'Acre

Jérusalem

Cairo

Alexandria

- ⊙ Ghettoes which Napoleon freed, with dates These ghettoes were all restored after Napoleon's fall in 1815

↑ Napoleon's march on Constantinople, checked by the British in 1799

Jews of Westphalia fully emancipated in 1807 by Napoleon's brother, Jerome

Jews of Hamburg, Mecklenburg, Lübeck and Bremen granted full civil rights by France in 1811

0    300
Miles

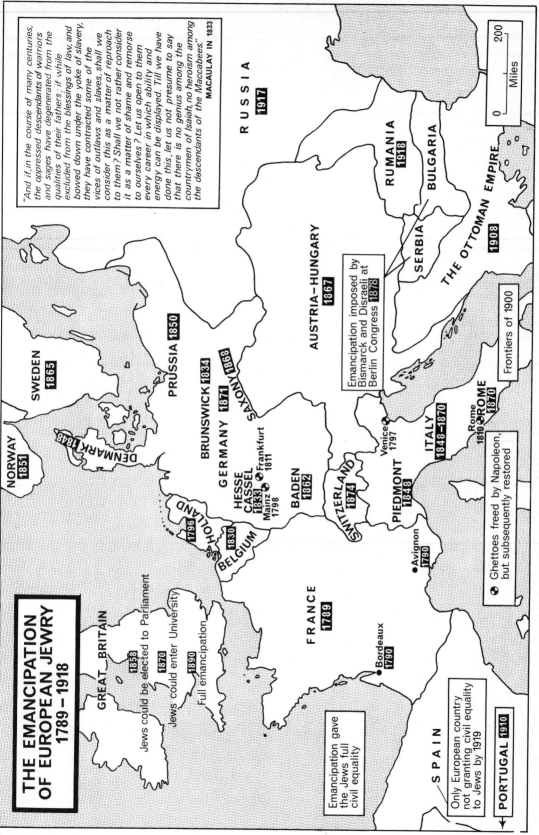

# THE EMANCIPATION OF EUROPEAN JEWRY 1789–1918

"And if, in the course of many centuries, the oppressed descendants of warriors and sages have degenerated from the qualities of their fathers; if while excluded from the blessings of law, and bowed down under the yoke of slavery, they have contracted some of the vices of outlaws and slaves, shall we consider this as a matter of reproach to them? Shall we not rather consider it as a matter of shame and remorse to ourselves? Let us open to them every career in which ability and energy can be displayed. Till we have done this, let us not presume to say that there is no genius among the countrymen of Isaiah, no heroism among the descendants of the Maccabees."

MACAULAY IN 1833

R U S S I A **1917**

NORWAY **1851**

SWEDEN **1865**

DENMARK **1848**

PRUSSIA **1850**

BRUNSWICK **1834**

SAXONY **1868**

GERMANY **1871**

HESSE CASSEL **1833**

Mainz **1798**

Frankfurt **1811**

BADEN **1862**

HOLLAND **1796**

BELGIUM **1830**

SWITZERLAND **1874**

PIEDMONT **1848**

ITALY **1848–1870**

Venice **1797**

Rome **1810** ROME **1870**

AUSTRIA–HUNGARY **1867**

Emancipation imposed by Bismarck and Disraeli at Berlin Congress **1878**

RUMANIA **1918**

SERBIA

BULGARIA

THE OTTOMAN EMPIRE **1908**

Frontiers of 1900

Ghettoes freed by Napoleon, but subsequently restored

Avignon **1790**

F R A N C E **1789**

Bordeaux **1790**

GREAT BRITAIN

**1858** Jews could be elected to Parliament

**1870** Jews could enter University

**1890** Full emancipation

Emancipation gave the Jews full civil equality

S P A I N

Only European country not granting civil equality to Jews by 1919

PORTUGAL **1910**

0 200 Miles

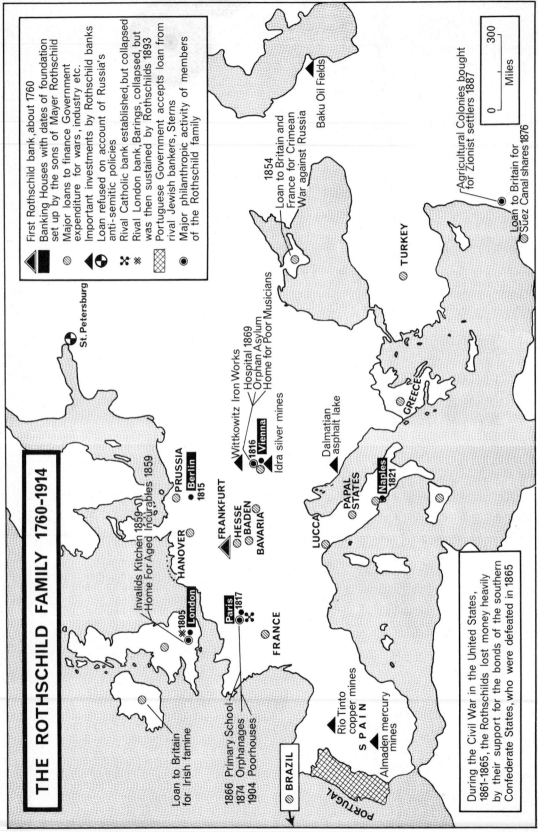

# THE ROTHSCHILD FAMILY 1760-1914

First Rothschild bank, about 1760

Banking Houses with dates of foundation set up by the sons of Mayer Rothschild

Major loans to finance Government expenditure for wars, industry etc.

Important investments by Rothschild banks

Loan refused on account of Russia's anti-semitic policies

Rival Catholic bank established, but collapsed

Rival London bank, Barings, collapsed, but was then sustained by Rothschilds 1893

Portuguese Government accepts loan from rival Jewish bankers, Sterns

Major philanthropic activity of members of the Rothschild family

St. Petersburg

PRUSSIA
Berlin
1815

FRANKFURT

HESSE
BADEN
BAVARIA

HANOVER

Invalids Kitchen 1859
Home For Aged Incurables 1859

London
1805

Paris
1817

FRANCE

1866 Primary School
1874 Orphanages
1904 Poorhouses

Loan to Britain for Irish famine

SPAIN

Rio Tinto copper mines

Almaden mercury mines

BRAZIL

PORTUGAL

Wittkowitz Iron Works

Hospital 1869
Orphan Asylum
Home for Poor Musicians

1816 Vienna

Idra silver mines

Dalmatian asphalt lake

LUCCA

PAPAL
STATES

Naples
1821

GREECE

TURKEY

Baku Oil Fields

1854
Loan to Britain and France for Crimean War against Russia

Agricultural Colonies bought for Zionist settlers 1887

Loan to Britain for Suez Canal shares 1876

0          300
Miles

During the Civil War in the United States, 1861-1865, the Rothschilds lost money heavily by their support for the bonds of the southern Confederate States, who were defeated in 1865

57

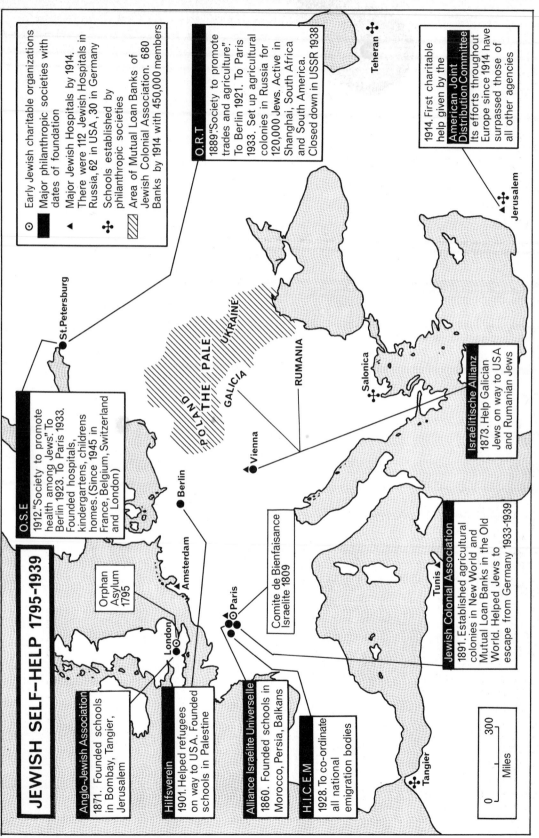

# JEWISH SELF–HELP 1795-1939

**Anglo-Jewish Association**
1871. Founded schools in Bombay, Tangier, Jerusalem

**Hilfsverein**
1901. Helped refugees on way to USA. Founded schools in Palestine

**Alliance Israélite Universelle**
1860. Founded schools in Morocco, Persia, Balkans

**H.I.C.E.M**
1928. To co-ordinate all national emigration bodies

**O.S.E**
1912. "Society to promote health among Jews". To Berlin 1923. To Paris 1933. Founded hospitals, kindergartens, childrens homes. (Since 1945 in France, Belgium, Switzerland and London)

**O.R.T**
1889. "Society to promote trades and agriculture". To Berlin 1921. To Paris 1933. Set up agricultural colonies in Russia for 120,000 Jews. Active in Shanghai, South Africa and South America. Closed down in USSR 1938

**American Joint Distribution Committee**
1914. First charitable help given by the American Joint Distribution Committee Its efforts throughout Europe since 1914 have surpassed those of all other agencies

**Israëlitische Allianz**
1873. Help Galician Jews on way to USA and Rumanian Jews

**Jewish Colonial Association**
1891. Established agricultural colonies in New World and Mutual Loan Banks in the Old World. Helped Jews to escape from Germany 1933-1939

Comité de Bienfaisance Israelite 1809

Orphan Asylum 1795

### Legend

⊙ Early Jewish charitable organizations

▮ Major philanthropic societies with dates of foundation

▲ Major Jewish Hospitals by 1914. There were 112 Jewish Hospitals in Russia, 62 in USA, 30 in Germany

✣ Schools established by philanthropic societies

▨ Area of Mutual Loan Banks of Jewish Colonial Association. 680 Banks by 1914 with 450,000 members

### Map labels

St.Petersburg
London
Amsterdam
Berlin
Paris
Vienna
POLAND THE PALE
GALICIA
UKRAINE
RUMANIA
Salonica
Jerusalem
Teheran
Tunis
Tangier

0 — 300 Miles

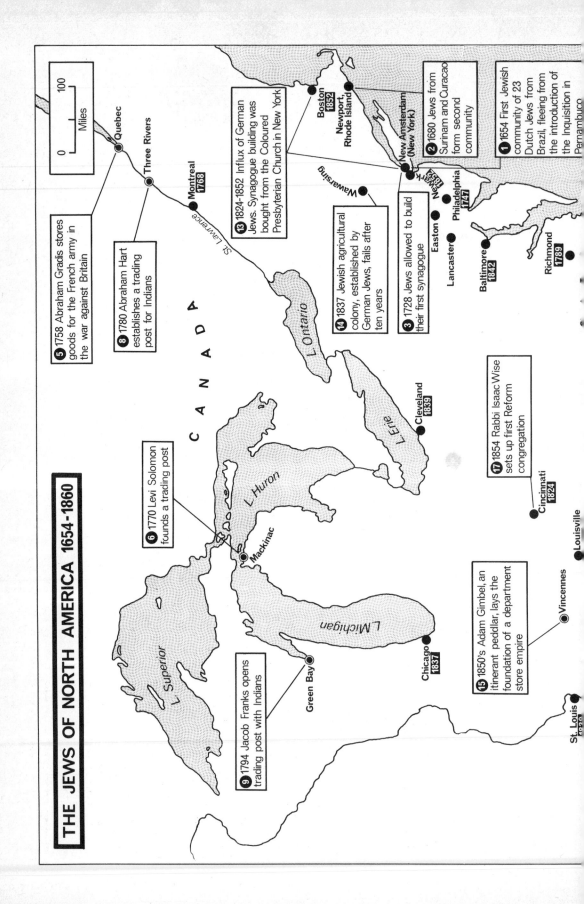

# THE JEWS OF NORTH AMERICA 1654-1860

0 — 100 Miles

**5** 1758 Abraham Gradis stores goods for the French army in the war against Britain

**8** 1780 Abraham Hart establishes a trading post for Indians

**6** 1770 Levi Solomon founds a trading post

**9** 1794 Jacob Franks opens trading post with Indians

**15** 1850's Adam Gimbel, an itinerant peddlar, lays the foundation of a department store empire

**17** 1854 Rabbi Isaac Wise sets up first Reform congregation

**13** 1824-1852 Influx of German Jews. Synagogue building was bought from the Coloured Presbyterian Church in New York

**14** 1837 Jewish agricultural colony, established by German Jews, fails after ten years

**3** 1728 Jews allowed to build their first synagogue

**2** 1680 Jews from Surinam and Curacao form second community

**1** 1654 First Jewish community of 23 Dutch Jews from Brazil, fleeing from the introduction of the Inquisition in Pernambuco

Quebec

Three Rivers

Montreal 1768

St. Lawrence

CANADA

L. Ontario

L. Erie

L. Huron

L. Superior

L. Michigan

Mackinac

Green Bay

Chicago 1837

St. Louis

Vincennes

Louisville

Cincinnati 1824

Cleveland 1839

Boston 1852

Newport, Rhode Island

New Amsterdam (New York)

New York

Wawarsing

Philadelphia 1747

Easton

Lancaster

Baltimore 1842

Richmond 1789

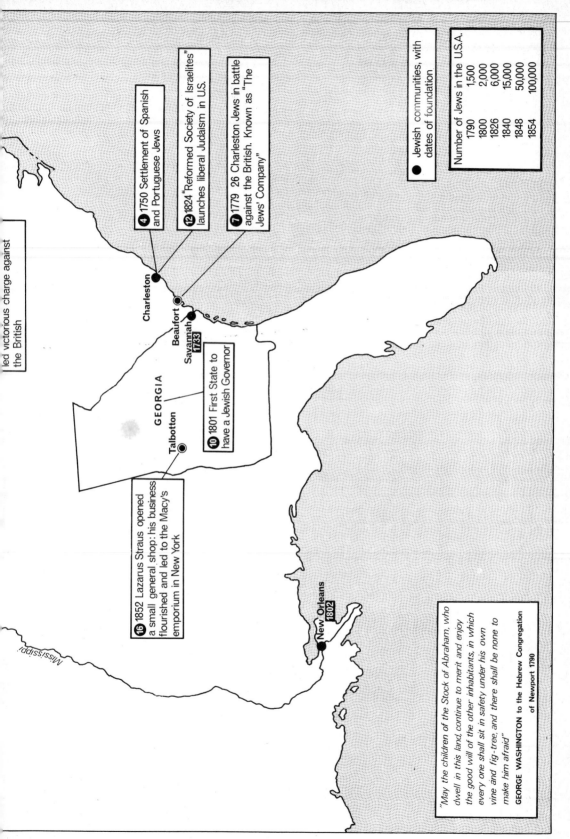

led victorious charge against the British

**④ 1750** Settlement of Spanish and Portuguese Jews

**⑫ 1824** "Reformed Society of Israelites" launches liberal Judaism in U.S.

**⑦ 1779** 26 Charleston Jews in battle against the British. Known as "The Jews' Company"

Charleston

Beaufort

Savannah **1733**

**GEORGIA**

**⑩ 1801** First State to have a Jewish Governor

Talbotton

**⑯ 1852** Lazarus Straus opened a small general shop: his business flourished and led to the Macy's emporium in New York

Mississippi

New Orleans **1802**

● Jewish communities, with dates of foundation

Number of Jews in the U.S.A.
| | |
|---|---|
| 1790 | 1,500 |
| 1800 | 2,000 |
| 1826 | 6,000 |
| 1840 | 15,000 |
| 1848 | 50,000 |
| 1854 | 100,000 |

*"May the children of the Stock of Abraham, who dwell in this land, continue to merit and enjoy the good will of the other inhabitants, in which every one shall sit in safety under his own vine and fig-tree, and there shall be none to make him afraid"*

**GEORGE WASHINGTON** to the Hebrew Congregation of Newport 1790

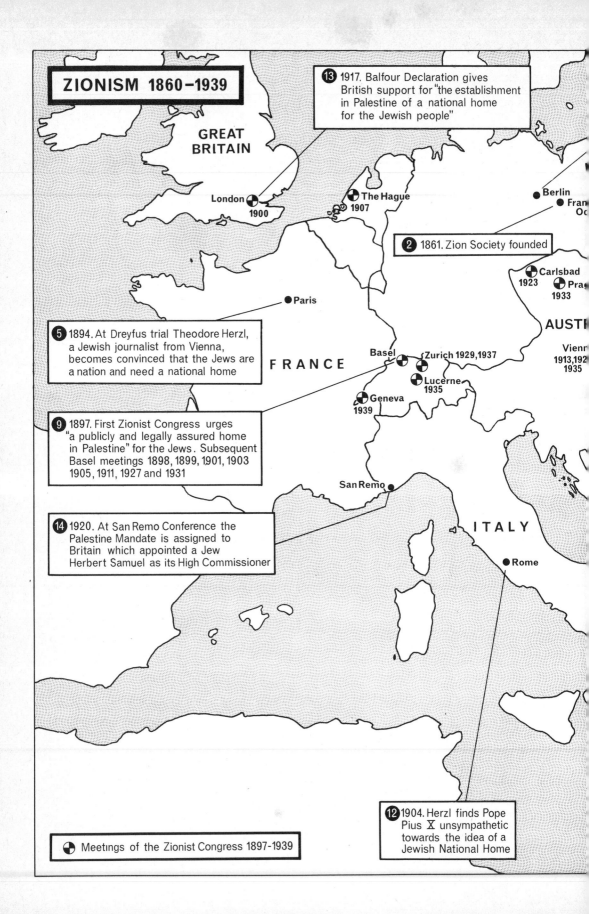

# ZIONISM 1860-1939

**GREAT BRITAIN**

London ⦿ 1900

⓭ 1917. Balfour Declaration gives British support for "the establishment in Palestine of a national home for the Jewish people"

The Hague 1907

● Berlin
● Fran
Oc

② 1861. Zion Society founded

⦿ Carlsbad 1923 ⦿ Pra 1933

● Paris

⑤ 1894. At Dreyfus trial Theodore Herzl, a Jewish journalist from Vienna, becomes convinced that the Jews are a nation and need a national home

**FRANCE**

Basel ⦿

⦿ Zurich 1929,1937

**AUST**

Vienn 1913,192 1935

⦿ Lucerne 1935

⦿ Geneva 1939

⑨ 1897. First Zionist Congress urges "a publicly and legally assured home in Palestine" for the Jews. Subsequent Basel meetings 1898, 1899, 1901, 1903 1905, 1911, 1927 and 1931

San Remo ●

⑭ 1920. At San Remo Conference the Palestine Mandate is assigned to Britain which appointed a Jew Herbert Samuel as its High Commissioner

**ITALY**

● Rome

⑫ 1904. Herzl finds Pope Pius Ⅹ unsympathetic towards the idea of a Jewish National Home

⦿ Meetings of the Zionist Congress 1897-1939

1882. Leo Pinsker in "Auto-Emancipation" urged Jews to seek a national retreat, preferably on the banks of the Jordan

● Vilna

**11** 1903. Herzl acclaimed "Herzl the King" during visit to Russia

● Thorn

**1** 1860. Conference discusses possibility of a Jewish home in Palestine

● Kattowitz

**R U S S I A**

**4** 1884. "Lovers of Zion" movement holds conference

**UNGARY**

Odessa ●

**6** 1896. Herzl publishes his "Jews' State" urging the Jews to seek their national home in Palestine. Its immediate impact was on Russian Jewry

**8** 1897. "Lovers of Zion" revitalized by Herzl, and by its new President, Ussishkin, a disciple of Ahad Ha-am, the spiritual prophet of Zionism

**B U L G A R I A**

Constantinople ●

T U R K E Y

**7** 1896. Herzl acclaimed as the Messiah

**10** 1901 Herzl has audience with Sultan. Asks in vain for Palestine as a Jewish national home

0        200
Miles

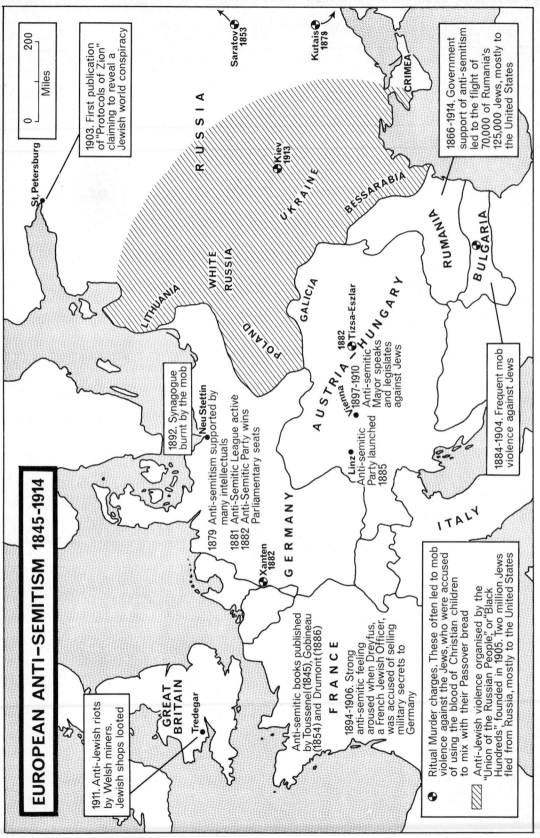

# EUROPEAN ANTI–SEMITISM 1845–1914

0 200
Miles

1903. First publication of "Protocols of Zion" claiming to reveal a Jewish world conspiracy

Saratov 1853

Kutais 1878

St. Petersburg

R U S S I A

Kiev 1913

U K R A I N E

WHITE RUSSIA

BESSARABIA

CRIMEA

LITHUANIA

POLAND

GALICIA

RUMANIA

BULGARIA

1866-1914. Government support of anti-semitism led to the flight of 70,000 of Rumania's 125,000 Jews, mostly to the United States

1892. Synagogue burnt by the mob

Neu Stettin

1879 Anti-semitism supported by many intellectuals
1881 Anti-Semitic League active
1882 Anti-Semitic Party wins Parliamentary seats

A U S T R I A 1882

Vienna Tizsa-Eszlar
1897-1910 Anti-semitic Mayor speaks and legislates against Jews

H U N G A R Y

Linz
Anti-semitic Party launched 1885

1884-1904. Frequent mob violence against Jews

Xanten 1882

G E R M A N Y

I T A L Y

Anti-semitic books published by Toussenel (1845), Gobineau (1854) and Drumont (1886)

F R A N C E

1894-1906. Strong anti-semitic feeling aroused when Dreyfus, a French Jewish Officer, was accused of selling military secrets to Germany

GREAT BRITAIN

Tredegar

1911. Anti-Jewish riots by Welsh miners. Jewish shops looted

Ritual Murder charges. These often led to mob violence against the Jews, who were accused of using the blood of Christian children to mix with their Passover bread

Anti-Jewish violence organised by the "Union of the Russian People," or "Black Hundreds" founded in 1905. Two million Jews fled from Russia, mostly to the United States

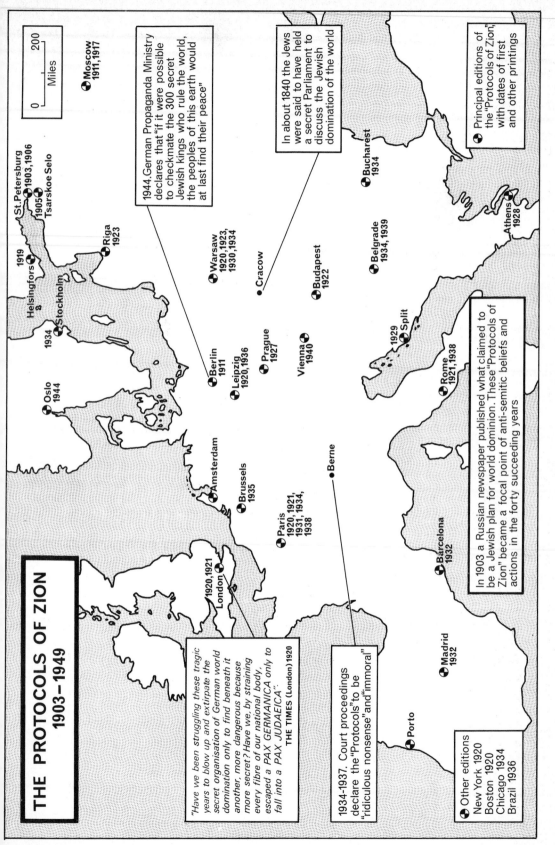

## THE PROTOCOLS OF ZION
### 1903–1949

0    200
Miles

Moscow
1911, 1917

St.Petersburg
1903, 1906
1905
Tsarskoe Selo

Helsingfors
1919

Riga
1923

Stockholm
1934

Oslo
1944

Berlin
1911

Leipzig
1920, 1936

Prague
1927

Warsaw
1920, 1923,
1930, 1934

Cracow

Vienna
1940

Budapest
1922

Belgrade
1934, 1939

Bucharest
1934

Athens
1928

Amsterdam

Brussels
1935

Paris
1920, 1921,
1931, 1934,
1938

Berne

Split
1929

Rome
1921, 1938

London
1920, 1921

Barcelona
1932

Madrid
1932

Porto

1944. German Propaganda Ministry declares that "if it were possible to checkmate the 300 secret Jewish kings who rule the world, the peoples of this earth would at last find their peace"

In about 1840 the Jews were said to have held a secret Parliament to discuss the Jewish domination of the world

In 1903 a Russian newspaper published what claimed to be a Jewish plan for world dominion. These "Protocols of Zion" became a focal point of anti-semitic beliefs and actions in the forty succeeding years

"Have we been struggling these tragic years to blow up and extirpate the secret organisation of German world domination only to find beneath it another, more dangerous because more secret? Have we, by straining every fibre of our national body, escaped a PAX GERMANICA only to fall into a PAX JUDAEICA".
**THE TIMES (London) 1920**

1934–1937. Court proceedings declare the "Protocols" to be "ridiculous nonsense" and "immoral"

Principal editions of the "Protocols of Zion," with dates of first and other printings

Other editions
New York 1920
Boston 1920
Chicago 1934
Brazil 1936

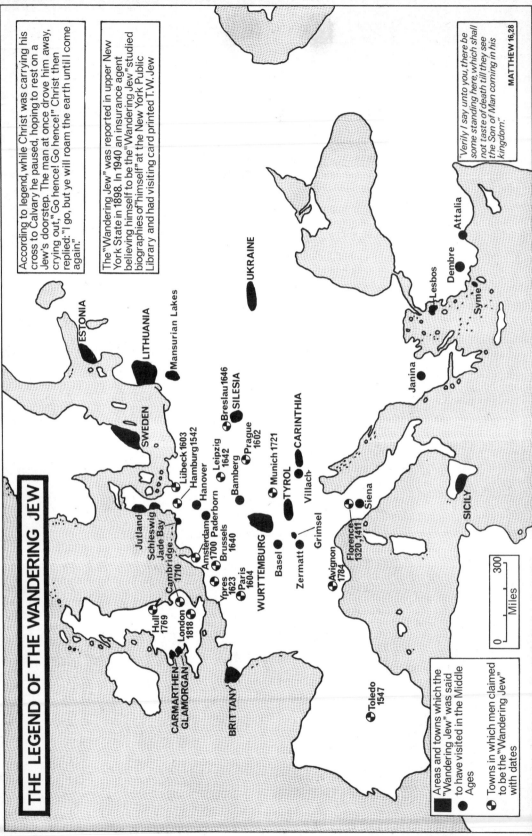

# THE LEGEND OF THE WANDERING JEW

According to legend, while Christ was carrying his cross to Calvary he paused, hoping to rest on a Jew's doorstep. The man at once drove him away, crying out, "Go hence! Go hence!" Christ then replied: "I go, but ye will roam the earth untill come again."

The "Wandering Jew" was reported in upper New York State in 1898. In 1940 an insurance agent believing himself to be the "Wandering Jew" studied biographies of "himself" at the New York Public Library and had visiting card printed T.W. Jew

"Verily I say unto you, there be some standing here, which shall not taste of death till they see the Son of Man coming in his kingdom."

MATTHEW 16,28

ESTONIA

LITHUANIA

Mansurian Lakes

SWEDEN

UKRAINE

Breslau1646
SILESIA

Lübeck 1603
Hamburg1542
Hanover
Leipzig 1642
Bamberg
Prague 1602

Munich 1721
TYROL
CARINTHIA
Villach

Jutland
Schleswig
Jade Bay
Amsterdam
1700 Paderborn
Brussels
1640

Janina

Lesbos
Dembre   Attalia
Syme

Cambridge
1710

Ypres
1623
Paris
1604

WURTTEMBURG

Basel
Grimsel
Zermatt

Siena

Hull
1769
London
1818

Avignon
1784

Florence
1320,1411

SICILY

CARMARTHEN
GLAMORGAN

BRITTANY

Toledo
1547

0    Miles    300

Areas and towns which the "Wandering Jew" was said to have visited in the Middle Ages

Towns in which men claimed to be the "Wandering Jew" with dates

63

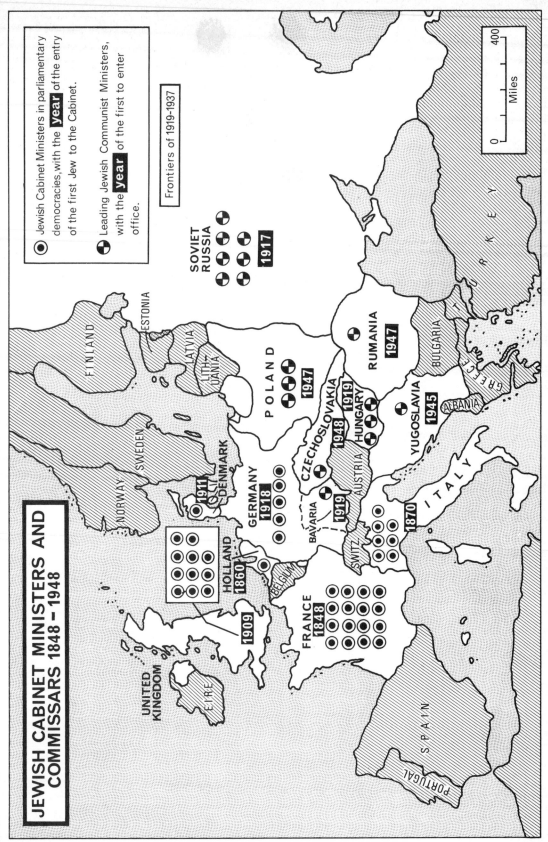

# JEWISH CABINET MINISTERS AND COMMISSARS 1848–1948

Jewish Cabinet Ministers in parliamentary democracies, with the **year** of the entry of the first Jew to the Cabinet.

Leading Jewish Communist Ministers, with the **year** of the first to enter office.

Frontiers of 1919–1937

SOVIET RUSSIA 1917

FINLAND

ESTONIA

LATVIA

LITH-UANIA

NORWAY

SWEDEN

DENMARK 1911

POLAND 1947

RUMANIA 1947

CZECHOSLOVAKIA 1948

HUNGARY 1919

BULGARIA

GREECE

TURKEY

ALBANIA 1945

YUGOSLAVIA 1945

AUSTRIA 1919

BAVARIA 1919

GERMANY 1918

SWITZ.

ITALY 1870

BELGIUM

FRANCE 1848

HOLLAND 1860

UNITED KINGDOM 1909

EIRE

SPAIN

PORTUGAL

0        400
Miles

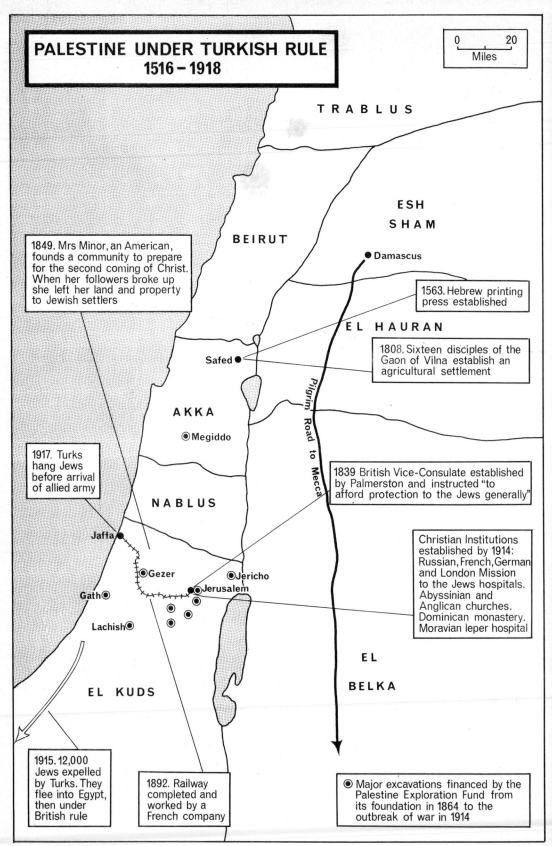

# PALESTINE UNDER TURKISH RULE 1516–1918

0    20
Miles

T R A B L U S

E S H
S H A M

B E I R U T

● Damascus

1849. Mrs Minor, an American, founds a community to prepare for the second coming of Christ. When her followers broke up she left her land and property to Jewish settlers

1563. Hebrew printing press established

E L   H A U R A N

1808. Sixteen disciples of the Gaon of Vilna establish an agricultural settlement

Safed ●

A K K A

◉ Megiddo

1917. Turks hang Jews before arrival of allied army

N A B L U S

1839 British Vice-Consulate established by Palmerston and instructed "to afford protection to the Jews generally"

Christian Institutions established by 1914: Russian, French, German and London Mission to the Jews hospitals. Abyssinian and Anglican churches. Dominican monastery. Moravian leper hospital

Jaffa ●

◉ Gezer

◉ Jericho

◉ Jerusalem

Gath ◉

◉
◉ ◉
◉

E L
B E L K A

Lachish ◉

E L   K U D S

1915. 12,000 Jews expelled by Turks. They flee into Egypt, then under British rule

1892. Railway completed and worked by a French company

◉ Major excavations financed by the Palestine Exploration Fund from its foundation in 1864 to the outbreak of war in 1914

Pilgrim Road to Mecca

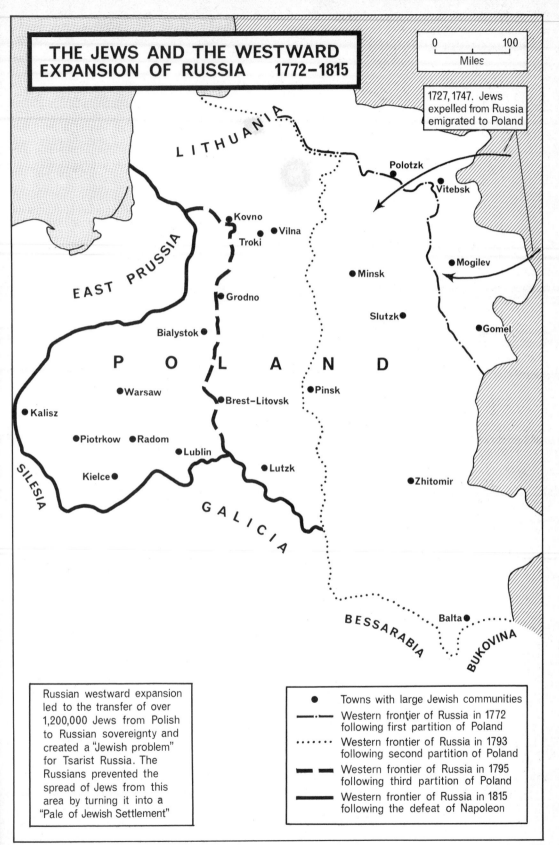

# THE JEWS AND THE WESTWARD EXPANSION OF RUSSIA    1772–1815

0 — 100
Miles

1727, 1747. Jews expelled from Russia emigrated to Poland

LITHUANIA

Polotzk

Vitebsk

EAST PRUSSIA

Kovno

Vilna

Troki

Mogilev

Grodno

Minsk

Bialystok

Slutzk●

Gomel

P   O   L   A   N   D

Warsaw

Brest–Litovsk

Pinsk

Kalisz

Piotrkow   ●Radom

Lublin

Lutzk

Kielce●

Zhitomir

SILESIA

GALICIA

BESSARABIA

Balta●

BUKOVINA

Russian westward expansion led to the transfer of over 1,200,000 Jews from Polish to Russian sovereignty and created a "Jewish problem" for Tsarist Russia. The Russians prevented the spread of Jews from this area by turning it into a "Pale of Jewish Settlement"

●       Towns with large Jewish communities
—·—   Western frontier of Russia in 1772 following first partition of Poland
·······   Western frontier of Russia in 1793 following second partition of Poland
▬ ▬   Western frontier of Russia in 1795 following third partition of Poland
▬▬▬   Western frontier of Russia in 1815 following the defeat of Napoleon

66

## THE PALE 1835–1917

0 — 200
Miles

Baltic Sea

● St.Petersburg

1891. 2,000 Jews deported,
many of them in chains

1865. Open to Jews

● Moscow

1891. 20,000 Jews expelled

KOVNO

VITEBSK

GERMANY

SUWALKI

VILNA

MOGILEV

PLOCK

LOMZA

GRODNO

WARSAW

KALISZ

SYEDLITZ

MINSK

PIOTRKOW

RADOM

SYEDLITZ

KIELCE

LUBLIN

CHERNIGOV

Brody ●

VOLHYNIA

Kiev ●

AUSTRIA-HUNGARY

POLTAVA

KIEV

PODOLIA

EKATERINOSLAV

BESSARABIA

RUMANIA

KHERSON

Nikolaev ●

T A U R I D A

Principal town from which in
1880 began the exodus of
over two million Jews from
the Pale to the United States,
Britain, Europe, South America,
and Palestine

Sebastopol ● ● Yalta

Black Sea

In 1882 500,000 Jews living in rural areas
of the Pale were forced to leave their
homes and live in towns or townlets (shtetls)
in the Pale. 250,000 Jews living along the
western frontier of Russia were also moved
into the Pale. 700,000 Jews living east of
the Pale were driven into the Pale by 1891

☐ The Pale of Settlement. Russian
Jews confined to this area
by laws of 1795 and 1835. By 1885
there were over 4 million Jews
living in the Pale

● Towns within the Pale barred
to Jews without special residence
permits

# POVERTY AND CHARITY AMONG RUSSIAN JEWS IN 1900

Legend:

- 22% of Jews in receipt of poor relief from the Jewish community
- 20% on receipt of poor relief. No province in the Pale had less than 14% of its Jews on relief
- ● Cities in which over one in every four of all Jews received free fuel from the Fuel Charities organised by the Jewish community
- Principal houses of shelter for poor vagrants

*"Fully 80% of the Jewish population of Vilna do not know in the evening where they will obtain food the next morning"*
**BAER RATNER 1906**

R U S S I A

Dvinsk
Kovno
Vilna
Minsk
Warsaw
Zhitomir
Berdychev
Poltava
Kremenchug
Ekaterinoslav
Elizavetgrad
Nikolaev
Kherson
Odessa

Among the charitable societies organised by the Jews were those to supply poor students with clothes, soldiers with kosher food, the poor with free medical treatment, poor brides with dowries and orphans with technical education

At the cheap eating house in Odessa 400 dinners were provided daily, over 150 without charge

0    100
Miles

68

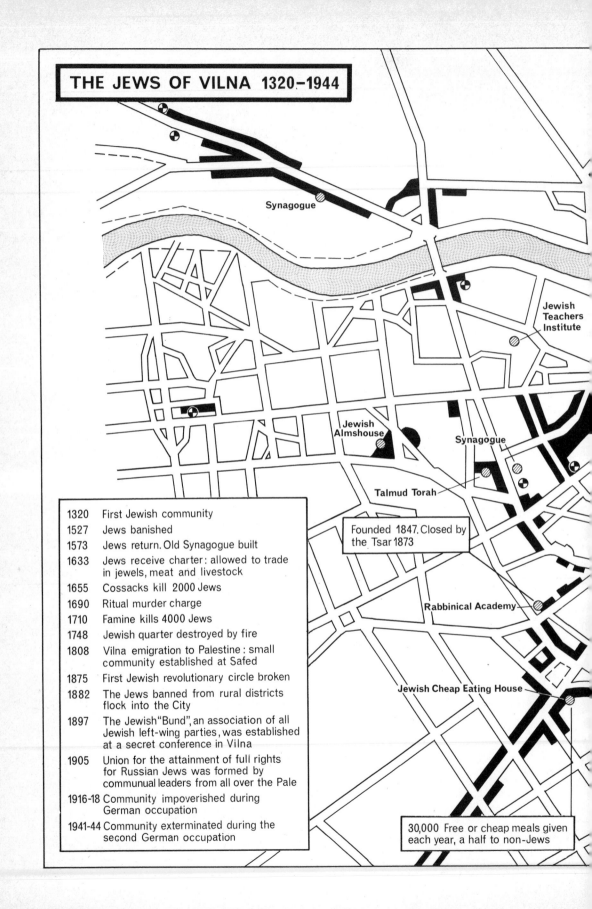

# THE JEWS OF VILNA 1320-1944

Synagogue

Jewish
Teachers
Institute

Jewish
Almshouse

Synagogue

Talmud Torah

Founded 1847. Closed by
the Tsar 1873

Rabbinical Academy

Jewish Cheap Eating House

| 1320 | First Jewish community |
|------|------------------------|
| 1527 | Jews banished |
| 1573 | Jews return. Old Synagogue built |
| 1633 | Jews receive charter: allowed to trade in jewels, meat and livestock |
| 1655 | Cossacks kill 2000 Jews |
| 1690 | Ritual murder charge |
| 1710 | Famine kills 4000 Jews |
| 1748 | Jewish quarter destroyed by fire |
| 1808 | Vilna emigration to Palestine: small community established at Safed |
| 1875 | First Jewish revolutionary circle broken |
| 1882 | The Jews banned from rural districts flock into the City |
| 1897 | The Jewish "Bund", an association of all Jewish left-wing parties, was established at a secret conference in Vilna |
| 1905 | Union for the attainment of full rights for Russian Jews was formed by communal leaders from all over the Pale |
| 1916-18 | Community impoverished during German occupation |
| 1941-44 | Community exterminated during the second German occupation |

30,000 Free or cheap meals given
each year, a half to non-Jews

From the time of the Vilna Gaon (1720-1797) Vilna was a centre of Jewish intellectual, cultural and political life. It was known as "The Citadel of Culture". In 1900 it had 150,000 Jewish inhabitants.

New
Jewish Cemetery

Old
Jewish
Cemetery

anical Gardens

hedral

Public Library

Old
Synagogue

Jewish
Hospital

to St.Petersburg→

New Synagogue

to Warsaw

Station

Jewish quarter by 1655
Jewish quarters by 1914
Schools of adult religious instruction in 1914

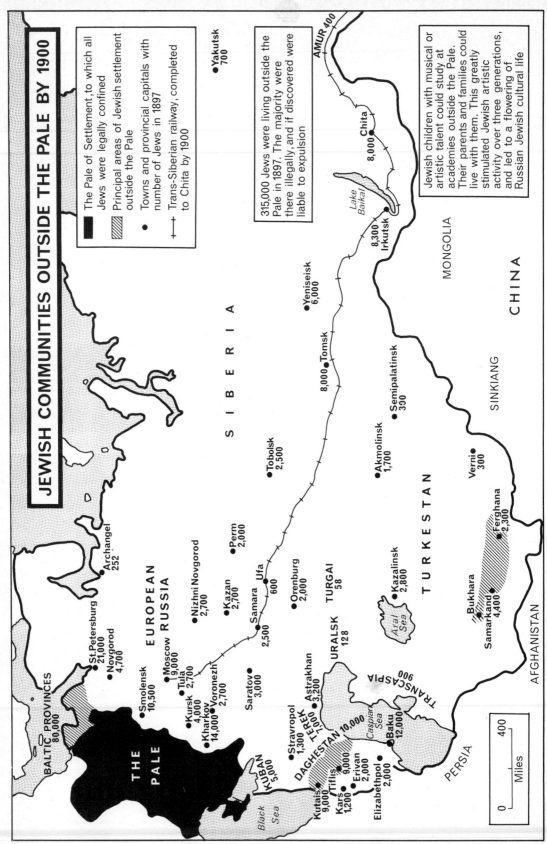

# JEWISH COMMUNITIES OUTSIDE THE PALE BY 1900

The Pale of Settlement, to which all Jews were legally confined

Principal areas of Jewish settlement outside the Pale

Towns and provincial capitals with number of Jews in 1897

Trans-Siberian railway, completed to Chita by 1900

315,000 Jews were living outside the Pale in 1897. The majority were there illegally, and if discovered were liable to expulsion

Jewish children with musical or artistic talent could study at academies outside the Pale. Their parents and families could live with them. This greatly stimulated Jewish artistic activity over three generations, and led to a flowering of Russian Jewish cultural life

EUROPEAN RUSSIA

SIBERIA

THE PALE

BALTIC PROVINCES 80,000

St. Petersburg 21,000

Novgorod 4,700

Archangel 252

Smolensk 10,500

Moscow 9,000

Tula 2,700

Kursk 4,000

Kharkov 14,000

Voronezh 2,700

Nizhni Novgorod 2,700

Kazan 2,700

Samara 2,500

Perm 2,000

Ufa 600

Orenburg 2,000

Saratov 3,000

URALSK 128

TURGAI 58

Kazalinsk 2,800

Aral Sea

Tobolsk 2,500

Akmolinsk 1,700

Semipalatinsk 300

Tomsk 8,000

Yeniseisk 6,000

Irkutsk 8,300

Lake Baikal

Chita 8,000

AMUR 400

Yakutsk 700

MONGOLIA

CHINA

SINKIANG

TURKESTAN

Bukhara

Samarkand 4,400

Ferghana 2,300

Verni 300

AFGHANISTAN

PERSIA

TRANSCASPIA 900

Baku 12,000

Caspian Sea

Astrakhan 3,200

Stravropol 1,300

TEREK 7,000

DAGHESTAN 10,000

KUBAN 5,000

Kutais 9,000

Tiflis 9,000

Kars 1,200

Erivan 9,000

Elizabethpol 2,000

Black Sea

0    400
Miles

70

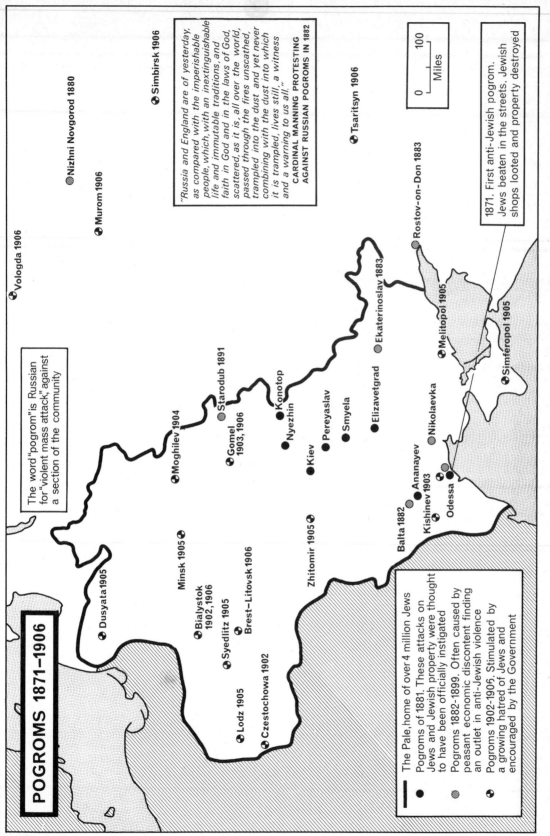

# POGROMS 1871–1906

The word "pogrom" is Russian for "violent mass attack," against a section of the community

"Russia and England are of yesterday, as compared with the imperishable people, which, with an inextinguishable life and immutable traditions, and faith in God and in the laws of God, scattered, as it is, all over the world, passed through the fires unscathed, trampled into the dust and yet never combining with the dust into which it is trampled, lives still, a witness and a warning to us all."
CARDINAL MANNING PROTESTING AGAINST RUSSIAN POGROMS IN 1882

1871. First anti-Jewish pogrom. Jews beaten in the streets. Jewish shops looted and property destroyed

Vologda 1906
Nizhni Novgorod 1880
Murom 1906
Simbirsk 1906
Tsaritsyn 1906
Rostov-on-Don 1883
Dusyata 1905
Minsk 1905
Moghilev 1904
Starodub 1891
Bialystok 1902, 1906
Syedlitz 1905
Brest–Litovsk 1906
Gomel 1903, 1906
Konotop
Nyezhin
Lodz 1905
Czestochowa 1902
Zhitomir 1905
Kiev
Pereyaslav
Smyela
Elizavetgrad
Ekaterinoslav 1883
Melitopol 1905
Simferopol 1905
Balta 1882
Ananayev
Kishinev 1903
Nikolaevka
Odessa

0    100
Miles

The Pale, home of over 4 million Jews

Pogroms of 1881. These attacks on Jews and Jewish property were thought to have been officially instigated

Pogroms 1882-1899. Often caused by peasant economic discontent finding an outlet in anti-Jewish violence

Pogroms 1902-1906. Stimulated by a growing hatred of Jews and encouraged by the Government

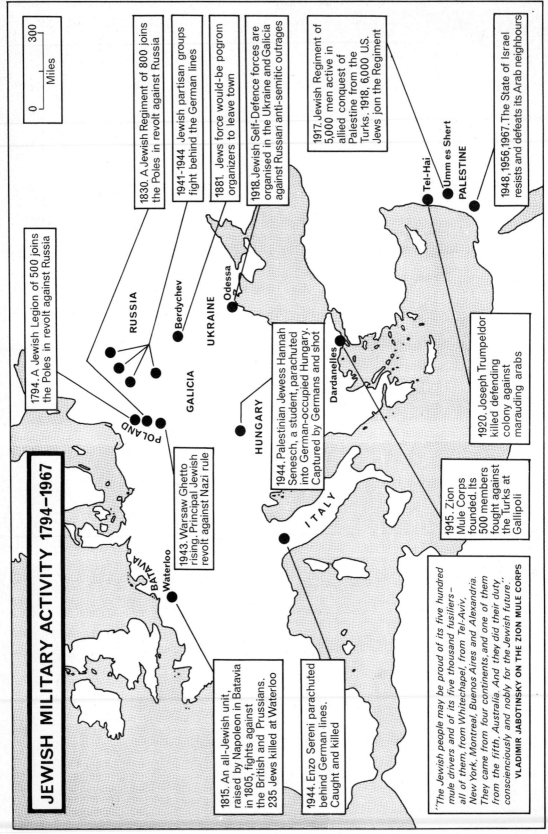

# JEWISH MILITARY ACTIVITY 1794–1967

0    300
Miles

1794. A Jewish Legion of 500 joins the Poles in revolt against Russia

1830. A Jewish Regiment of 800 joins the Poles in revolt against Russia

1941-1944. Jewish partisan groups fight behind the German lines

1881. Jews force would-be pogrom organizers to leave town

1918. Jewish Self-Defence forces are organised in the Ukraine and Galicia against Russian anti-semitic outrages

1917. Jewish Regiment of 5,000 men active in allied conquest of Palestine from the Turks. 1918, 6,000 U.S. Jews join the Regiment

1948, 1956, 1967. The State of Israel resists and defeats its Arab neighbours

1943. Warsaw Ghetto rising. Principal Jewish revolt against Nazi rule

1944. Palestinian Jewess Hannah Senesch, a student, parachuted into German-occupied Hungary. Captured by Germans and shot

1920. Joseph Trumpeldor killed defending colony against marauding arabs

1815. An all-Jewish unit, raised by Napoleon in Batavia in 1805, fights against the British and Prussians. 235 Jews killed at Waterloo

1944. Enzo Sereni parachuted behind German lines. Caught and killed

1915. Zion Mule Corps founded. Its 500 members fought against the Turks at Gallipoli

"The Jewish people may be proud of its five hundred mule drivers and of its five thousand fusiliers – all of them, from Whitechapel, from Tel-Aviv, New York, Montreal, Buenos Aires and Alexandria. They came from four continents, and one of them from the fifth, Australia. And they did their duty, conscienciously and nobly for the Jewish future."
VLADIMIR JABOTINSKY ON THE ZION MULE CORPS

RUSSIA

Berdychev

UKRAINE

Odessa

GALICIA

POLAND

Waterloo

BATAVIA

HUNGARY

ITALY

Dardanelles

Tel-Hai
Umm es Shert
PALESTINE

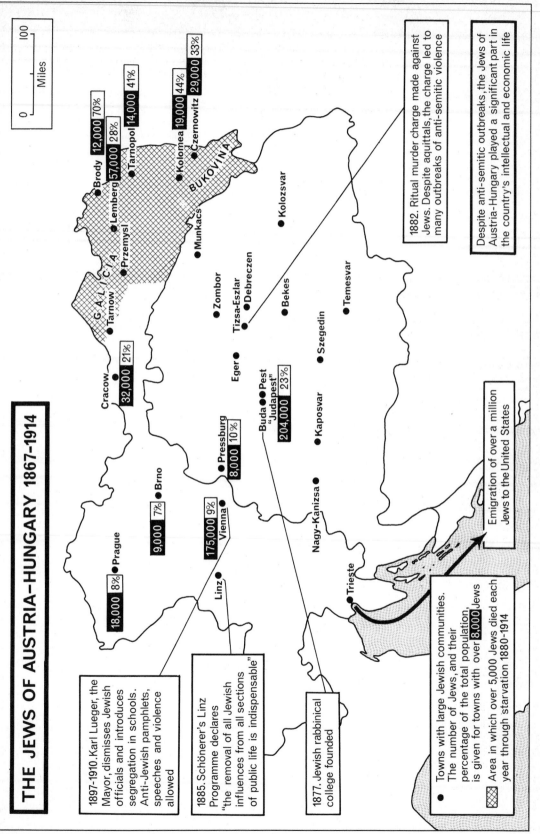

# THE JEWS OF AUSTRIA–HUNGARY 1867-1914

0 — 100 Miles

**Brody** 12,000 70%
**Lemberg** 57,000 28%
**Tarnopol** 14,000 41%
**Kolomea** 19,000 44%
**Czernowitz** 29,000 33%

Przemysl
GALICIA
BUKOVINA
Munkacs
Kolozsvar

Cracow 32,000 21%
Tarnow

Zombor
Tizsa-Eszlar
Debreczen
Bekes
Temesvar
Eger
Szegedin
Kaposvar

Prague 18,000 8%
Brno 9,000 7%
Pressburg 8,000 10%
Vienna 175,000 9%
Linz

Buda ● ● Pest
"Judapest"
204,000 23%

Nagy-Kanizsa

Trieste

1897-1910. Karl Lueger, the Mayor, dismisses Jewish officials and introduces segregation in schools. Anti-Jewish pamphlets, speeches and violence allowed

1885. Schönerer's Linz Programme declares "the removal of all Jewish influences from all sections of public life is indispensable"

1877. Jewish rabbinical college founded

1882. Ritual murder charge made against Jews. Despite aquittals, the charge led to many outbreaks of anti-semitic violence

Despite anti-semitic outbreaks, the Jews of Austria-Hungary played a significant part in the country's intellectual and economic life

Emigration of over a million Jews to the United States

● Towns with large Jewish communities. The number of Jews, and their percentage of the total population, is given for towns with over 8,000 Jews

▨ Area in which over 5,000 Jews died each year through starvation 1880-1914

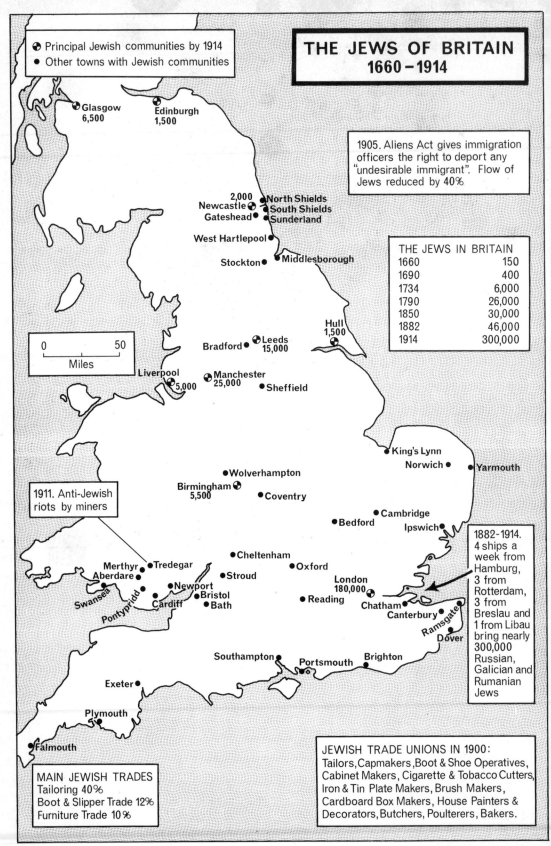

# THE JEWS OF BRITAIN
# 1660–1914

● Principal Jewish communities by 1914
• Other towns with Jewish communities

1905. Aliens Act gives immigration officers the right to deport any "undesirable immigrant". Flow of Jews reduced by 40%

THE JEWS IN BRITAIN
| | |
|---|---:|
| 1660 | 150 |
| 1690 | 400 |
| 1734 | 6,000 |
| 1790 | 26,000 |
| 1850 | 30,000 |
| 1882 | 46,000 |
| 1914 | 300,000 |

Glasgow 6,500
Edinburgh 1,500

Newcastle 2,000
North Shields
South Shields
Gateshead
Sunderland
West Hartlepool
Stockton
Middlesborough

Hull 1,500

Bradford
Leeds 15,000

Liverpool 5,000
Manchester 25,000
Sheffield

0    50
Miles

King's Lynn
Norwich
Yarmouth

Wolverhampton
Birmingham 5,500
Coventry

Cambridge
Bedford
Ipswich

1911. Anti-Jewish riots by miners

Cheltenham
Oxford

Merthyr
Tredegar
Aberdare
Stroud
Newport
Swansea
Pontypridd
Cardiff
Bristol
Bath
Reading

London 180,000
Chatham
Canterbury
Ramsgate
Dover

1882–1914. 4 ships a week from Hamburg, 3 from Rotterdam, 3 from Breslau and 1 from Libau bring nearly 300,000 Russian, Galician and Rumanian Jews

Southampton
Portsmouth
Brighton

Exeter

Plymouth

Falmouth

MAIN JEWISH TRADES
Tailoring 40%
Boot & Slipper Trade 12%
Furniture Trade 10%

JEWISH TRADE UNIONS IN 1900:
Tailors, Capmakers, Boot & Shoe Operatives, Cabinet Makers, Cigarette & Tobacco Cutters, Iron & Tin Plate Makers, Brush Makers, Cardboard Box Makers, House Painters & Decorators, Butchers, Poulterers, Bakers.

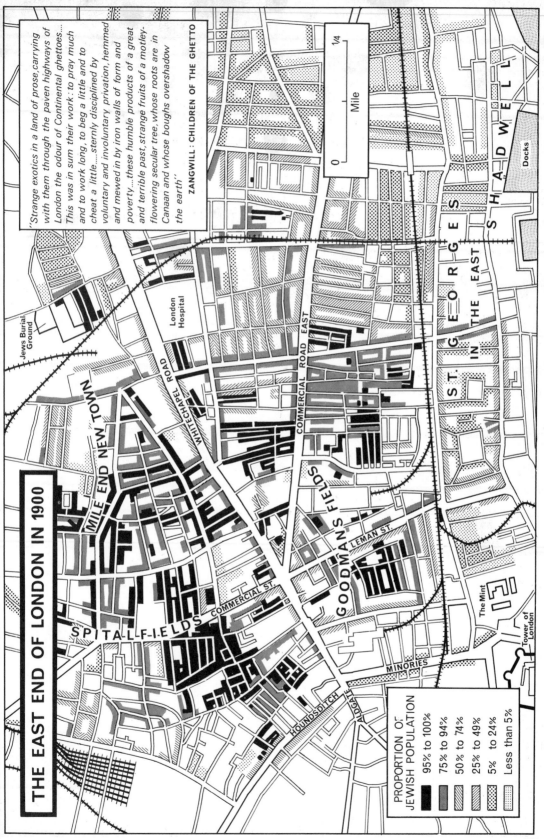

# THE EAST END OF LONDON IN 1900

SPITALFIELDS

MILE END NEW TOWN

Jews Burial Ground

WHITECHAPEL ROAD

London Hospital

COMMERCIAL ROAD EAST

COMMERCIAL ST

GOODMANS FIELDS

LEMAN ST.

ST. GEORGES IN THE EAST

SHADWELL

Docks

The Mint

Tower of London

MINORIES

ALDGATE

HOUNDSDITCH

*"Strange exotics in a land of prose, carrying with them through the paven highways of London the odour of Continental ghettoes.... This was in sum their work : to pray much and to work long, to beg a little and to cheat a little....sternly disciplined by voluntary and involuntary privation, hemmed and mewed in by iron walls of form and poverty....these humble products of a great and terrible past, strange fruits of a motley-flowering secular tree, whose roots are in Canaan and whose boughs overshadow the earth"*

**ZANGWILL : CHILDREN OF THE GHETTO**

0 — ¼ — Mile

PROPORTION OF JEWISH POPULATION

- 95% to 100%
- 75% to 94%
- 50% to 74%
- 25% to 49%
- 5% to 24%
- Less than 5%

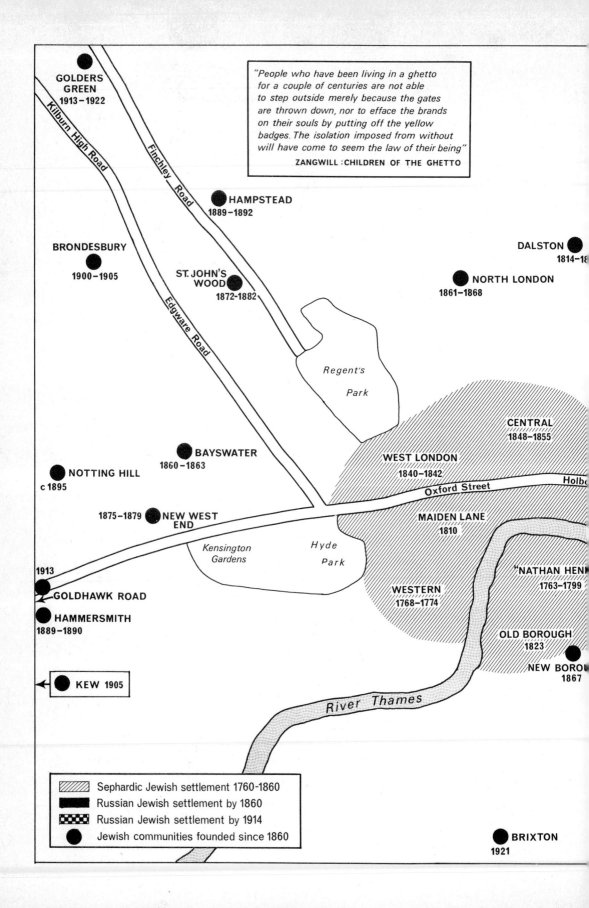

GOLDERS
GREEN
1913–1922

Kilburn High Road

Finchley Road

HAMPSTEAD
1889–1892

BRONDESBURY
1900–1905

ST. JOHN'S
WOOD
1872–1882

Edgware Road

*"People who have been living in a ghetto
for a couple of centuries are not able
to step outside merely because the gates
are thrown down, nor to efface the brands
on their souls by putting off the yellow
badges. The isolation imposed from without
will have come to seem the law of their being"*
ZANGWILL : CHILDREN OF THE GHETTO

DALSTON
1814–18

NORTH LONDON
1861–1868

*Regent's
Park*

CENTRAL
1848–1855

BAYSWATER
1860–1863

NOTTING HILL
c 1895

WEST LONDON
1840–1842

Oxford Street

Holb

1875–1879 NEW WEST
END

*Kensington
Gardens*

*Hyde
Park*

MAIDEN LANE
1810

1913

GOLDHAWK ROAD

HAMMERSMITH
1889–1890

WESTERN
1768–1774

"NATHAN HENR
1763–1799

OLD BOROUGH
1823

NEW BORO
1867

KEW 1905

*River Thames*

Sephardic Jewish settlement 1760-1860
Russian Jewish settlement by 1860
Russian Jewish settlement by 1914
Jewish communities founded since 1860

BRIXTON
1921

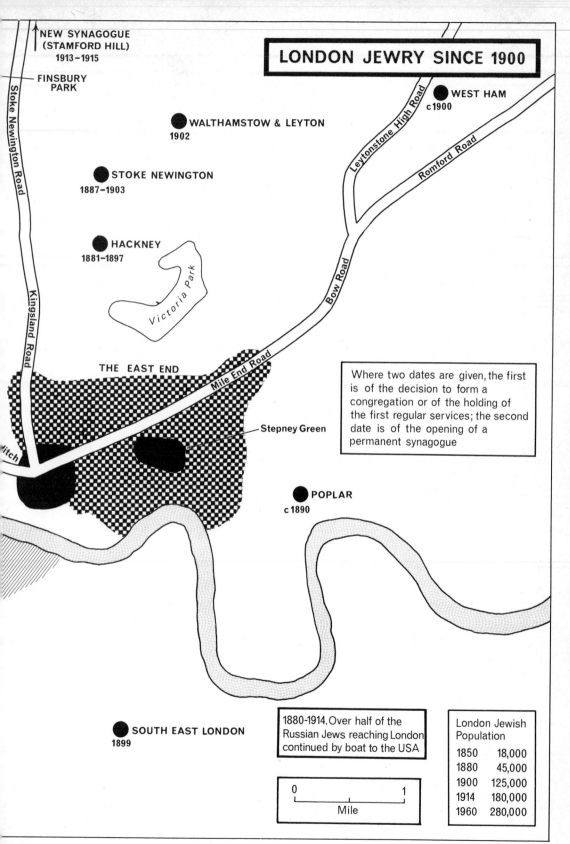

NEW SYNAGOGUE
(STAMFORD HILL)
1913–1915

FINSBURY
PARK

Stoke Newington Road

Kingsland Road

## LONDON JEWRY SINCE 1900

WEST HAM
c 1900

Leytonstone High Road

Romford Road

WALTHAMSTOW & LEYTON
1902

STOKE NEWINGTON
1887–1903

HACKNEY
1881–1897

Victoria Park

Bow Road

THE EAST END

Mile End Road

Stepney Green

itch

Where two dates are given, the first
is of the decision to form a
congregation or of the holding of
the first regular services; the second
date is of the opening of a
permanent synagogue

POPLAR
c 1890

SOUTH EAST LONDON
1899

1880-1914. Over half of the
Russian Jews reaching London
continued by boat to the USA

| 0 | 1 |
|---|---|
| Mile | |

| London Jewish Population | |
|---|---|
| 1850 | 18,000 |
| 1880 | 45,000 |
| 1900 | 125,000 |
| 1914 | 180,000 |
| 1960 | 280,000 |

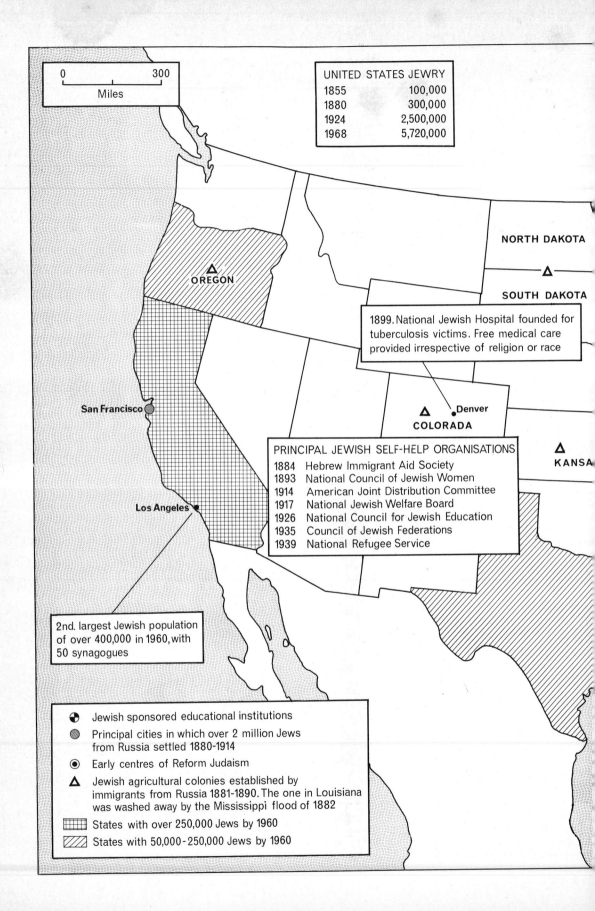

0                  300
Miles

| UNITED STATES JEWRY | |
|---|---|
| 1855 | 100,000 |
| 1880 | 300,000 |
| 1924 | 2,500,000 |
| 1968 | 5,720,000 |

NORTH DAKOTA

SOUTH DAKOTA

1899. National Jewish Hospital founded for tuberculosis victims. Free medical care provided irrespective of religion or race

OREGON

San Francisco

Los Angeles

Denver
COLORADA

KANSA

PRINCIPAL JEWISH SELF-HELP ORGANISATIONS
| 1884 | Hebrew Immigrant Aid Society |
| 1893 | National Council of Jewish Women |
| 1914 | American Joint Distribution Committee |
| 1917 | National Jewish Welfare Board |
| 1926 | National Council for Jewish Education |
| 1935 | Council of Jewish Federations |
| 1939 | National Refugee Service |

2nd. largest Jewish population of over 400,000 in 1960, with 50 synagogues

- ◕ Jewish sponsored educational institutions
- ◓ Principal cities in which over 2 million Jews from Russia settled 1880-1914
- ◉ Early centres of Reform Judaism
- △ Jewish agricultural colonies established by immigrants from Russia 1881-1890. The one in Louisiana was washed away by the Mississippi flood of 1882
- ▦ States with over 250,000 Jews by 1960
- ▨ States with 50,000-250,000 Jews by 1960

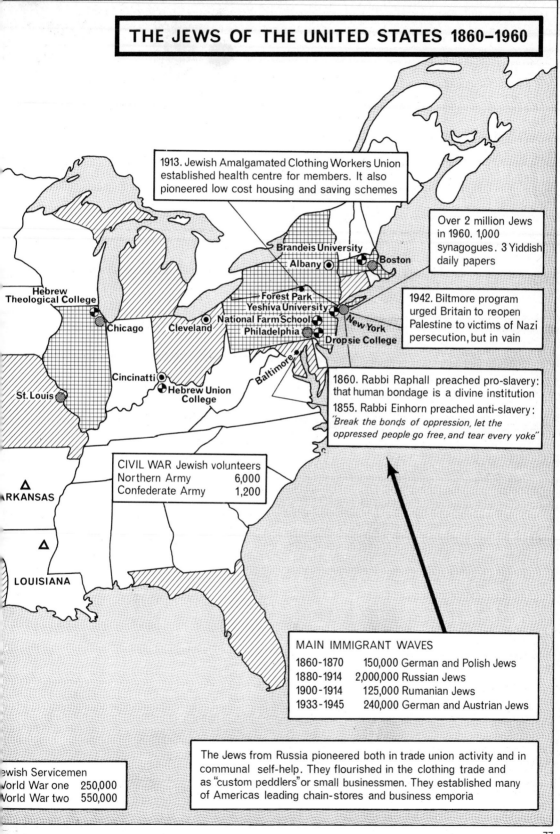

# THE JEWS OF THE UNITED STATES 1860–1960

**1913.** Jewish Amalgamated Clothing Workers Union established health centre for members. It also pioneered low cost housing and saving schemes

Over 2 million Jews in 1960. 1,000 synagogues. 3 Yiddish daily papers

Brandeis University

Albany

Boston

Hebrew Theological College

Forest Park
Yeshiva University
National Farm School
Philadelphia

Chicago

Cleveland

New York

Dropsie College

**1942.** Biltmore program urged Britain to reopen Palestine to victims of Nazi persecution, but in vain

Cincinatti

Hebrew Union College

Baltimore

St. Louis

**1860.** Rabbi Raphall preached pro-slavery: that human bondage is a divine institution

**1855.** Rabbi Einhorn preached anti-slavery: "Break the bonds of oppression, let the oppressed people go free, and tear every yoke"

CIVIL WAR Jewish volunteers
Northern Army        6,000
Confederate Army     1,200

△
ARKANSAS

△

LOUISIANA

MAIN IMMIGRANT WAVES

| 1860-1870 | 150,000 German and Polish Jews |
| 1880-1914 | 2,000,000 Russian Jews |
| 1900-1914 | 125,000 Rumanian Jews |
| 1933-1945 | 240,000 German and Austrian Jews |

Jewish Servicemen
World War one    250,000
World War two    550,000

The Jews from Russia pioneered both in trade union activity and in communal self-help. They flourished in the clothing trade and as "custom peddlers" or small businessmen. They established many of Americas leading chain-stores and business emporia

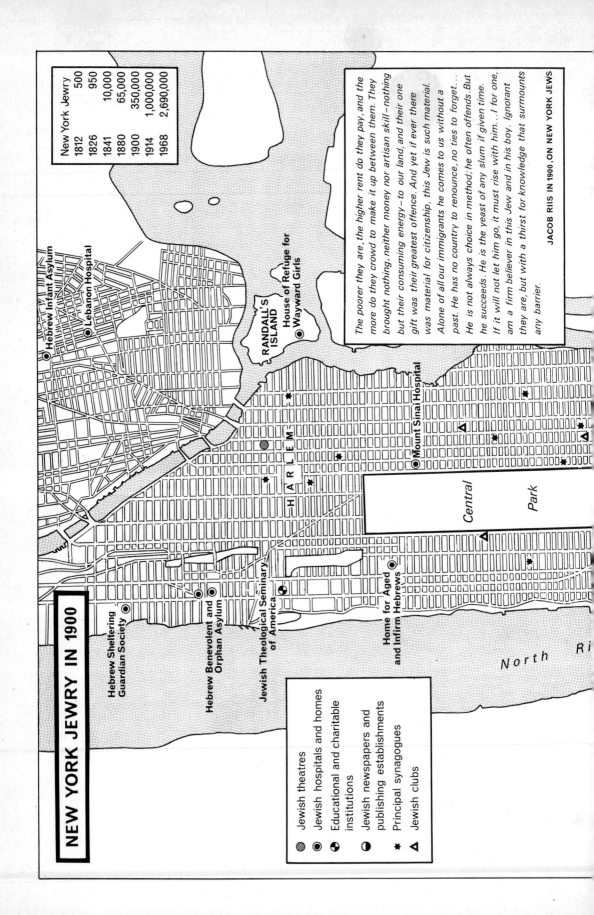

# NEW YORK JEWRY IN 1900

| New York Jewry | |
|---|---|
| 1812 | 500 |
| 1826 | 950 |
| 1841 | 10,000 |
| 1880 | 65,000 |
| 1900 | 350,000 |
| 1914 | 1,000,000 |
| 1968 | 2,690,000 |

Hebrew Infant Asylum

Lebanon Hospital

RANDALL'S ISLAND

House of Refuge for Wayward Girls

Mount Sinai Hospital

HARLEM

Central

Park

Home for Aged and Infirm Hebrews

Jewish Theological Seminary of America

Hebrew Benevolent and Orphan Asylum

Hebrew Sheltering Guardian Society

North Ri

*The poorer they are, the higher rent do they pay, and the more do they crowd to make it up between them. They brought nothing, neither money nor artisan skill – nothing but their consuming energy – to our land, and their one gift was their greatest offence. And yet if ever there was material for citizenship, this Jew is such material. Alone of all our immigrants he comes to us without a past. He has no country to renounce, no ties to forget... He is not always choice in method: he often offends. But he succeeds. He is the yeast of any slum if given time. If it will not let him go, it must rise with him...I for one, am a firm believer in this Jew and in his boy. Ignorant they are, but with a thirst for knowledge that surmounts any barrier.*

JACOB RIIS IN 1900, ON NEW YORK JEWS

**Legend:**
- ◓ Jewish theatres
- ◉ Jewish hospitals and homes
- ◑ Educational and charitable institutions
- ◐ Jewish newspapers and publishing establishments
- ★ Principal synagogues
- △ Jewish clubs

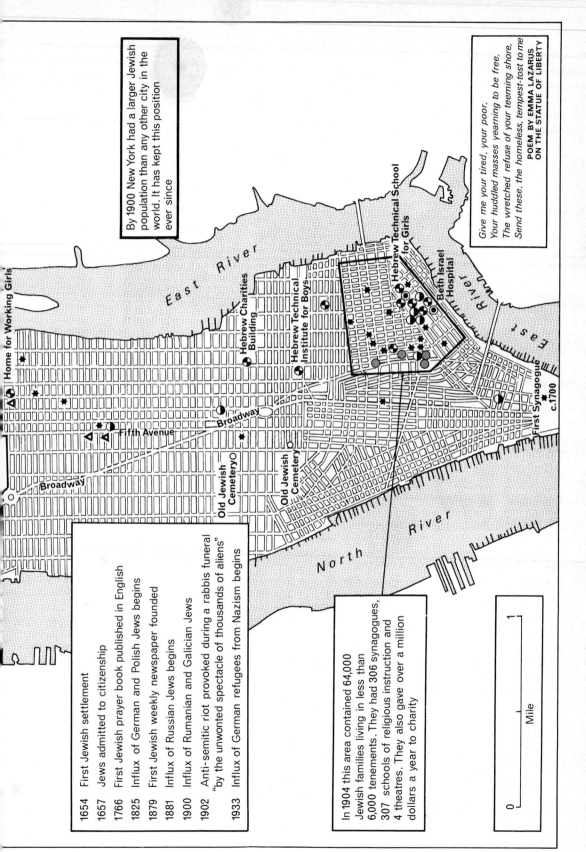

Home for Working Girls

By 1900 New York had a larger Jewish population than any other city in the world. It has kept this position ever since

Hebrew Technical School for Girls

Beth Israel Hospital

East River

Give me your tired, your poor,
Your huddled masses yearning to be free,
The wretched refuse of your teeming shore,
Send these, the homeless, tempest-tost to me

POEM BY EMMA LAZARUS
ON THE STATUE OF LIBERTY

East River

Hebrew Charities Building

Hebrew Technical Institute for Boys

Broadway

First Synagogue
c.1700

Fifth Avenue

Broadway

Old Jewish Cemetery

Old Jewish Cemetery

North River

| 1654 | First Jewish settlement |
| 1657 | Jews admitted to citizenship |
| 1766 | First Jewish prayer book published in English |
| 1825 | Influx of German and Polish Jews begins |
| 1879 | First Jewish weekly newspaper founded |
| 1881 | Influx of Russian Jews begins |
| 1900 | Influx of Rumanian and Galician Jews |
| 1902 | Anti-semitic riot provoked during a rabbis funeral "by the unwonted spectacle of thousands of aliens" |
| 1933 | Influx of German refugees from Nazism begins |

In 1904 this area contained 64,000 Jewish families living in less than 6,000 tenements. They had 306 synagogues, 307 schools of religious instruction and 4 theatres. They also gave over a million dollars a year to charity

0       Mile       1

78

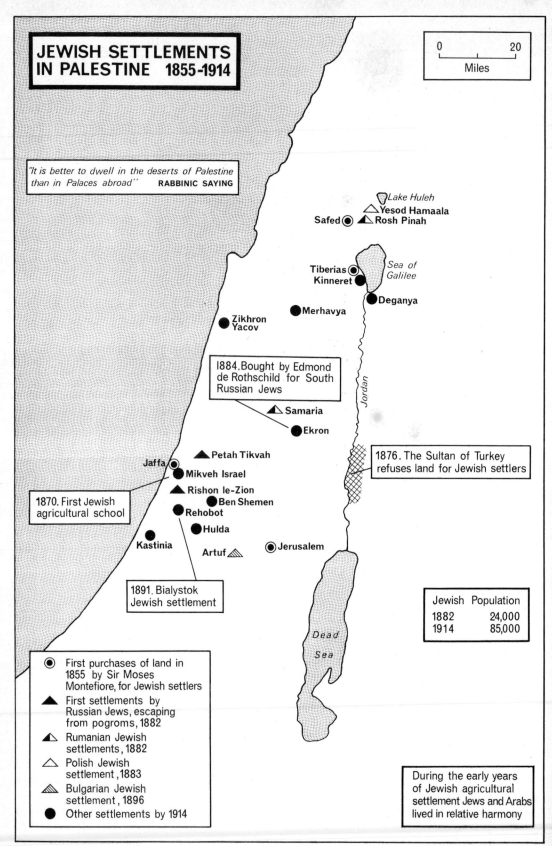

# JEWISH SETTLEMENTS IN PALESTINE 1855-1914

0       20
Miles

*"It is better to dwell in the deserts of Palestine than in Palaces abroad"* **RABBINIC SAYING**

*Lake Huleh*
△ *Yesod Hamaala*
Safed ◉ ▲ **Rosh Pinah**

*Sea of Galilee*
**Tiberias** ◉
**Kinneret**
**Deganya** ●

● **Merhavya**

**Zikhron Yacov** ●

1884. Bought by Edmond de Rothschild for South Russian Jews

▲ **Samaria**
● **Ekron**

1876. The Sultan of Turkey refuses land for Jewish settlers

▲ **Petah Tikvah**
**Jaffa** ◉
● **Mikveh Israel**
▲ **Rishon le-Zion**
● **Ben Shemen**
● **Rehobot**
● **Hulda**

1870. First Jewish agricultural school

● **Kastinia**
**Artuf** ◮

◉ **Jerusalem**

1891. Bialystok Jewish settlement

*Jordan*

**Jewish Population**
1882     24,000
1914     85,000

*Dead Sea*

◉ First purchases of land in 1855 by Sir Moses Montefiore, for Jewish settlers
▲ First settlements by Russian Jews, escaping from pogroms, 1882
◭ Rumanian Jewish settlements, 1882
△ Polish Jewish settlement, 1883
◮ Bulgarian Jewish settlement, 1896
● Other settlements by 1914

During the early years of Jewish agricultural settlement Jews and Arabs lived in relative harmony

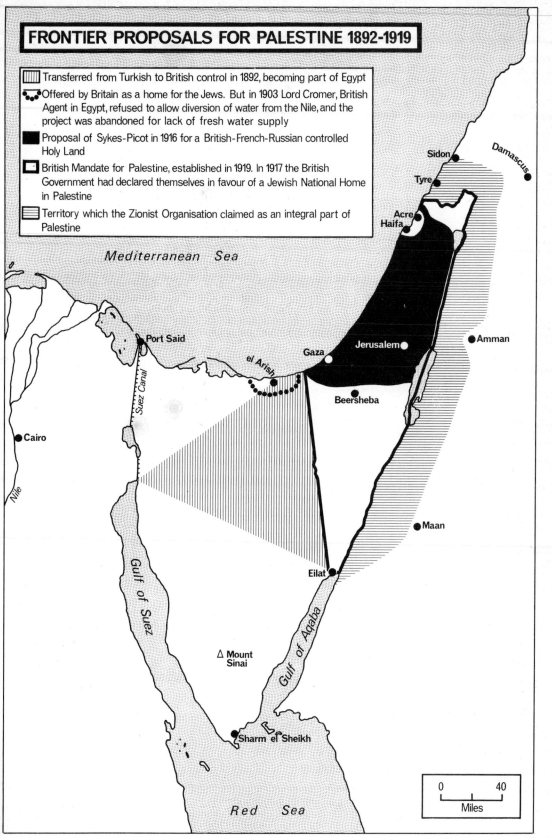

# FRONTIER PROPOSALS FOR PALESTINE 1892-1919

Transferred from Turkish to British control in 1892, becoming part of Egypt

Offered by Britain as a home for the Jews. But in 1903 Lord Cromer, British Agent in Egypt, refused to allow diversion of water from the Nile, and the project was abandoned for lack of fresh water supply

Proposal of Sykes-Picot in 1916 for a British-French-Russian controlled Holy Land

British Mandate for Palestine, established in 1919. In 1917 the British Government had declared themselves in favour of a Jewish National Home in Palestine

Territory which the Zionist Organisation claimed as an integral part of Palestine

Mediterranean Sea

Damascus

Sidon

Tyre

Acre
Haifa

Port Said

Gaza

Jerusalem

Amman

el Arish

Beersheba

Cairo

Nile

Suez Canal

Maan

Eilat

Gulf of Suez

Gulf of Aqaba

△ Mount
Sinai

Sharm el Sheikh

0    40
Miles

Red Sea

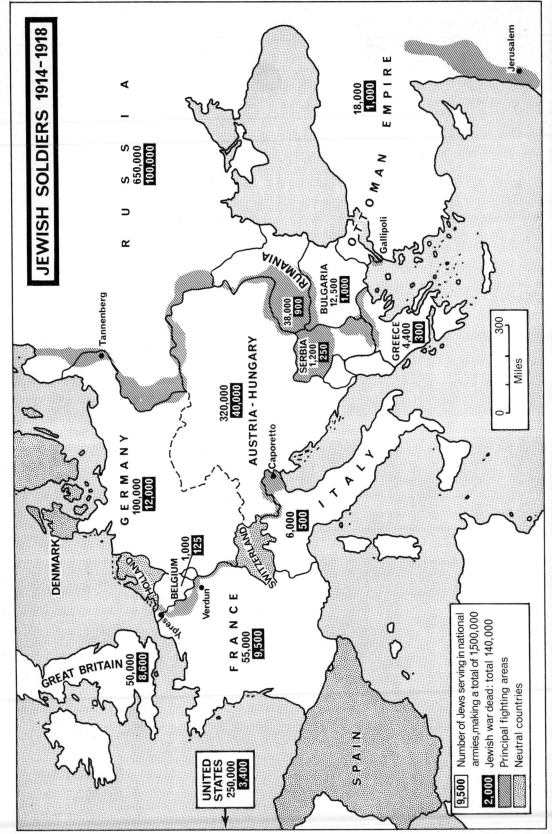

# JEWISH SOLDIERS 1914–1918

**RUSSIA**
650,000
**100,000**

**OTTOMAN EMPIRE**
18,000
**1,000**

Jerusalem

Gallipoli

**RUMANIA**
38,000
**900**

**BULGARIA**
12,500
**1,000**

**SERBIA**
1,200
**250**

**GREECE**
4,400
**300**

Tannenberg

**AUSTRIA–HUNGARY**
320,000
**40,000**

Caporetto

**GERMANY**
100,000
**12,000**

**ITALY**
6,000
**500**

**BELGIUM**
1,000
**125**

DENMARK

HOLLAND

SWITZERLAND

Verdun

Ypres

**FRANCE**
55,000
**9,500**

**GREAT BRITAIN**
50,000
**3,600**

**UNITED STATES**
250,000
**3,400**

**SPAIN**

| 0 | | 300 |
|---|---|---|

Miles

**9,500** Number of Jews serving in national armies, making a total of 1,500,000

**2,000** Jewish war dead: total 140,000

Principal fighting areas

Neutral countries

81

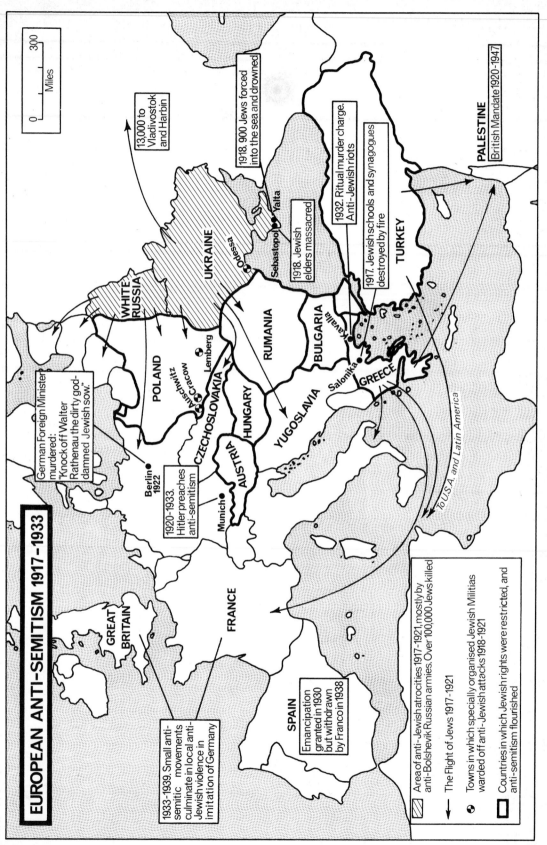

# EUROPEAN ANTI-SEMITISM 1917–1933

German Foreign Minister murdered: "Knock off Walter Rathenau the dirty god-damned Jewish sow."

13,000 to Vladivostok and Harbin

1918. 900 Jews forced into the sea and drowned

1918. Jewish elders massacred

1932. Ritual murder charge. Anti-Jewish riots

1917. Jewish schools and synagogues destroyed by fire

PALESTINE British Mandate 1920–1947

WHITE RUSSIA

UKRAINE

Odessa

Sebastopol · Yalta

POLAND

Auschwitz · Cracow · Lemberg

CZECHOSLOVAKIA

RUMANIA

BULGARIA

Kavalla

TURKEY

1920–1933. Hitler preaches anti-semitism

Berlin 1922

HUNGARY

AUSTRIA

Munich

YUGOSLAVIA

Salonika

GREECE

GREAT BRITAIN

FRANCE

To U.S.A. and Latin America

1933–1939. Small anti-semitic movements culminate in local anti-Jewish violence in imitation of Germany

SPAIN
Emancipation granted in 1930 but withdrawn by Franco in 1938

Miles
0    300

Area of anti-Jewish atrocities 1917–1921, mostly by anti-Bolshevik Russian armies. Over 100,000 Jews killed

The Flight of Jews 1917–1921

Towns in which specially organised Jewish Militias warded off anti-Jewish attacks 1918–1921

Countries in which Jewish rights were restricted, and anti-semitism flourished

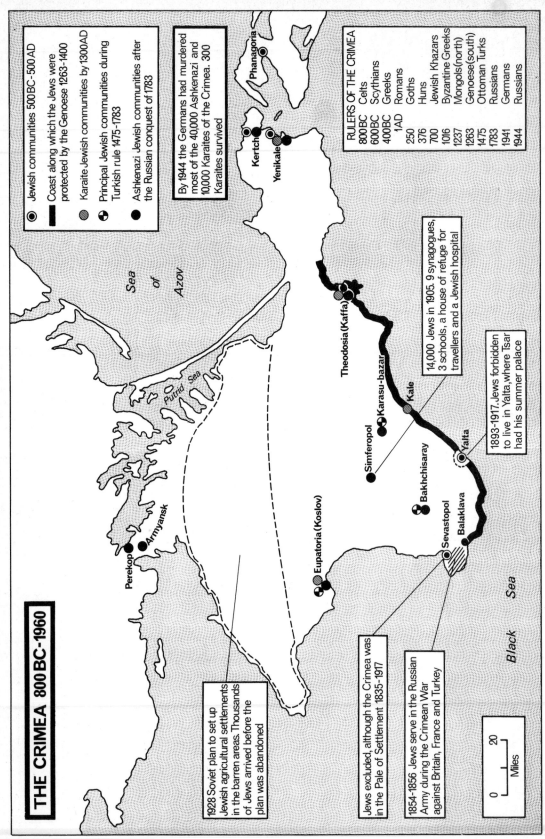

# THE CRIMEA 800 BC-1960

## Legend

- ◉ Jewish communities 500BC - 500 AD
- ▬ Coast along which the Jews were protected by the Genoese 1263-1400
- ◍ Karaite Jewish communities by 1300AD
- ✪ Principal Jewish communities during Turkish rule 1475-1783
- ● Ashkenazi Jewish communities after the Russian conquest of 1783

By 1944 the Germans had murdered most of the 40,000 Ashkenazi and 10,000 Karaites of the Crimea. 300 Karaites survived

## RULERS OF THE CRIMEA

| | |
|---|---|
| 800BC | Celts |
| 600BC | Scythians |
| 400BC | Greeks |
| 1AD | Romans |
| 250 | Goths |
| 376 | Huns |
| 700 | Jewish Khazars |
| 1016 | Byzantine Greeks |
| 1237 | Mongols(north) |
| 1263 | Genoese(south) |
| 1475 | Ottoman Turks |
| 1783 | Russians |
| 1941 | Germans |
| 1944 | Russians |

Sea of Azov

Putrid Sea

14,000 Jews in 1905. 9 synagogues, 3 schools, a house of refuge for travellers and a Jewish hospital

1893-1917. Jews forbidden to live in Yalta, where Tsar had his summer palace

Phanagoria

Kertch

Yenikale

Theodosia (Kaffa)

Karasu-bazar

Kale

Simferopol

Bakhchisaray

Yalta

Balaklava

Sevastopol

Eupatoria (Koslov)

Perekop

Armyansk

1928 Soviet plan to set up Jewish agricultural settlements in the barren areas. Thousands of Jews arrived before the plan was abandoned

Jews excluded, although the Crimea was in the Pale of Settlement 1835-1917

1854-1856 Jews serve in the Russian Army during the Crimean War against Britain, France and Turkey

Black Sea

0    20
Miles

83

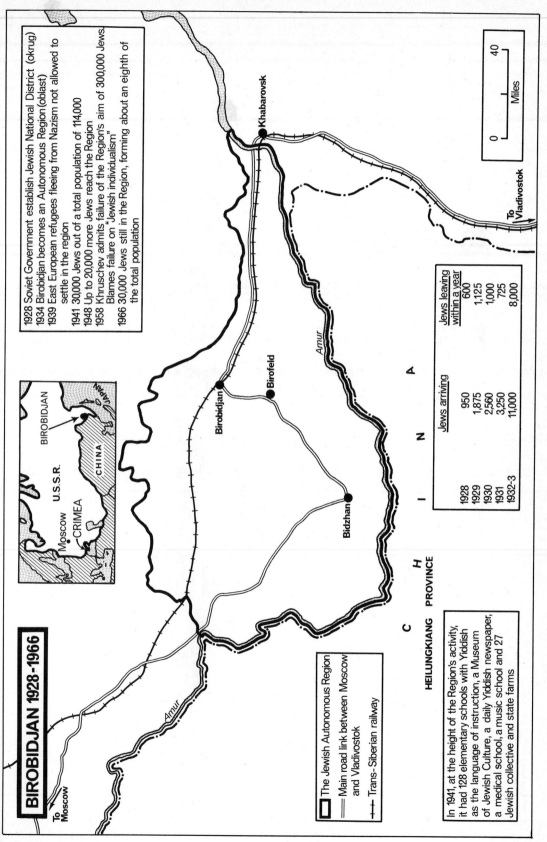

# BIROBIDJAN 1928-1966

To Moscow

BIROBIDJAN

U.S.S.R.

Moscow
CRIMEA

CHINA

Amur

Khabarovsk

Birobidjan

Birofeld

Bidzhan

Amur

To Vladivostok

CHINA

HEILUNGKIANG PROVINCE

1928 Soviet Government establish Jewish National District (okrug)
1934 Birobidjan becomes an Autonomous Region (oblast)
1939 East European refugees fleeing from Nazism not allowed to settle in the region
1941 30,000 Jews out of a total population of 114,000
1948 Up to 20,000 more Jews reach the Region
1958 Khruschev admits failure of the Region's aim of 300,000 Jews. Blames failure on "Jewish individualism"
1966 30,000 Jews still in the Region, forming about an eighth of the total population

| | Jews arriving | Jews leaving within a year |
|---|---|---|
| 1928 | 950 | 600 |
| 1929 | 1,875 | 1,125 |
| 1930 | 2,560 | 1,000 |
| 1931 | 3,250 | 725 |
| 1932-3 | 11,000 | 8,000 |

The Jewish Autonomous Region

Main road link between Moscow and Vladivostok

Trans-Siberian railway

In 1941, at the height of the Region's activity, it had 128 elementary schools with Yiddish as the language of instruction, a Museum of Jewish Culture, a daily Yiddish newspaper, a medical school, a music school and 27 Jewish collective and state farms

0        40
Miles

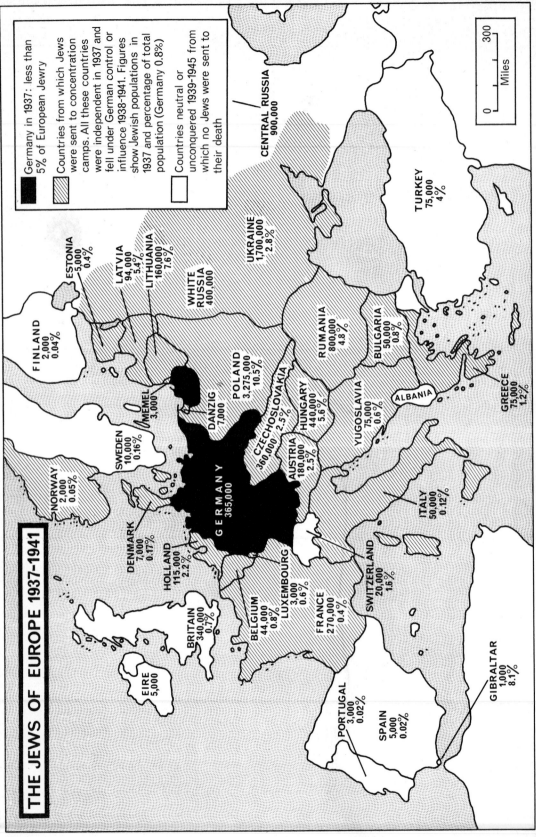

## THE JEWS OF EUROPE 1937-1941

**Legend:**

Germany in 1937: less than 5% of European Jewry

Countries from which Jews were sent to concentration camps. All these countries were independent in 1937 and fell under German control or influence 1938-1941. Figures show Jewish populations in 1937 and percentage of total population (Germany 0.8%)

Countries neutral or unconquered 1939-1945 from which no Jews were sent to their death

0     300
Miles

CENTRAL RUSSIA
900,000

TURKEY
75,000
4%

ESTONIA
5,000
0.4%

LATVIA
94,000
5.4%

LITHUANIA
160,000
7.6%

UKRAINE
1,700,000
2.8%

WHITE RUSSIA
400,000

FINLAND
2,000
0.04%

RUMANIA
800,000
4.8%

BULGARIA
50,000
0.8%

MEMEL
3,000

SWEDEN
10,000
0.16%

POLAND
3,275,000
10.5%

DANZIG
7,000

CZECHOSLOVAKIA
360,000
2.5%

HUNGARY
440,000
5.6%

YUGOSLAVIA
75,000
0.6%

ALBANIA

GREECE
75,000
1.2%

NORWAY
2,000
0.05%

GERMANY
365,000

AUSTRIA
180,000
2.5%

ITALY
50,000
0.12%

DENMARK
7,000
0.17%

HOLLAND
115,000
2.2%

LUXEMBOURG
3,000
0.6%

FRANCE
270,000
0.4%

SWITZERLAND
20,000
1.6%

BRITAIN
340,000
0.7%

BELGIUM
44,000
0.8%

EIRE
5,000

PORTUGAL
3,000
0.02%

SPAIN
5,000
0.02%

GIBRALTAR
1,000
8.1%

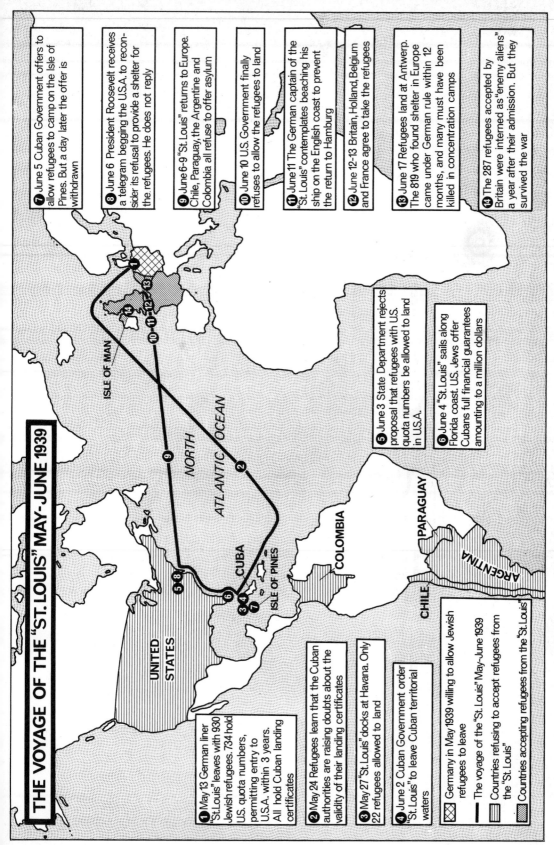

# THE VOYAGE OF THE "ST. LOUIS" MAY-JUNE 1939

**1** May 13 German liner "St.Louis" leaves with 930 Jewish refugees. 734 hold U.S. quota numbers, permitting entry to U.S.A. within 3 years. All hold Cuban landing certificates

**2** May 24 Refugees learn that the Cuban authorities are raising doubts about the validity of their landing certificates

**3** May 27 "St.Louis" docks at Havana. Only 22 refugees allowed to land

**4** June 2 Cuban Government order "St. Louis" to leave Cuban territorial waters

**5** June 3 State Department rejects proposal that refugees with U.S. quota numbers be allowed to land in U.S.A.

**6** June 4 "St.Louis" sails along Florida coast. U.S. Jews offer Cubans full financial guarantees amounting to a million dollars

**7** June 5 Cuban Government offers to allow refugees to camp on the Isle of Pines. But a day later the offer is withdrawn

**8** June 6 President Roosevelt receives a telegram begging the U.S.A. to reconsider its refusal to provide a shelter for the refugees. He does not reply

**9** June 6-9 "St. Louis" returns to Europe. Chile, Paraguay, the Argentine and Colombia all refuse to offer asylum

**10** June 10 U.S. Government finally refuses to allow the refugees to land

**11** June 11 The German captain of the "St. Louis" contemplates beaching his ship on the English coast to prevent the return to Hamburg

**12** June 12-13 Britain, Holland, Belgium and France agree to take the refugees

**13** June 17 Refugees land at Antwerp. The 819 who found shelter in Europe came under German rule within 12 months, and many must have been killed in concentration camps

**14** The 287 refugees accepted by Britain were interned as "enemy aliens" a year after their admission. But they survived the war

UNITED STATES

NORTH ATLANTIC OCEAN

CUBA

ISLE OF PINES

COLOMBIA

CHILE

PARAGUAY

ARGENTINA

ISLE OF MAN

⬚⬚ Germany in May 1939 willing to allow Jewish refugees to leave

— The voyage of the "St. Louis" May-June 1939

▤ Countries refusing to accept refugees from the "St. Louis"

▥ Countries accepting refugees from the "St. Louis"

86

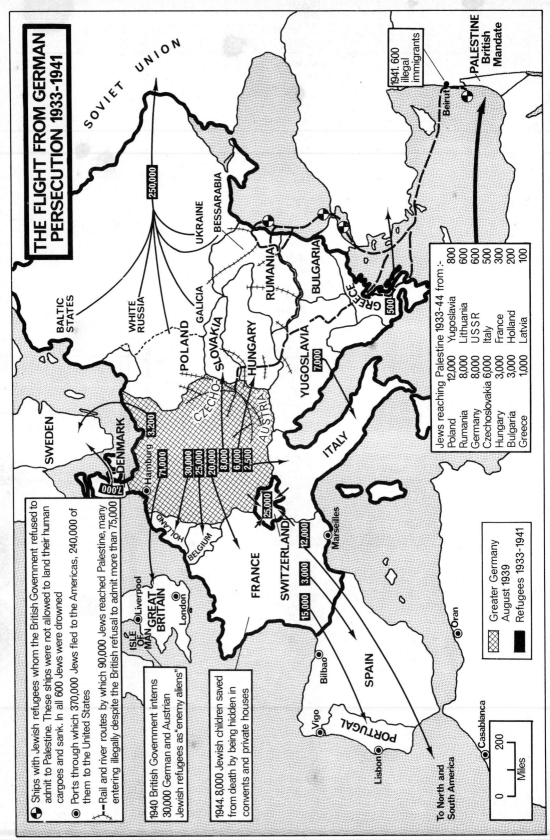

# THE FLIGHT FROM GERMAN PERSECUTION 1933-1941

SOVIET UNION

UKRAINE

BESSARABIA

250,000

BALTIC STATES

WHITE RUSSIA

POLAND

GALICIA

SLOVAKIA

HUNGARY

RUMANIA

BULGARIA

CZECHO.

AUSTRIA

YUGOSLAVIA

GREECE

500

SWEDEN

DENMARK

Hamburg 3,200

71,000

30,000

25,000

20,000

8,000

6,000

2,500

7,000

ITALY

7,000

25,000

HOLLAND

BELGIUM

SWITZERLAND

12,000

FRANCE

3,000

Marseilles

15,000

Liverpool

ISLE OF MAN GREAT BRITAIN

London

SPAIN

Bilbao

Vigo

PORTUGAL

Lisbon

Oran

Casablanca

To North and South America

Beirut

PALESTINE
British
Mandate

1941. 600 illegal immigrants

| Jews reaching Palestine 1933-44 from :- | | | |
|---|---|---|---|
| Poland | 12,000 | Yugoslavia | 800 |
| Rumania | 8,000 | Lithuania | 600 |
| Germany | 8,000 | USSR | 600 |
| Czechoslovakia | 6,000 | Italy | 500 |
| Hungary | 3,000 | France | 300 |
| Bulgaria | 3,000 | Holland | 200 |
| Greece | 500 | Latvia | 100 |

Ships with Jewish refugees whom the British Government refused to admit to Palestine. These ships were not allowed to land their human cargoes and sank. In all 600 Jews were drowned

Ports through which 370,000 Jews fled to the Americas, 240,000 of them to the United States

Rail and river routes by which 90,000 Jews reached Palestine, many entering illegally despite the British refusal to admit more than 75,000

1940 British Government interns 30,000 German and Austrian Jewish refugees as "enemy aliens"

1944. 8,000 Jewish children saved from death by being hidden in convents and private houses

| | |
|---|---|
| Greater Germany August 1939 | |
| Refugees 1933-1941 | |

0    200
Miles

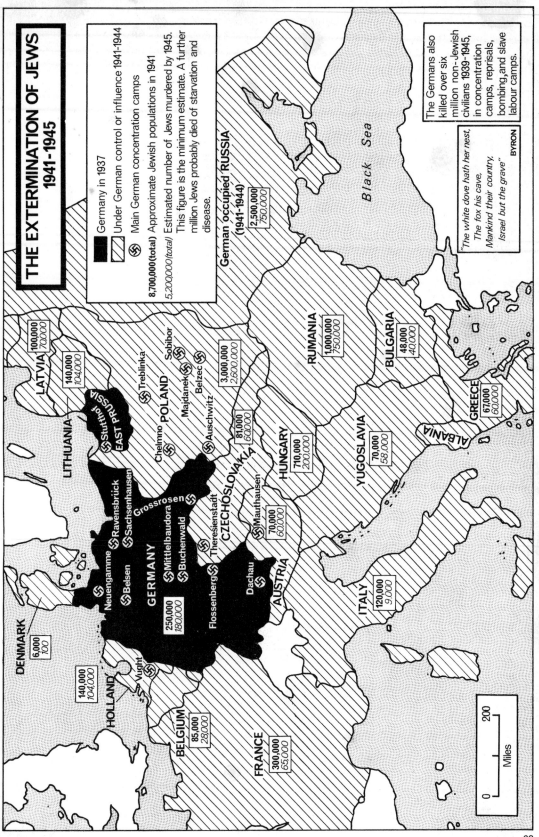

# THE EXTERMINATION OF JEWS 1941-1945

**Legend:**
- ■ Germany in 1937
- ▨ Under German control or influence 1941-1944
- ⚕ Main German concentration camps
- **8,700,000(total)** Approximate Jewish populations in 1941
- *5,200,000(total)* Estimated number of Jews murdered by 1945. This figure is the minimum estimate. A further million Jews probably died of starvation and disease.

The Germans also killed over six million non-Jewish civilians 1939-1945, in concentration camps, reprisals, bombing, and slave labour camps.

"The white dove hath her nest,
The fox his cave.
Mankind their country.
Israel but the grave"
**BYRON**

German occupied RUSSIA (1941-1944) **2,500,000** *750,000*

*Black Sea*

RUMANIA **1,000,000** *750,000*

BULGARIA **48,000** *40,000*

GREECE **67,000** *60,000*

ALBANIA

LATVIA **100,000** *70,000*

**140,000** *104,000*

Treblinka

Sobibor

Chelmno POLAND

Majdanek Belzec **3,000,000** *2,600,000*

Auschwitz

LITHUANIA

Stutthof EAST PRUSSIA

Ravensbrück Sachsenhausen

Grossrosen

Mittlelbaudora Buchenwald

CZECHOSLOVAKIA Theresienstadt **81,000** *60,000*

Mauthausen

HUNGARY **710,000** *200,000*

YUGOSLAVIA **70,000** *58,000*

Neuengamme Belsen

GERMANY **250,000** *180,000*

Flossenberg Dachau

AUSTRIA **70,000** *60,000*

ITALY **120,000** *9,000*

DENMARK **6,000** *100*

Vught

HOLLAND **140,000** *104,000*

BELGIUM **85,000** *28,000*

FRANCE **300,000** *65,000*

0        200
Miles

88

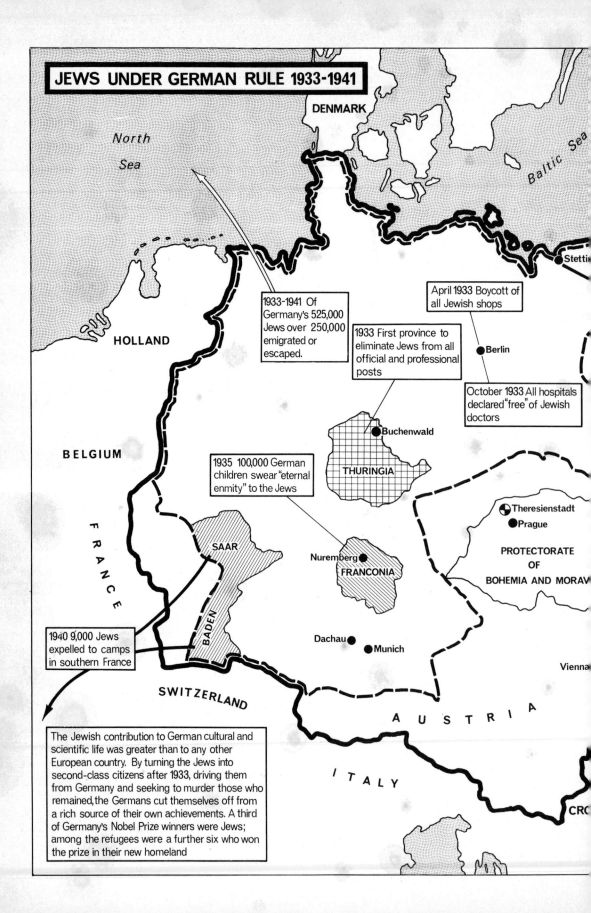

# JEWS UNDER GERMAN RULE 1933-1941

DENMARK

*North Sea*

*Baltic Sea*

Stettin

HOLLAND

1933-1941 Of Germany's 525,000 Jews over 250,000 emigrated or escaped.

April 1933 Boycott of all Jewish shops

1933 First province to eliminate Jews from all official and professional posts

● Berlin

October 1933 All hospitals declared "free" of Jewish doctors

BELGIUM

1935 100,000 German children swear "eternal enmity" to the Jews

● Buchenwald

THURINGIA

● Theresienstadt
● Prague

F R A N C E

SAAR

Nuremberg ●

FRANCONIA

PROTECTORATE
OF
BOHEMIA AND MORAV

1940 9,000 Jews expelled to camps in southern France

BADEN

Dachau ●
● Munich

Vienna

SWITZERLAND

A U S T R I A

The Jewish contribution to German cultural and scientific life was greater than to any other European country. By turning the Jews into second-class citizens after 1933, driving them from Germany and seeking to murder those who remained, the Germans cut themselves off from a rich source of their own achievements. A third of Germany's Nobel Prize winners were Jews; among the refugees were a further six who won the prize in their new homeland

I T A L Y

CRO

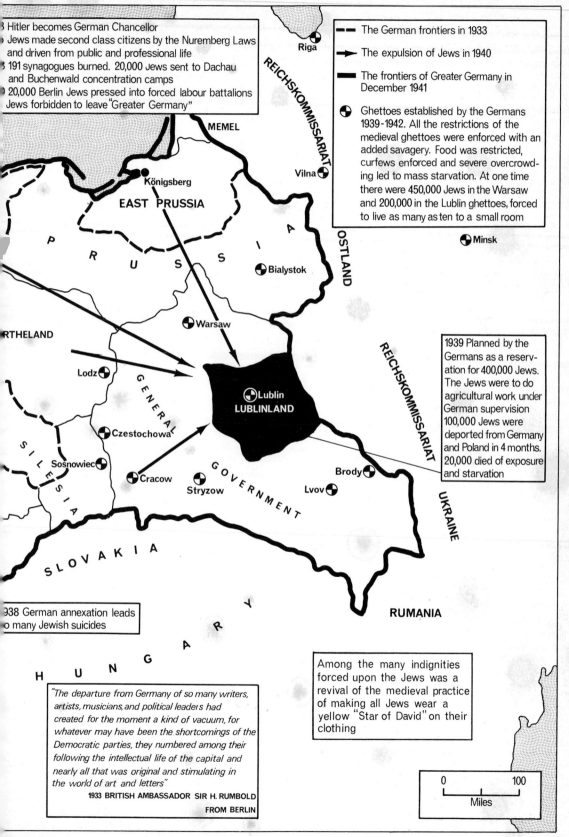

Hitler becomes German Chancellor
Jews made second class citizens by the Nuremberg Laws and driven from public and professional life
191 synagogues burned. 20,000 Jews sent to Dachau and Buchenwald concentration camps
20,000 Berlin Jews pressed into forced labour battalions
Jews forbidden to leave "Greater Germany"

- - - The German frontiers in 1933

→ The expulsion of Jews in 1940

━━━ The frontiers of Greater Germany in December 1941

✦ Ghettoes established by the Germans 1939-1942. All the restrictions of the medieval ghettoes were enforced with an added savagery. Food was restricted, curfews enforced and severe overcrowding led to mass starvation. At one time there were 450,000 Jews in the Warsaw and 200,000 in the Lublin ghettoes, forced to live as many as ten to a small room

REICHSKOMMISSARIAT

Riga

MEMEL

Vilna ✦

Königsberg

EAST PRUSSIA

OSTLAND

P R U S S I A

Bialystok ✦

Minsk ✦

Warsaw ✦

RTHELAND

Lodz ✦

G E N E R A L

REICHSKOMMISSARIAT

Lublin ✦
LUBLINLAND

1939 Planned by the Germans as a reservation for 400,000 Jews. The Jews were to do agricultural work under German supervision 100,000 Jews were deported from Germany and Poland in 4 months. 20,000 died of exposure and starvation

Czestochowa ✦

S I L E S I A

Sosnowiec ✦

Cracow ✦
Stryzow ✦

G O V E R N M E N T

Brody ✦

Lvov ✦

UKRAINE

S L O V A K I A

RUMANIA

938 German annexation leads o many Jewish suicides

H U N G A R Y

"The departure from Germany of so many writers, artists, musicians, and political leaders had created for the moment a kind of vacuum, for whatever may have been the shortcomings of the Democratic parties, they numbered among their following the intellectual life of the capital and nearly all that was original and stimulating in the world of art and letters"
1933 BRITISH AMBASSADOR SIR H. RUMBOLD
FROM BERLIN

Among the many indignities forced upon the Jews was a revival of the medieval practice of making all Jews wear a yellow "Star of David" on their clothing

0        100
Miles

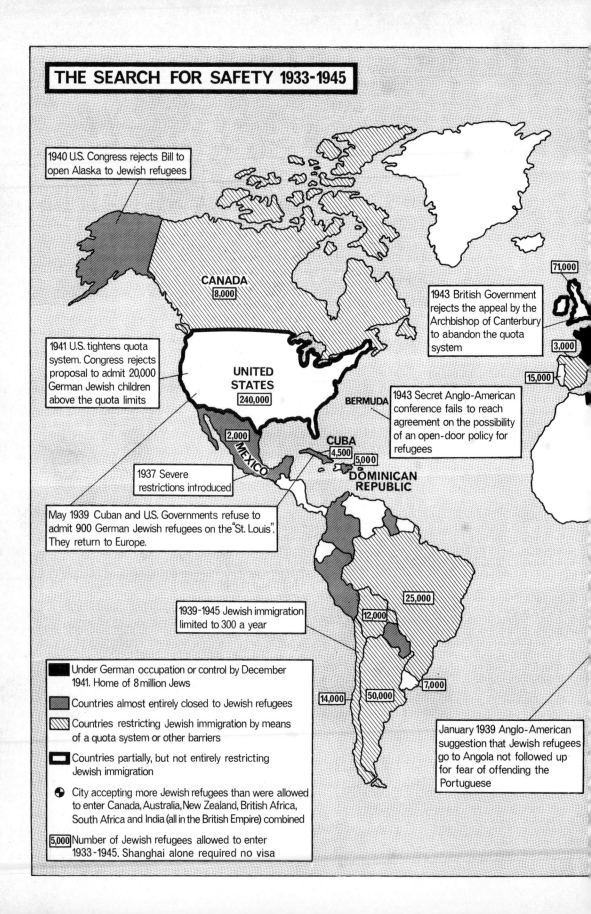

# THE SEARCH FOR SAFETY 1933-1945

1940 U.S. Congress rejects Bill to open Alaska to Jewish refugees

1943 British Government rejects the appeal by the Archbishop of Canterbury to abandon the quota system

1941 U.S. tightens quota system. Congress rejects proposal to admit 20,000 German Jewish children above the quota limits

1943 Secret Anglo-American conference fails to reach agreement on the possibility of an open-door policy for refugees

1937 Severe restrictions introduced

May 1939 Cuban and U.S. Governments refuse to admit 900 German Jewish refugees on the "St. Louis". They return to Europe.

1939-1945 Jewish immigration limited to 300 a year

January 1939 Anglo-American suggestion that Jewish refugees go to Angola not followed up for fear of offending the Portuguese

CANADA 8,000

UNITED STATES 240,000

BERMUDA

MEXICO 2,000

CUBA 4,500

5,000 DOMINICAN REPUBLIC

71,000

3,000

15,000

25,000

12,000

14,000

50,000

7,000

■ Under German occupation or control by December 1941. Home of 8 million Jews

▨ Countries almost entirely closed to Jewish refugees

▧ Countries restricting Jewish immigration by means of a quota system or other barriers

▭ Countries partially, but not entirely restricting Jewish immigration

◉ City accepting more Jewish refugees than were allowed to enter Canada, Australia, New Zealand, British Africa, South Africa and India (all in the British Empire) combined

5,000 Number of Jewish refugees allowed to enter 1933-1945. Shanghai alone required no visa

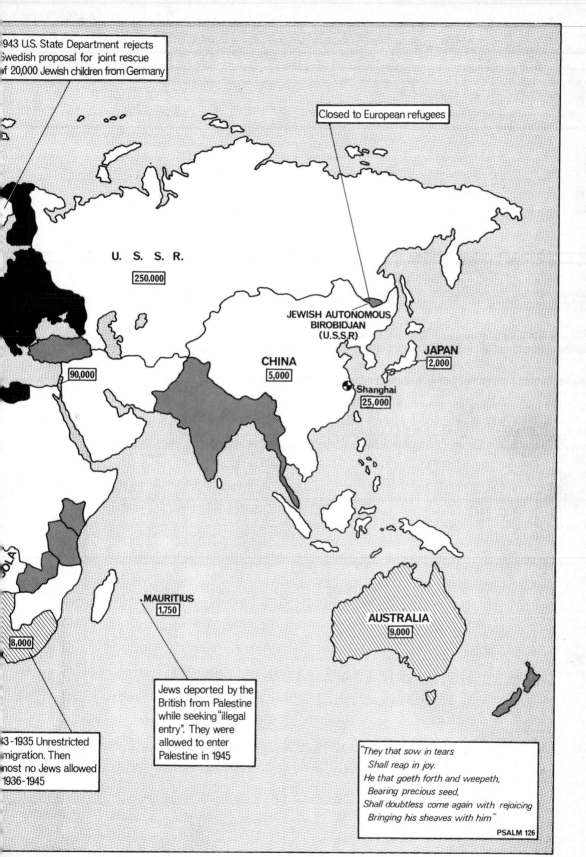

1943 U.S. State Department rejects Swedish proposal for joint rescue of 20,000 Jewish children from Germany

Closed to European refugees

U. S. S. R.
250,000

JEWISH AUTONOMOUS BIROBIDJAN (U.S.S.R)

CHINA
5,000

JAPAN
2,000

Shanghai
25,000

MAURITIUS
1,750

AUSTRALIA
9,000

...GOLA

8,000

Jews deported by the British from Palestine while seeking "illegal entry". They were allowed to enter Palestine in 1945

3-1935 Unrestricted migration. Then most no Jews allowed 1936-1945

"They that sow in tears
Shall reap in joy.
He that goeth forth and weepeth,
Bearing precious seed,
Shall doubtless come again with rejoicing
Bringing his sheaves with him"

PSALM 126

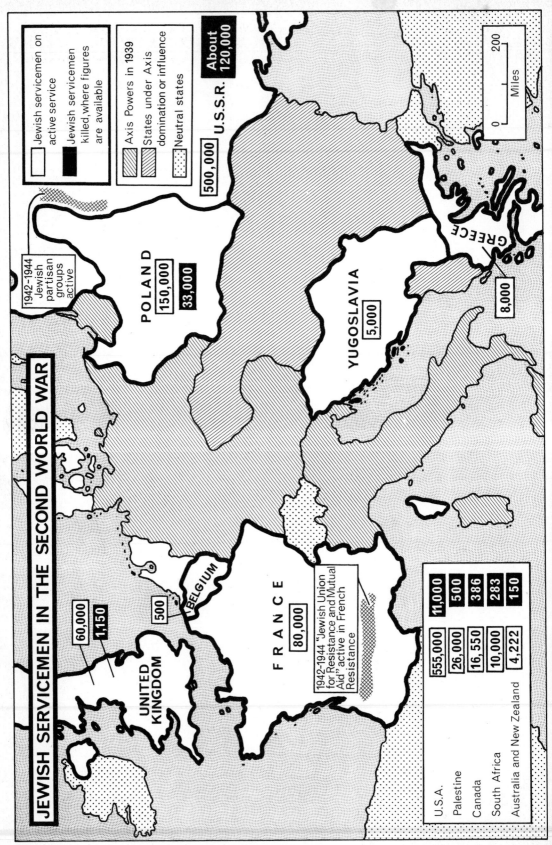

# JEWISH SERVICEMEN IN THE SECOND WORLD WAR

Jewish servicemen on active service

Jewish servicemen killed, where figures are available

Axis Powers in 1939

States under Axis domination or influence

Neutral states

About 120,000

U.S.S.R.
500,000

1942-1944 Jewish partisan groups active

POLAND
150,000
33,000

YUGOSLAVIA
5,000

GREECE
8,000

UNITED KINGDOM
60,000
1150

BELGIUM
500

FRANCE
80,000

1942-1944 "Jewish Union for Resistance and Mutual Aid" active in French Resistance

| | |
|---|---|
| U.S.A. | 555,000 | 11,000 |
| Palestine | 26,000 | 500 |
| Canada | 16,550 | 386 |
| South Africa | 10,000 | 283 |
| Australia and New Zealand | 4,222 | 150 |

0    200
Miles

# JEWISH RESISTANCE 1940-1944

*Baltic Sea*

Riga

1942-1944 "Vilna Avengers". Jewish partisans active in anti-German sabotage.

1943-1944 The "Tobias Bielski" Division: about 1,000 Jewish partisans.

LITHUANIA

*Niemen*

Vilna

Minsk

Mir

Lida

WHITE RUSSIA

Bialystok

"Jerusalem"

1943-1944 A Jewish "Free City" in the woods of White Russia, a haven for partisans and refugees.

*Vistula*

P O L A N D

*Bug*

Treblinka

Warsaw

*Vistula*

Sobibor

Lublin

Lutzk

UKRAINE

Czestochowa

Koniecpol

Zhitomir

Sosnowica

Sielce

Bendzin

Brody

Tarnow

Lvov

Cracow

Tarnopol

*Auschwitz*

Stryzow

● Ghettoes in which the Jews organised risings against the Germans, despite the brutality and severity of German rule

▨ Jewish partisan groups in German occupied territory

★ Concentration camps in which Jewish risings took place

0        50
Miles

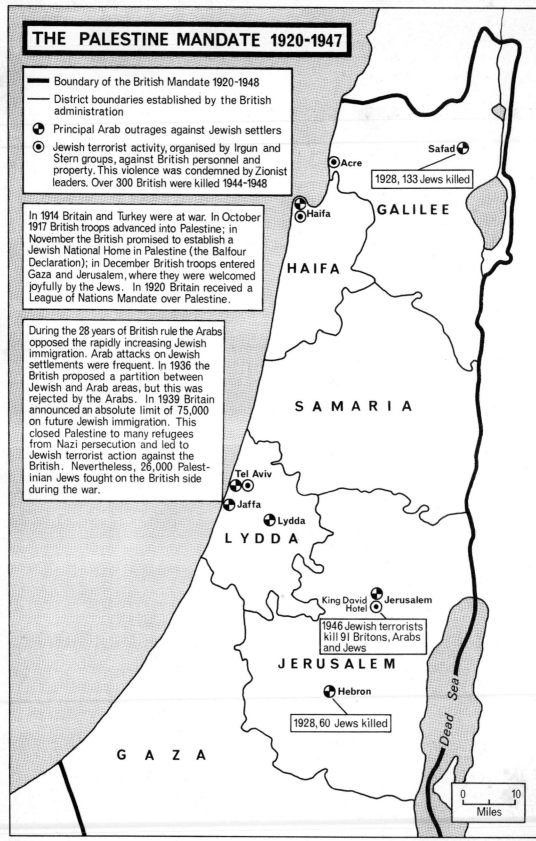

# THE PALESTINE MANDATE 1920-1947

**▬** Boundary of the British Mandate 1920-1948

**—** District boundaries established by the British administration

**⊕** Principal Arab outrages against Jewish settlers

**⊙** Jewish terrorist activity, organised by Irgun and Stern groups, against British personnel and property. This violence was condemned by Zionist leaders. Over 300 British were killed 1944-1948

In 1914 Britain and Turkey were at war. In October 1917 British troops advanced into Palestine; in November the British promised to establish a Jewish National Home in Palestine (the Balfour Declaration); in December British troops entered Gaza and Jerusalem, where they were welcomed joyfully by the Jews. In 1920 Britain received a League of Nations Mandate over Palestine.

During the 28 years of British rule the Arabs opposed the rapidly increasing Jewish immigration. Arab attacks on Jewish settlements were frequent. In 1936 the British proposed a partition between Jewish and Arab areas, but this was rejected by the Arabs. In 1939 Britain announced an absolute limit of 75,000 on future Jewish immigration. This closed Palestine to many refugees from Nazi persecution and led to Jewish terrorist action against the British. Nevertheless, 26,000 Palestinian Jews fought on the British side during the war.

Safad

**1928, 133 Jews killed**

Acre

Haifa

GALILEE

HAIFA

SAMARIA

Tel Aviv

Jaffa

Lydda

LYDDA

King David Hotel — Jerusalem

**1946 Jewish terrorists kill 91 Britons, Arabs and Jews**

JERUSALEM

Hebron

**1928, 60 Jews killed**

GAZA

Dead Sea

0    10
Miles

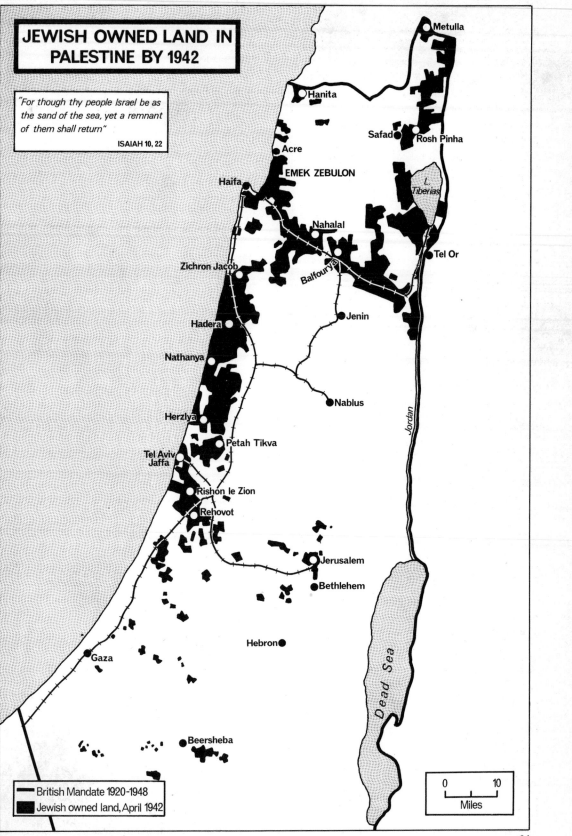

# JEWISH OWNED LAND IN PALESTINE BY 1942

*"For though thy people Israel be as the sand of the sea, yet a remnant of them shall return"*

ISAIAH 10, 22

Metulla

Hanita

Safad

Rosh Pinha

Acre

EMEK ZEBULON

Haifa

L. Tiberias

Nahalal

Zichron Jacob

Balfouryal

Tel Or

Jenin

Hadera

Nathanya

Nablus

Herzlya

Petah Tikva

Tel Aviv
Jaffa

Rishon le Zion

Rehovot

Jerusalem

Bethlehem

Hebron

Gaza

Dead Sea

Jordan

Beersheba

— British Mandate 1920-1948

■ Jewish owned land, April 1942

0        10

Miles

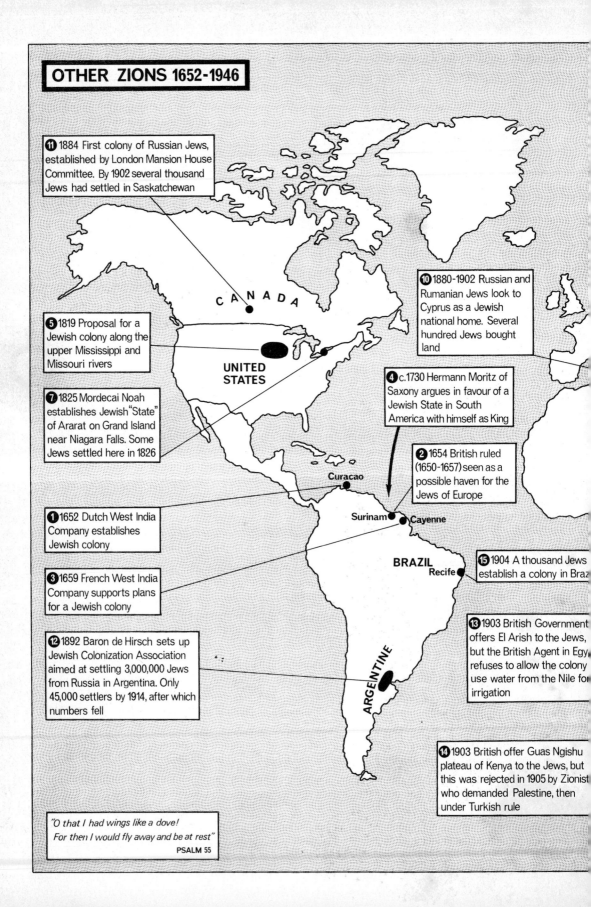

# OTHER ZIONS 1652-1946

**11** 1884 First colony of Russian Jews, established by London Mansion House Committee. By 1902 several thousand Jews had settled in Saskatchewan

**10** 1880-1902 Russian and Rumanian Jews look to Cyprus as a Jewish national home. Several hundred Jews bought land

**5** 1819 Proposal for a Jewish colony along the upper Mississippi and Missouri rivers

**4** c.1730 Hermann Moritz of Saxony argues in favour of a Jewish State in South America with himself as King

**7** 1825 Mordecai Noah establishes Jewish "State" of Ararat on Grand Island near Niagara Falls. Some Jews settled here in 1826

**2** 1654 British ruled (1650-1657) seen as a possible haven for the Jews of Europe

**1** 1652 Dutch West India Company establishes Jewish colony

**3** 1659 French West India Company supports plans for a Jewish colony

**15** 1904 A thousand Jews establish a colony in Braz

**13** 1903 British Government offers El Arish to the Jews, but the British Agent in Egyp refuses to allow the colony use water from the Nile for irrigation

**12** 1892 Baron de Hirsch sets up Jewish Colonization Association aimed at settling 3,000,000 Jews from Russia in Argentina. Only 45,000 settlers by 1914, after which numbers fell

**14** 1903 British offer Guas Ngishu plateau of Kenya to the Jews, but this was rejected in 1905 by Zionist who demanded Palestine, then under Turkish rule

CANADA

UNITED STATES

Curacao

Surinam · Cayenne

BRAZIL
Recife

ARGENTINE

"O that I had wings like a dove! For then I would fly away and be at rest"
PSALM 55

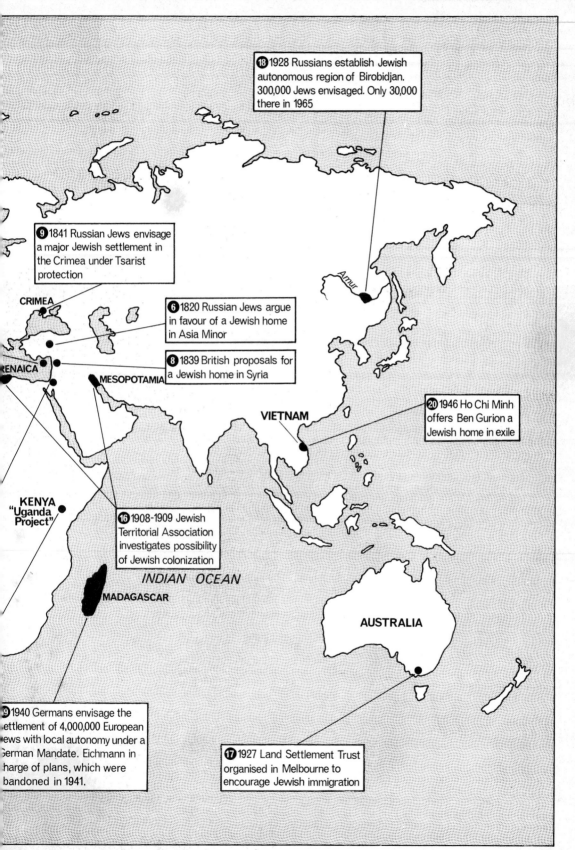

**18** 1928 Russians establish Jewish autonomous region of Birobidjan. 300,000 Jews envisaged. Only 30,000 there in 1965

**9** 1841 Russian Jews envisage a major Jewish settlement in the Crimea under Tsarist protection

CRIMEA

Amur

**6** 1820 Russian Jews argue in favour of a Jewish home in Asia Minor

**8** 1839 British proposals for a Jewish home in Syria

RENAICA

MESOPOTAMIA

VIETNAM

**20** 1946 Ho Chi Minh offers Ben Gurion a Jewish home in exile

KENYA "Uganda Project"

**16** 1908-1909 Jewish Territorial Association investigates possibility of Jewish colonization

*INDIAN OCEAN*

MADAGASCAR

AUSTRALIA

**19** 1940 Germans envisage the settlement of 4,000,000 European Jews with local autonomy under a German Mandate. Eichmann in charge of plans, which were abandoned in 1941.

**17** 1927 Land Settlement Trust organised in Melbourne to encourage Jewish immigration

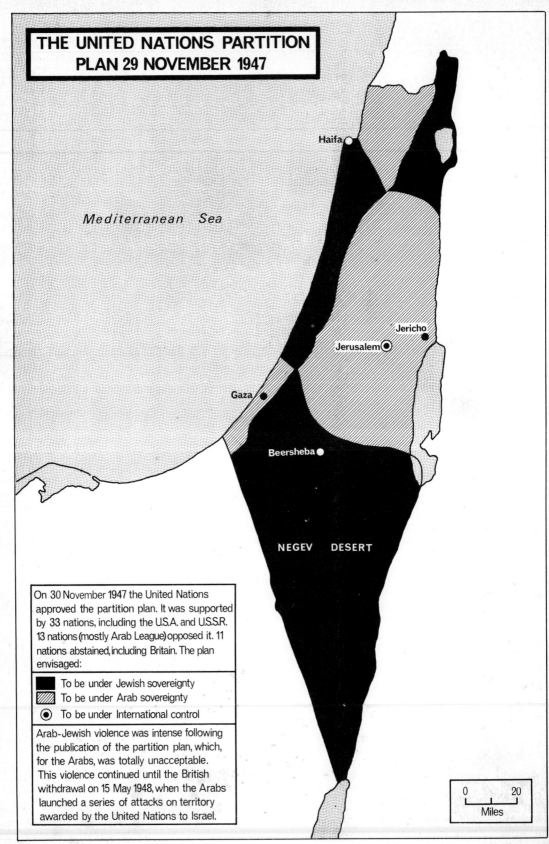

# THE UNITED NATIONS PARTITION PLAN 29 NOVEMBER 1947

*Mediterranean  Sea*

Haifa

Jericho

Jerusalem

Gaza

Beersheba

**NEGEV   DESERT**

On 30 November 1947 the United Nations
approved the partition plan. It was supported
by 33 nations, including the U.S.A. and U.S.S.R.
13 nations (mostly Arab League) opposed it. 11
nations abstained, including Britain. The plan
envisaged:

To be under Jewish sovereignty
To be under Arab sovereignty
To be under International control

Arab-Jewish violence was intense following
the publication of the partition plan, which,
for the Arabs, was totally unacceptable.
This violence continued until the British
withdrawal on 15 May 1948, when the Arabs
launched a series of attacks on territory
awarded by the United Nations to Israel.

0        20
Miles

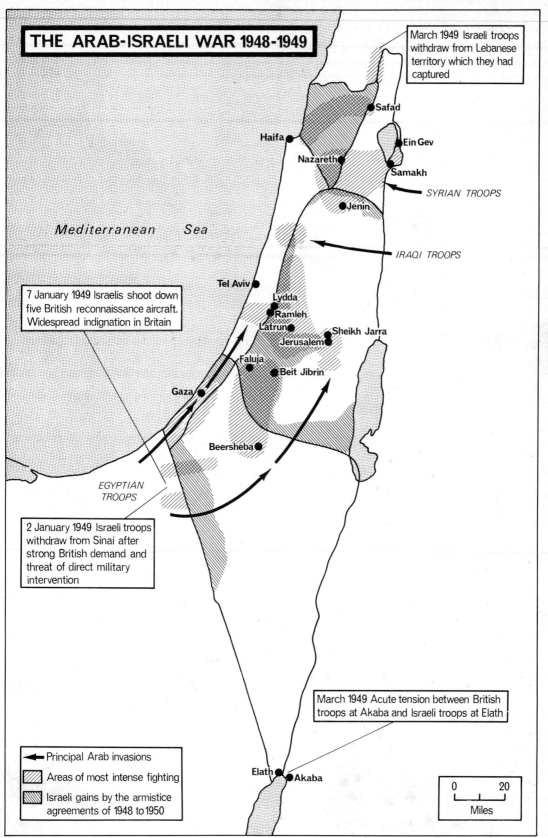

# THE ARAB-ISRAELI WAR 1948-1949

March 1949 Israeli troops withdraw from Lebanese territory which they had captured

*Mediterranean Sea*

●Safad

Haifa●

Nazareth● ●Ein Gev

●Samakh

*SYRIAN TROOPS*

●Jenin

*IRAQI TROOPS*

7 January 1949 Israelis shoot down five British reconnaissance aircraft. Widespread indignation in Britain

Tel Aviv●

Lydda●
●Ramleh
Latrun●
●Sheikh Jarra
●Jerusalem
Faluja●
●Beit Jibrin
Gaza●

Beersheba●

*EGYPTIAN TROOPS*

2 January 1949 Israeli troops withdraw from Sinai after strong British demand and threat of direct military intervention

March 1949 Acute tension between British troops at Akaba and Israeli troops at Elath

Elath● ●Akaba

Principal Arab invasions

Areas of most intense fighting

Israeli gains by the armistice agreements of 1948 to 1950

0    20
Miles

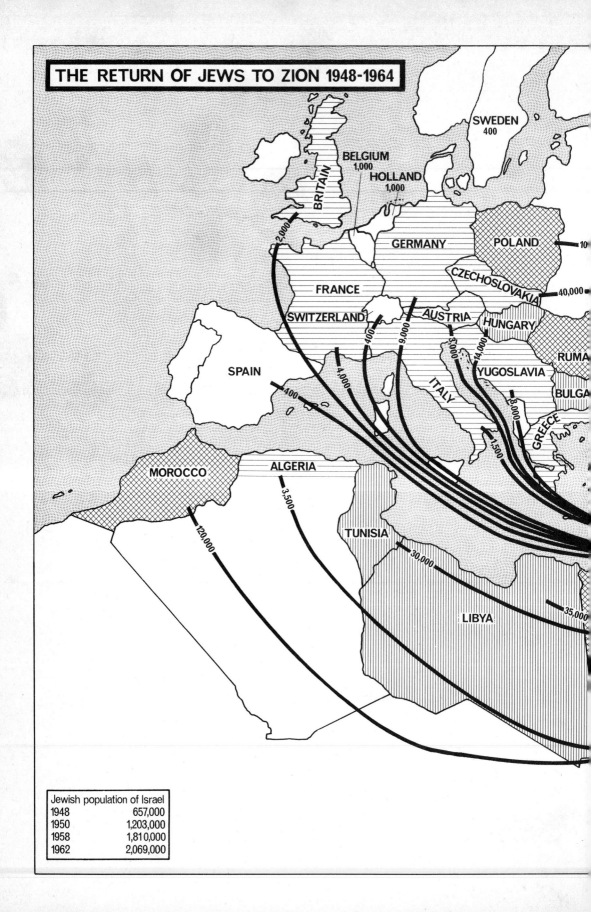

# THE RETURN OF JEWS TO ZION 1948-1964

SWEDEN
400

BELGIUM
1,000

HOLLAND
1,000

BRITAIN

GERMANY

POLAND

10

CZECHOSLOVAKIA

40,000

FRANCE

SWITZERLAND

AUSTRIA

HUNGARY

RUMA

YUGOSLAVIA

BULGA

2,000

400

9,000

3,000

14,000

ITALY

SPAIN

400

4,000

8,000

GREECE

1,500

MOROCCO

ALGERIA

3,500

120,000

TUNISIA

30,000

LIBYA

35,000

| Jewish population of Israel | |
|---|---|
| 1948 | 657,000 |
| 1950 | 1,203,000 |
| 1958 | 1,810,000 |
| 1962 | 2,069,000 |

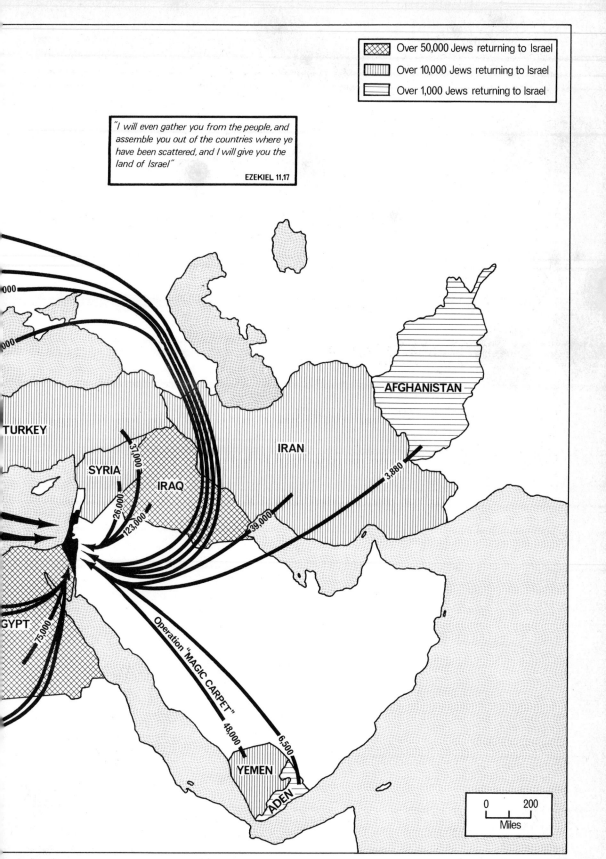

Over 50,000 Jews returning to Israel

Over 10,000 Jews returning to Israel

Over 1,000 Jews returning to Israel

"I will even gather you from the people, and
assemble you out of the countries where ye
have been scattered, and I will give you the
land of Israel"

EZEKIEL 11,17

AFGHANISTAN

TURKEY

SYRIA

IRAQ

IRAN

31,000

26,000

123,000

39,000

3,880

EGYPT

75,000

Operation "MAGIC CARPET"

48,000

6,500

YEMEN

ADEN

0    200
Miles

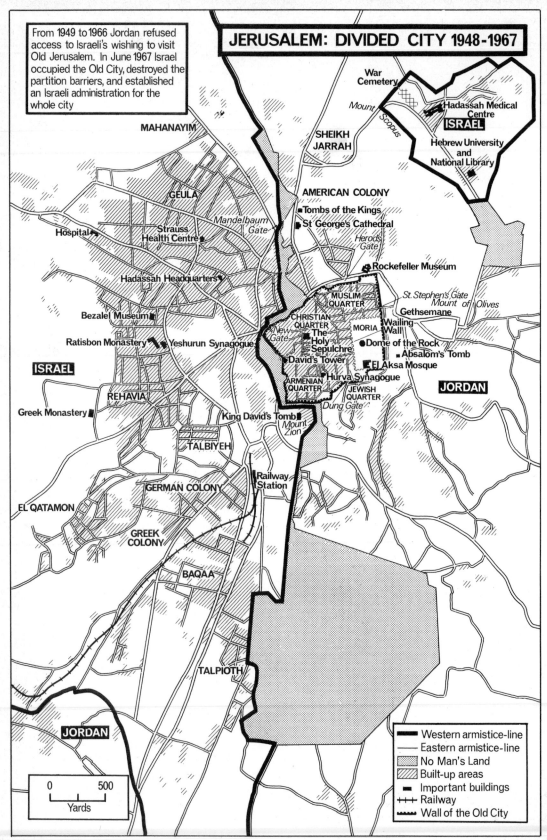

**JERUSALEM: DIVIDED CITY 1948-1967**

From 1949 to 1966 Jordan refused access to Israeli's wishing to visit Old Jerusalem. In June 1967 Israel occupied the Old City, destroyed the partition barriers, and established an Israeli administration for the whole city

War Cemetery

Mount Scopus

**ISRAEL**

Hadassah Medical Centre

Hebrew University and National Library

MAHANAYIM

SHEIKH JARRAH

AMERICAN COLONY

Tombs of the Kings

St George's Cathedral

*Herod's Gate*

GEULA

*Mandelbaum Gate*

Hospital

Strauss Health Centre

Rockefeller Museum

Hadassah Headquarters

MUSLIM QUARTER

*St. Stephen's Gate*
*Mount of Olives*

Gethsemane

Bezalel Museum

CHRISTIAN QUARTER

MORIA

Wailing Wall

Ratisbon Monastery

Yeshurun Synagogue

*New Gate*

The Holy Sepulchre

Dome of the Rock

Absalom's Tomb

David's Tower

El Aksa Mosque

**ISRAEL**

Hurva Synagogue

**JORDAN**

REHAVIA

ARMENIAN QUARTER

JEWISH QUARTER

Greek Monastery

King David's Tomb

*Dung Gate*

*Mount Zion*

TALBIYEH

GERMAN COLONY

Railway Station

EL QATAMON

GREEK COLONY

BAQAA

TALPIOTH

**JORDAN**

| 0 | 500 |
|---|---|

Yards

— Western armistice-line
— Eastern armistice-line
▨ No Man's Land
▨ Built-up areas
▬ Important buildings
+++ Railway
∿∿∿ Wall of the Old City

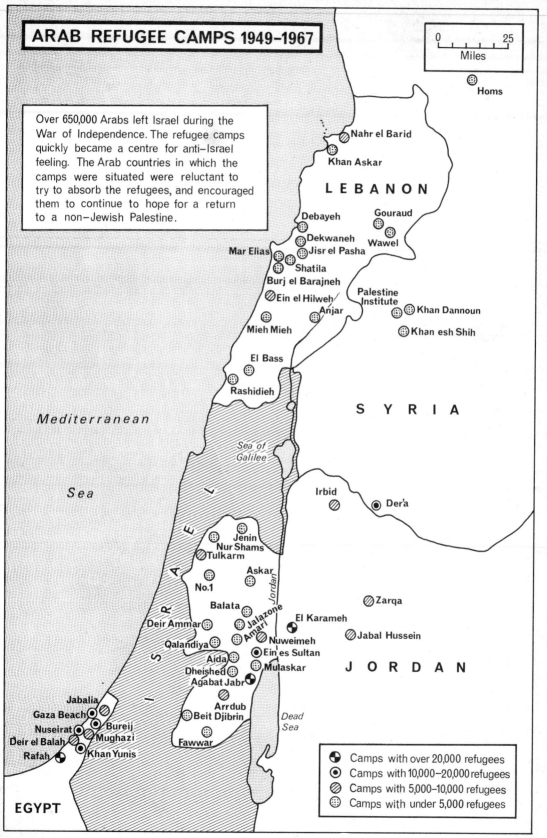

# ARAB REFUGEE CAMPS 1949-1967

Over 650,000 Arabs left Israel during the War of Independence. The refugee camps quickly became a centre for anti-Israel feeling. The Arab countries in which the camps were situated were reluctant to try to absorb the refugees, and encouraged them to continue to hope for a return to a non-Jewish Palestine.

0 — 25 Miles

Homs

Nahr el Barid

Khan Askar

**LEBANON**

Debayeh

Gouraud

Dekwaneh

Wawel

Mar Elias — Jisr el Pasha

Shatila

Burj el Barajneh

Ein el Hilweh

Anjar

Palestine Institute

Khan Dannoun

Mieh Mieh

Khan esh Shih

El Bass

Rashidieh

**SYRIA**

Mediterranean

Sea of Galilee

Sea

Irbid

Der'a

Jenin

Nur Shams

Tulkarm

Askar

No.1

Balata

Jalazone

Zarqa

Deir Ammar

Amari

El Karameh

Jabal Hussein

Qalandiya

Nuweimeh

Aida

Ein es Sultan

Dheished

Mulaskar

**JORDAN**

Agabat Jabr

Jabalia

Arrdub

Gaza Beach

Beit Djibrin

Dead Sea

Nuseirat

Bureij

Deir el Balah

Mughazi

Fawwar

Rafah

Khan Yunis

**ISRAEL**

Jordan

**EGYPT**

⊕ Camps with over 20,000 refugees
⊙ Camps with 10,000–20,000 refugees
⊘ Camps with 5,000–10,000 refugees
⊛ Camps with under 5,000 refugees

# ISRAELI IMPORTS AND EXPORTS 1958–1959

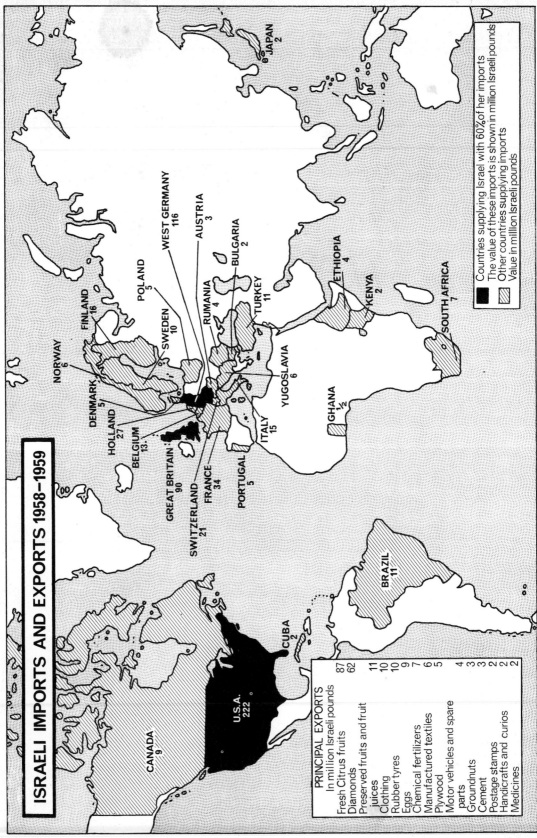

JAPAN 2

WEST GERMANY 116

AUSTRIA 3

BULGARIA 2

POLAND 5

RUMANIA 4

TURKEY 11

ETHIOPIA 4

FINLAND 16

SWEDEN 10

KENYA 2

NORWAY 6

YUGOSLAVIA 6

SOUTH AFRICA 7

DENMARK 5

HOLLAND 27

GHANA 1½

BELGIUM 13

GREAT BRITAIN 90

ITALY 15

SWITZERLAND 21

FRANCE 34

PORTUGAL 5

CANADA 9

U.S.A. 222

CUBA 2

BRAZIL 11

Countries supplying Israel with 60% of her imports
The value of these imports is shown in million Israeli pounds
Other countries supplying imports
Value in million Israeli pounds

## PRINCIPAL EXPORTS
In million Israeli pounds

| | |
|---|---|
| Fresh Citrus fruits | 87 |
| Diamonds | 62 |
| Preserved fruits and fruit juices | 11 |
| Clothing | 10 |
| Rubber tyres | 10 |
| Eggs | 9 |
| Chemical fertilizers | 7 |
| Manufactured textiles | 6 |
| Plywood | 5 |
| Motor vehicles and spare parts | 4 |
| Groundnuts | 3 |
| Cement | 3 |
| Postage stamps | 2 |
| Handicrafts and curios | 2 |
| Medicines | 2 |

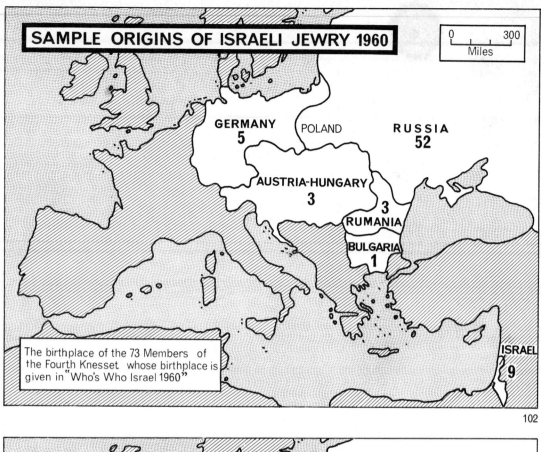

# SAMPLE ORIGINS OF ISRAELI JEWRY 1960

0  300
Miles

GERMANY
5

POLAND

RUSSIA
52

AUSTRIA-HUNGARY
3

3
RUMANIA

BULGARIA
1

ISRAEL
9

The birthplace of the 73 Members of the Fourth Knesset whose birthplace is given in "Who's Who Israel 1960"

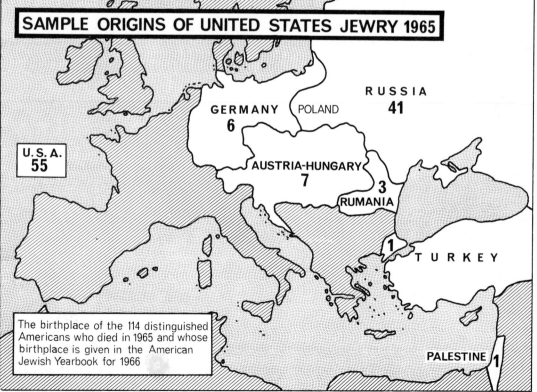

# SAMPLE ORIGINS OF UNITED STATES JEWRY 1965

GERMANY
6

POLAND

RUSSIA
41

U.S.A.
55

AUSTRIA-HUNGARY
7

3
RUMANIA

1

T U R K E Y

The birthplace of the 114 distinguished Americans who died in 1965 and whose birthplace is given in the American Jewish Yearbook for 1966

PALESTINE 1

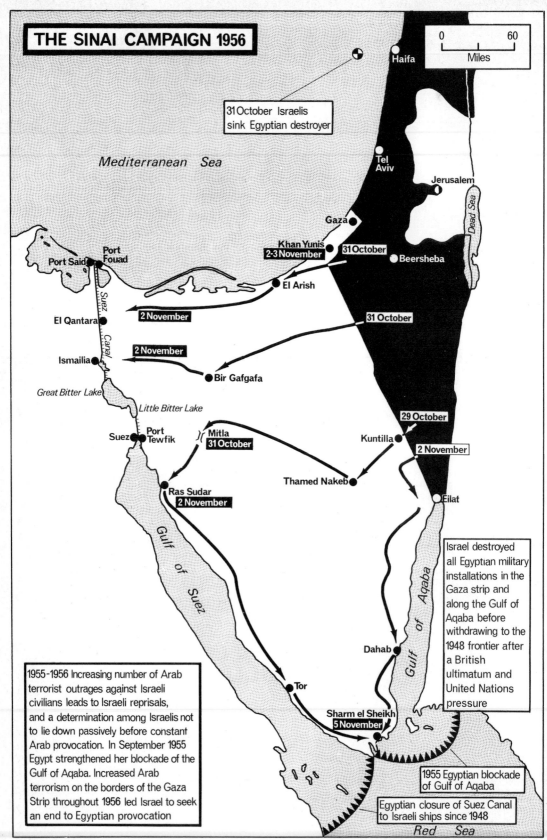

# THE SINAI CAMPAIGN 1956

0    60
Miles

Mediterranean Sea

31 October Israelis sink Egyptian destroyer

Haifa

Tel Aviv

Jerusalem

Dead Sea

Gaza

Khan Yunis
2-3 November

31 October

Beersheba

El Arish

Port Said
Port Fouad

2 November

El Qantara

31 October

Suez Canal

2 November

Ismailia

Bir Gafgafa

Great Bitter Lake

Little Bitter Lake

29 October

Suez
Port Tewfik

Mitla
31 October

Kuntilla

2 November

Thamed Nakeb

Ras Sudar
2 November

Eilat

Gulf of Suez

Gulf of Aqaba

Dahab

Israel destroyed all Egyptian military installations in the Gaza strip and along the Gulf of Aqaba before withdrawing to the 1948 frontier after a British ultimatum and United Nations pressure

Tor

Sharm el Sheikh
5 November

1955-1956 Increasing number of Arab terrorist outrages against Israeli civilians leads to Israeli reprisals, and a determination among Israelis not to lie down passively before constant Arab provocation. In September 1955 Egypt strengthened her blockade of the Gulf of Aqaba. Increased Arab terrorism on the borders of the Gaza Strip throughout 1956 led Israel to seek an end to Egyptian provocation

1955 Egyptian blockade of Gulf of Aqaba

Egyptian closure of Suez Canal to Israeli ships since 1948

Red Sea

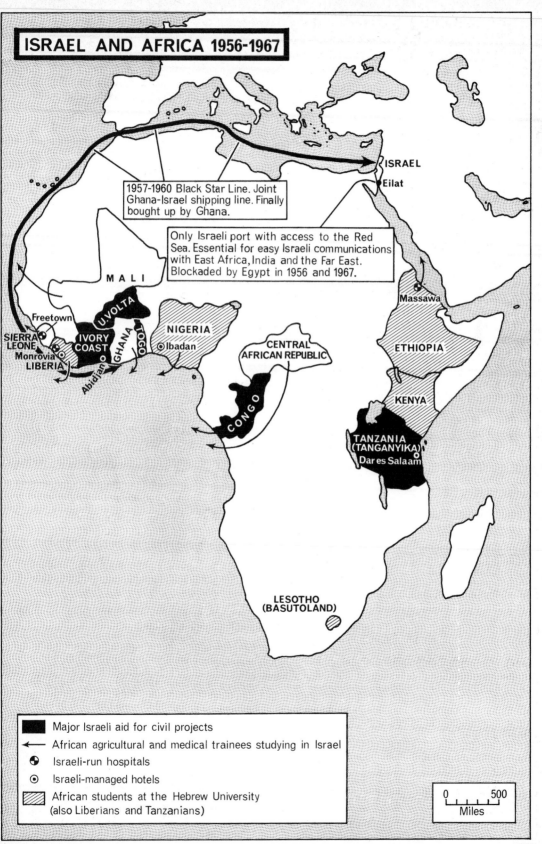

# ISRAEL AND AFRICA 1956-1967

1957-1960 Black Star Line. Joint Ghana-Israel shipping line. Finally bought up by Ghana.

Only Israeli port with access to the Red Sea. Essential for easy Israeli communications with East Africa, India and the Far East. Blockaded by Egypt in 1956 and 1967.

ISRAEL

Eilat

Massawa

MALI

U.VOLTA

Freetown

SIERRA LEONE

IVORY COAST

GHANA

TOGO

Abidjan

Monrovia

LIBERIA

NIGERIA

Ibadan

CENTRAL AFRICAN REPUBLIC

ETHIOPIA

KENYA

CONGO

TANZANIA (TANGANYIKA)

Dar es Salaam

LESOTHO (BASUTOLAND)

■ Major Israeli aid for civil projects

← African agricultural and medical trainees studying in Israel

Israeli-run hospitals

Israeli-managed hotels

African students at the Hebrew University (also Liberians and Tanzanians)

0    500
Miles

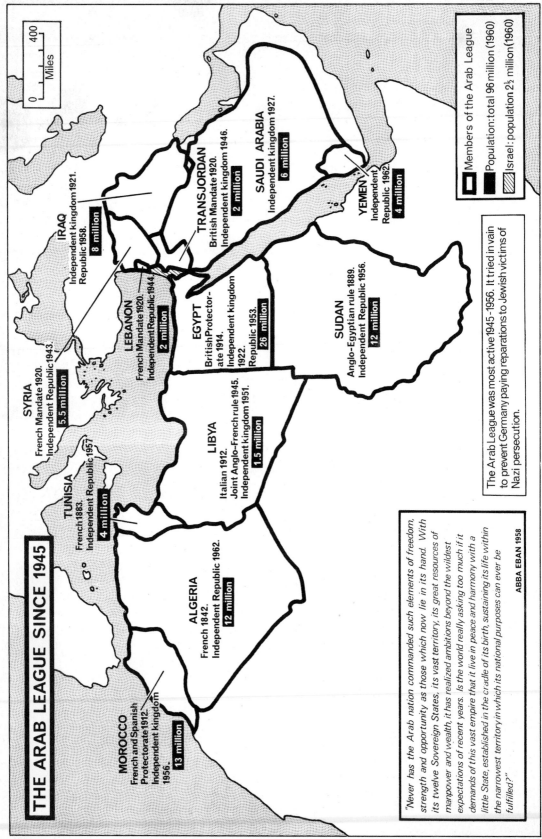

# THE ARAB LEAGUE SINCE 1945

## Scale
400 Miles

## SYRIA
French Mandate 1920.
Independent Republic 1943.
**5.5 million**

## IRAQ
Independent kingdom 1921.
Republic 1958.
**8 million**

## TRANSJORDAN
British Mandate 1920.
Independent kingdom 1946.
**2 million**

## SAUDI ARABIA
Independent kingdom 1927.
**6 million**

## YEMEN
Independent
Republic 1962.
**4 million**

## LEBANON
French Mandate 1920.
Independent Republic 1944.
**2 million**

## TUNISIA
French 1883.
Independent Republic 1957.
**4 million**

## EGYPT
British Protectorate 1914.
Independent kingdom 1922.
Republic 1953.
**26 million**

## SUDAN
Anglo-Egyptian rule 1889.
Independent Republic 1956.
**12 million**

## LIBYA
Italian 1912.
Joint Anglo-French rule 1945.
Independent kingdom 1951.
**1.5 million**

## ALGERIA
French 1842.
Independent Republic 1962.
**12 million**

## MOROCCO
French and Spanish
Protectorate 1912.
Independent Kingdom
1956.
**13 million**

Members of the Arab League

Population: total 96 million (1960)

Israel: population 2½ million (1960)

The Arab League was most active 1945-1956. It tried in vain to prevent Germany paying reparations to Jewish victims of Nazi persecution.

"Never has the Arab nation commanded such elements of freedom, strength and opportunity as those which now lie in its hand. With its twelve Sovereign States, its vast territory, its great resources of manpower and wealth, it has realized ambitions beyond the wildest expectations of recent years. Is the world really asking too much if it demands of this vast empire that it live in peace and harmony with a little State, established in the cradle of its birth, sustaining its life within the narrowest territory in which its national purposes can ever be fulfilled?"

**ABBA EBAN 1958**

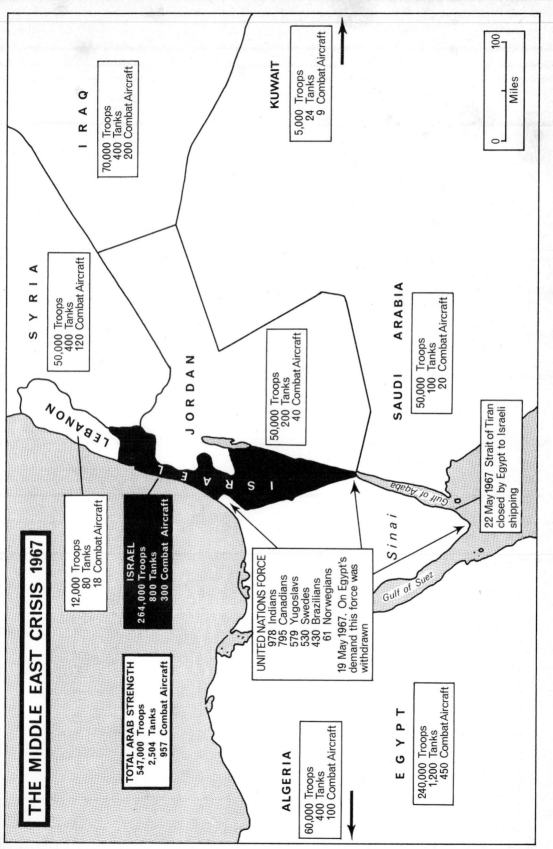

# THE MIDDLE EAST CRISIS 1967

**IRAQ**
70,000 Troops
400 Tanks
200 Combat Aircraft

**KUWAIT**
5,000 Troops
24 Tanks
9 Combat Aircraft

0        100
Miles

**SYRIA**
50,000 Troops
400 Tanks
120 Combat Aircraft

**JORDAN**
50,000 Troops
200 Tanks
40 Combat Aircraft

**SAUDI ARABIA**
50,000 Troops
100 Tanks
20 Combat Aircraft

**LEBANON**
12,000 Troops
80 Tanks
18 Combat Aircraft

**ISRAEL**
264,000 Troops
800 Tanks
300 Combat Aircraft

**TOTAL ARAB STRENGTH**
547,000 Troops
2,504 Tanks
957 Combat Aircraft

**UNITED NATIONS FORCE**
978 Indians
795 Canadians
579 Yugoslavs
530 Swedes
430 Brazilians
61 Norwegians

19 May 1967. On Egypt's
demand this force was
withdrawn

22 May 1967 Strait of Tiran
closed by Egypt to Israeli
shipping

*Sinai*

*Gulf of Suez*

*Gulf of Aqaba*

**ALGERIA**
60,000 Troops
400 Tanks
100 Combat Aircraft

**EGYPT**
240,000 Troops
1,200 Tanks
450 Combat Aircraft

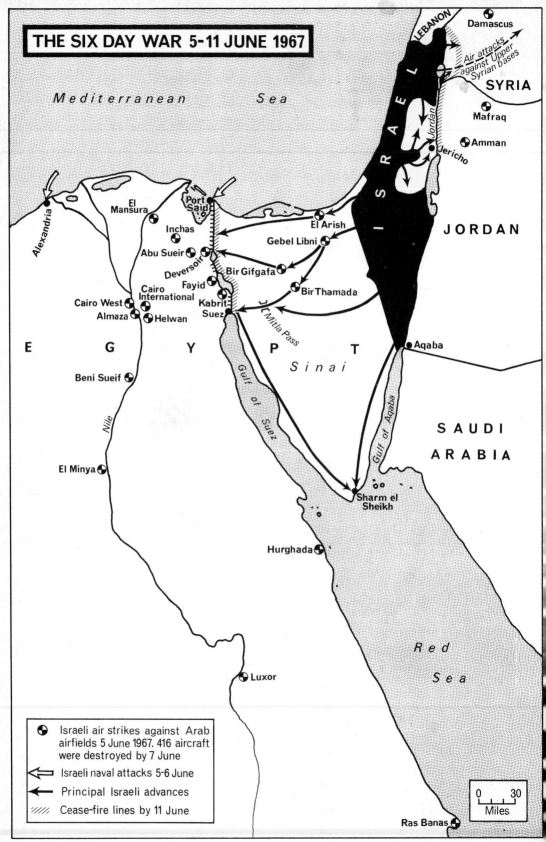

# THE SIX DAY WAR 5–11 JUNE 1967

Mediterranean Sea

SYRIA

Damascus

*Air attacks against Upper Syrian bases*

Mafraq

Amman

LEBANON

ISRAEL

Jordan

Jericho

JORDAN

Alexandria

El Mansura

Port Said

Inchas

El Arish

Abu Sueir

Gebel Libni

Deversoir

Bir Gifgafa

Cairo International

Fayid

Bir Thamada

Cairo West

Kabrit

Almaza

Suez

Helwan

Mitla Pass

Aqaba

E G Y P T

Sinai

SAUDI ARABIA

Beni Suef

Nile

Gulf of Suez

Gulf of Aqaba

El Minya

Sharm el Sheikh

Hurghada

Red Sea

Luxor

Ras Banas

Israeli air strikes against Arab airfields 5 June 1967. 416 aircraft were destroyed by 7 June

Israeli naval attacks 5–6 June

Principal Israeli advances

Cease-fire lines by 11 June

0    30
Miles

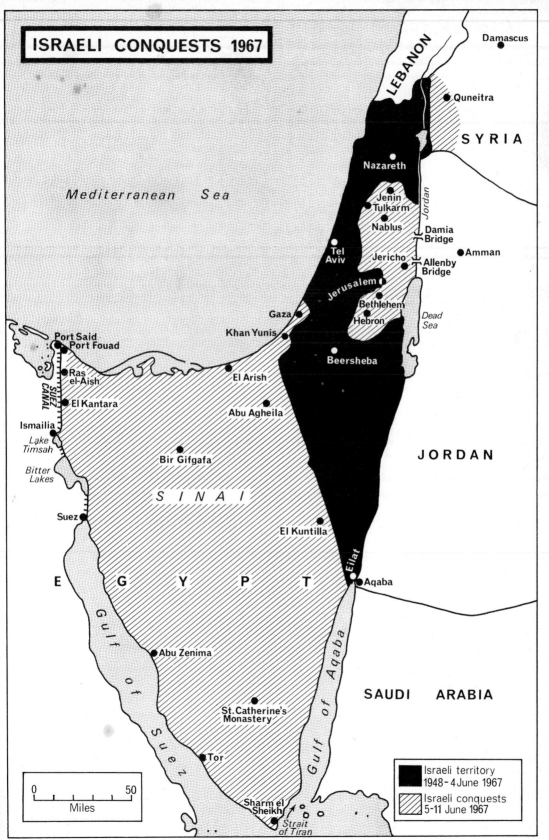

# ISRAELI CONQUESTS 1967

Damascus

● Quneitra

**SYRIA**

*Mediterranean Sea*

LEBANON

Nazareth

Jenin
Tulkarm

Nablus

Tel
Aviv

*Jordan*

Damia
Bridge

Jericho

● Amman

Jerusalem

Allenby
Bridge

Bethlehem

Gaza

Hebron

*Dead
Sea*

Khan Yunis

Beersheba

**JORDAN**

El Arish

Port Said
Port Fouad

Abu Agheila

Ras
el-Aish

SUEZ CANAL

El Kantara

Ismailia

Bir Gifgafa

*Lake
Timsah*

*Bitter
Lakes*

*S I N A I*

Suez

El Kuntilla

Eilat

Aqaba

**E        G        Y        P        T**

Gulf of Suez

Gulf of Aqaba

**SAUDI    ARABIA**

Abu Zenima

St. Catherine's
Monastery

Tor

0 ————————— 50
Miles

Sharm el
Sheikh

*Strait
of Tiran*

| ■ | Israeli territory 1948–4 June 1967 |
|---|---|
| ▨ | Israeli conquests 5–11 June 1967 |

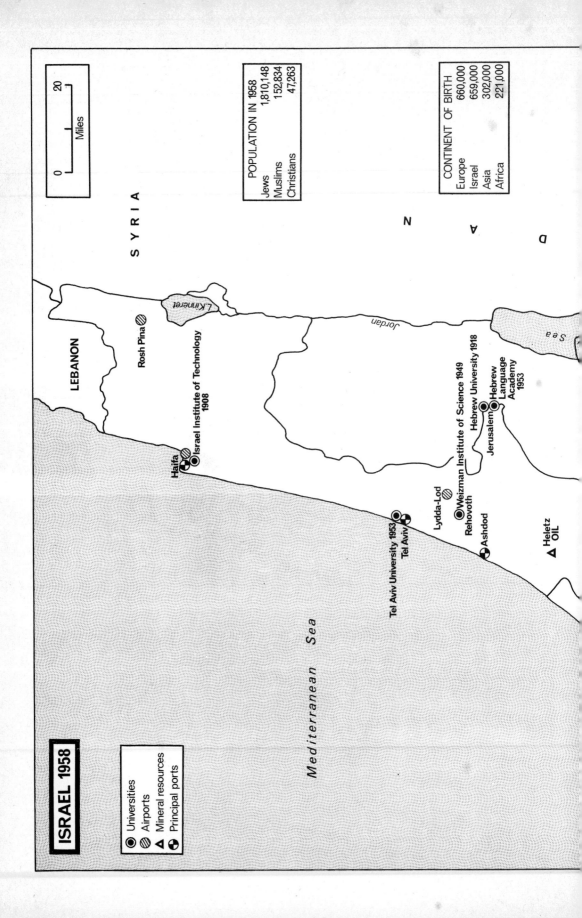

ISRAEL 1958

- ◉ Universities
- ◍ Airports
- ▲ Mineral resources
- ◕ Principal ports

Miles
0        20

POPULATION IN 1958
| | |
|---|---|
| Jews | 1,810,148 |
| Muslims | 152,834 |
| Christians | 47,263 |

CONTINENT OF BIRTH
| | |
|---|---|
| Europe | 660,000 |
| Israel | 659,000 |
| Asia | 302,000 |
| Africa | 221,000 |

S Y R I A

LEBANON

L. Kinneret

Rosh Pina ◍

Israel Institute of Technology 1908

Haifa ◍◕

Jordan

N

A

D

Sea

Weizman Institute of Science 1949

Hebrew University 1918

Jerusalem ◉

Hebrew Language Academy 1953

Lydda-Lod ◍

Rehovoth ◉

Tel Aviv University 1953 ◉
Tel Aviv ◕◕

Ashdod ◕

▲ Heletz OIL

Mediterranean Sea

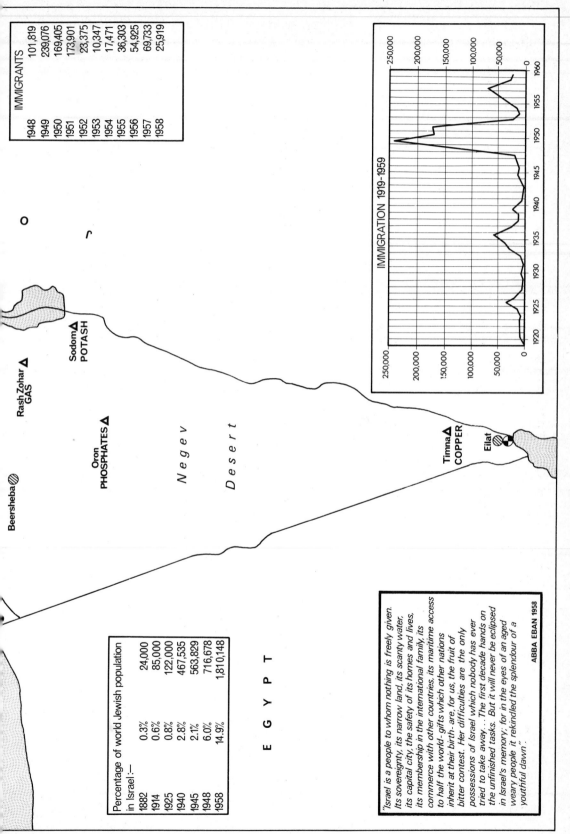

IMMIGRATION 1919-1959

Percentage of world Jewish population in Israel:–

| 1882 | 0.3% | 24,000 |
| --- | --- | --- |
| 1914 | 0.6% | 85,000 |
| 1925 | 0.8% | 122,000 |
| 1940 | 2.8% | 467,535 |
| 1945 | 2.1% | 563,829 |
| 1948 | 6.0% | 716,678 |
| 1958 | 14.9% | 1,810,148 |

Beersheba
Rash Zohar △ GAS
Sodom △ POTASH
Oron PHOSPHATES △
Negev Desert
Timna △ COPPER
Eilat

E G Y P T

"Israel is a people to whom nothing is freely given. Its sovereignty, its narrow land, its scanty water, its capital city, the safety of its homes and lives, its membership in the international family, its commerce with other countries, its maritime access to half the world- gifts which other nations inherit at their birth- are, for us, the fruit of bitter contest. Her difficulties are the only possessions of Israel which nobody has ever tried to take away... The first decade hands on the unfinished tasks. But it will never be eclipsed in Israel's memory; for in the eyes of an aged weary people it rekindled the splendour of a youthful dawn".

ABBA EBAN 1958

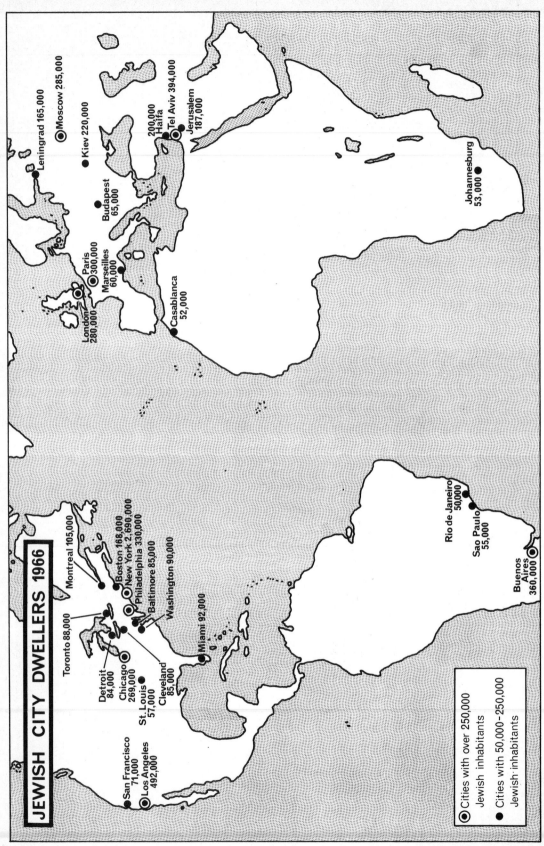

JEWISH CITY DWELLERS 1966

Leningrad 165,000
Moscow 285,000
Kiev 220,000
Tel Aviv 394,000
200,000 Haifa
Jerusalem 187,000
Johannesburg 53,000
Budapest 65,000
Paris 300,000
Marseilles 60,000
London 280,000
Casablanca 52,000

Montreal 105,000
Boston 168,000
New York 2,690,000
Philadelphia 330,000
Baltimore 85,000
Washington 90,000
Toronto 88,000
Detroit 84,000
Chicago 269,000
St. Louis 57,000
Cleveland 85,000
Miami 92,000
San Francisco 71,000
Los Angeles 492,000

Rio de Janeiro 50000
Sao Paulo 55,000
Buenos Aires 360,000

◉ Cities with over 250,000 Jewish inhabitants
● Cities with 50,000–250,000 Jewish inhabitants

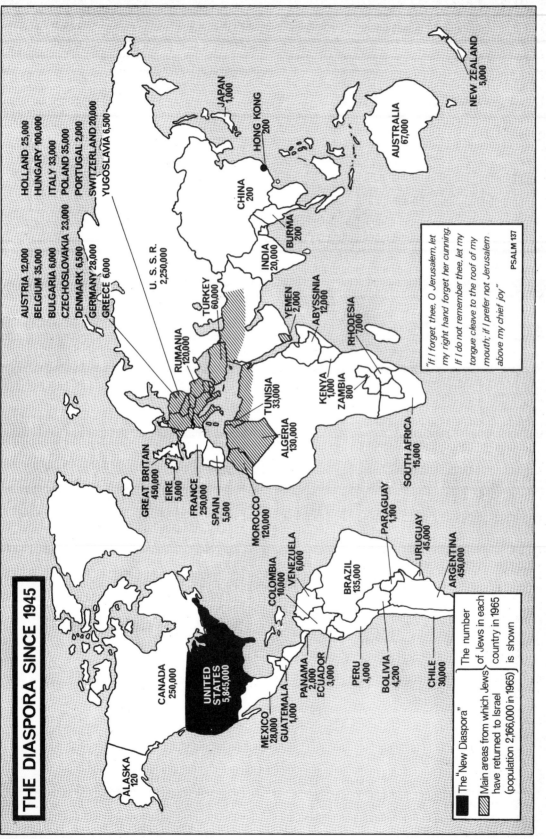

# THE DIASPORA SINCE 1945

AUSTRIA 12,000
BELGIUM 35,000
BULGARIA 6,000
CZECHOSLOVAKIA 23,000
DENMARK 6,500
GERMANY 28,000
GREECE 6,000

HOLLAND 25,000
HUNGARY 100,000
ITALY 33,000
POLAND 35,000
PORTUGAL 2,000
SWITZERLAND 20,000
YUGOSLAVIA 6,500

ALASKA 120

CANADA 250,000

UNITED STATES 5,845,000

MEXICO 28,000
GUATEMALA 1,000
PANAMA 2,000
ECUADOR 3,000
COLOMBIA 10,000
VENEZUELA 6,000
PERU 4,000
BOLIVIA 4,200
BRAZIL 135,000
PARAGUAY 1,100
URUGUAY 45,000
CHILE 30,000
ARGENTINA 450,000

GREAT BRITAIN 450,000
EIRE 5,000
FRANCE 250,000
SPAIN 5,500
MOROCCO 120,000
ALGERIA 130,000
TUNISIA 33,000

RUMANIA 120,000
U. S. S. R. 2,250,000
TURKEY 60,000
YEMEN 2,000
ABYSSINIA 12,000
KENYA 1,000
ZAMBIA 800
RHODESIA 7,000
SOUTH AFRICA 115,000

INDIA 20,000
BURMA 200
CHINA 200
HONG KONG 200
JAPAN 1,000

AUSTRALIA 67,000

NEW ZEALAND 5,000

*"If I forget thee, O Jerusalem, let my right hand forget her cunning. If I do not remember thee, let my tongue cleave to the roof of my mouth; if I prefer not Jerusalem above my chief joy"*

PSALM 137

The "New Diaspora"

Main areas from which Jews have returned to Israel (population 2,166,000 in 1965)

The number of Jews in each country in 1965 is shown

112

# Index

against German brutality, 92; against Arab terrorism in Palestine, 93; against Arab attacks on Israel, 97

JEWISH TRADERS  With Arabia, Africa and India, 5; in the Mediterranean and Black Seas, 10; in India, 12; in the Roman Empire, 15; from Europe to China, 21, 22; of Khazaria, 24; of Byzantium, 25; of France, 26; in Germany, 28; in Spain, 43; forbidden in Moscow, 46; spread out from Amsterdam throughout the world, 49; in North America, 59, 77; barred from the eastern half of Jerusalem, 99; creating a vigorous Israeli economy, 101

KARAITES  Jewish "heretics", 27; murdered by the Germans, 83

KHAZARIA  Jews trade through, 21; Jewish kingdom of, 22, 23; Jews flee to, 25; Jews flee to Russia from, 30

KHRUSCHEV  Soviet leader, critical of "Jewish individualism", 84

LITHUANIA  Jews settle in, 30; Jews expelled from, 44; Cossacks massacre Jews in, 53; anti-Jewish violence in, 61; the Wandering Jew said to have visited, 63; absorbed into Russia, 66; majority of Jews murdered in German concentration camps, 88

LONDON  Jews recorded in early medieval times, 38; Amsterdam Jews trade with, 49; Zevi's claim to be the messiah heard in, 51; Rothschilds active in, 57; Anglo-Jewish association founded, 58; Balfour declaration promises Jews a national home in Palestine, 60; *The Times* fears a Jewish plot to dominate the world, 62; man claims to be the Wandering Jew in, 63; London Mission to the Jews sets up hospital in Jerusalem, 65; 180,000 Jews settle in by 1914, 74; the pattern of Jewish settlement in the East End, 75; the spread of Jewish communities in, 76; over 280,000 Jewish inhabitants by 1966, 111

LUBLINLAND  Jewish agricultural reservation established by the Germans in 1939, 89

MACAULAY  British politician, urges emancipation of the Jews, 56

MADAGASCAR  Nazis consider as possible area of Jewish settlement, 95

MAHOZA  Independent Jewish kingdom of, 9; Rabbinical academy in, 20

MARCO POLO  Describes the Jews of China, 22

MASADA  Jewish resistance at crushed by Romans, 14

MASSACRES  In Jerusalem, 11; in India, 12; in China, 22; in Toulouse, 26; in Prague, 29; at Posen, 30; throughout the Rhineland, 35; in Jerusalem, 36; in Sicily, 37; throughout Spain, 43; in Russia, 46; throughout Poland, Galicia, White Russia and the Ukraine, 53; in Vilna, 69; in the Ukraine and the Crimea after the First World War, 82; throughout Europe under German supervision, 88; in Palestine, 93

converted to Zionism in, 60; Protocols of Zion published in, 62; man claims to be the Wandering Jew in, 63; 300,000 Jews in 1966, 111

# Bibliography

The following bibliography is strictly selective. It consists of some eighty
books which I myself have found useful while gathering material for the maps.
   In addition to the books listed below, I have made frequent use of a number
of general reference works, of which the most valuable were:

Isodore Singer (Managing Editor), *The Jewish Encyclopaedia*, 12 vols.,
   New York, 1901–1906, the most comprehensive of all encyclopaedias on
   Jewish affairs.

Y. L. Katzenelson (Editor), *Yevreyskaya Entsiklopediya*, 16 vols.,
   St. Petersburg, 1906–1913. An essential source for all problems of Russian
   Jewry.

Isaac Landman (Editor), *Universal Jewish Encyclopaedia*, 10 vols. (New York,
   1939–1943). The most recent complete multi-volume encyclopaedia of
   Jewish history.

Cecil Roth (Editor-in-Chief), *The Standard Jewish Encyclopaedia*, one volume
   (New York, 1962). The fullest single volume work of reference.

Israeli Department of Surveys and the Bialik Institute, *Atlas of Israel*
   (Jerusalem, 1956), contains an excellent bibliography of over a thousand
   cartographic sources relating to Israel.

## General works on Jewish History

Nathan Ausubel, *Pictorial History of the Jewish People* (New York, 1954)

Salo W. Baron, *A Social and Religious History of the Jews* (New York,
   1952–1960)

Edwyn R. Bevan and Charles Singer (editors), *The Legacy of Israel*
   (Oxford, 1927)

Max I. Dimont, *Jews, God and History* (New York, 1962)

Max L. Margolis and A. Marx, *A History of the Jewish People* (Philadelphia,
   1964)

James William Parkes, *A History of the Jewish People* (London, 1962)

Cecil Roth, *A Short History of the Jewish People* (London, 1959)

Cecil Roth, *Personalities and Events in Jewish History* (Philadelphia, 1961)

## Biblical and Classical Periods

W. F. Albright, *New Horizons in Biblical Research* (London, 1966)

M. Avi-Yonah, *Map of Roman Palestine* (Oxford, 1940)

Daniel-Rops, *Israel and the Ancient World* (Paris, 1943; London, 1949)

Luc Grollenberg, *Atlas de la Bible* (London, 1956)

James Hastings, *Dictionary of the Bible* (London, 1963)

Jean Juster, *Les Juifs dans l'empire romain* (Paris, 1914)

Harry J. Leon, *The Jews of Ancient Rome* (Philadelphia, 1960)

Benjamin Maisler, *Historical Atlas of Palestine* (Jerusalem, 1942)

W. O. E. Osterley, *The Jews and Judaism During the Greek Period* (London, 1941)

John William Parkes, *Jesus, Paul and the Jews* (London, 1936)

George Adam Smith, *Historical Geography of the Holy Land* (London, 1894)

John Stirling, *An Atlas of the Life of Christ* (London, 1954)

John Stirling, *An Atlas Illustrating the Acts of the Apostles and the Epistles* (London, 1954)


## Medieval Period

Marcus Nathan Adler, *The Itinery of Benjamin of Tudela* (London, 1907)

George K. Anderson, *The Legend of the Wandering Jew* (Providence, 1965)

Salo Baron, *The Jewish Community; Its History and Structure* (Philadelphia, 1942)

Herbert Ivan Bloom, *The Economic Activities of the Jews of Amsterdam* (Williamsport, 1937)

Claude Reignier Conder, *The Latin Kingdom of Jerusalem 1099–1291* (London, 1897)

D. M. Dunlop, *The History of the Jewish Khazars* (Princeton, 1954)

Louis Finkelstein, *Jewish Self-Government in the Middle Ages* (New York, 1924)

Walter Joseph Fischel, *Jews in the Economic and Political Life of Medieval Islam* (London, 1937)

Solomon Grayzel, *The Church and the Jews in the Thirteenth Century* (New York, 1966)

Julius H. Greenstone, *The Messianic Idea in Jewish History* (Philadelphia, 1906)

Henry Kamen, *The Spanish Inquisition* (London, 1965)

Robert S. Lopez and Irving W. Raymond (eds.), *Medieval Trade in the Mediterranean World* (New York, 1955)

Leon Nemoy, *Karaite Anthology* (New Haven, 1952)

Abraham A. Neuman, *The Jews in Spain* (Philadelphia, 1944)

James William Parkes, *The Conflict of the Church and the Synagogue* (London, 1934)

David Philipson, *Old European Jewries* (Harrisburg, 1894)

L. Rabinowitz, *Jewish Merchant Adventurers* (London, 1948)

Cecil Roth, *The History of the Jews of Italy* (Philadelphia, 1946)

Cecil Roth, *A History of the Marranos* (Philadelphia, 1942)

Cecil Roth, *A History of the Jews in England* (Oxford, 1941)

Cecil Roth, *The Jews of Medieval Oxford* (Oxford, 1951)

Steven Runciman, *A History of the Crusades* (Cambridge, 1951)

Abba Hillel Silver, *A History of Messianic Speculation in Israel* (New York, 1927)

Joshua Starr, *Jews in the Byzantine Empire 641–1204* (Athens, 1939)

Joshua Starr, *Romania, the Jews of the Levant After the Fourth Crusade* (Paris, 1949)

William Charles White, *Chinese Jews* (Toronto, 1942)

Louis Wirth, *The Ghetto* (Chicago, 1928)

### Modern Period

Karl Baedeker, *Austria-Hungary* (Leipzig, 1905)

Salo Baron, *The Russian Jew Under Tsars and Soviets* (New York, 1964)

Norman Bentwich, *They Found Refuge* (London, 1956)

Randolph S. Churchill and Winston S. Churchill, *The Six Day War* (London, 1967)

Israel Cohen, *A Short History of Zionism* (London, 1951)

Israel Cohen, *Contemporary Jewry* (London, 1950)

Israel Cohen, *Vilna* (Philadelphia, 1943)

Israel Cohen, *My Mission to Poland 1918–1919* (London, 1951)

Norman Cohn, *Warrant for Genocide* (London, 1967)

Moshe Dayan, *Diary of the Sinai Campaign* (London, 1966)

S. M. Dubnow, *History of the Jews in Russia and Poland* (Philadelphia, 1916–20)

Abba Eban, *Voice of Israel* (London, 1958)

Lloyd P. Gartner, *The Jewish Immigrant in England 1870–1914* (London, 1960)

Louis Greenberg, *The Jews in Russia: The Struggle for Emancipation* (New Haven 1944 and 1951)

Philip Guedalla, *Napoleon and Palestine* (London, 1925)

Vladimir Jabotinsky, *The Story of the Jewish Legion* (New York, 1954)

Leo Jung (ed.), *Jewish Leaders 1750–1940* (Jerusalem, 1964)

Roderick Kedward, *The Dreyfus Affair* (London, 1964)

Mordechai E. Kreinin, *Israel and Africa* (New York, 1964)

Harry S. Linfield, *Statistics of Jews 1931* (New York, 1931)

Vivian David Lipman, *Social History of the Jews in England 1850–1950* (London, 1954)

Macmillan (publishers), *Atlas of the Arab World and the Middle East* (London, 1960)

Arthur D. Morse, *While Six Million Died* (London, 1968)

Alfred Nossig, *Materialen Zur statistik der Judischen Stammes* (Vienna, 1897)

Edgar O'Ballance, *The Arab-Israeli War 1948* (London, 1956)

F. J. Pietri, *Napoléon et les Israélites* (Paris, 1965)

James William Parkes, *Arabs and Jews in the Middle East: a Tragedy of Errors* (London, 1967)

J. H. Patterson, *With the Judaeans in the Palestine Campaign* (London, 1922)

Leon Poliakov, *Harvest of Hate* (New York, 1954)

Malcolm J. Proudfoot, *European Refugees 1939–52* (London, 1957)

Peter George J. Pulzer, *The Rise of Political Anti-Semitism in Germany and Austria* (New York, 1964)

Gerald Reitlinger, *The Final Solution* (London, 1953)

Adolf Rudnicki, *Ascent to Heaven* (London, 1951)

Joseph B. Schechtman, *On Wings of Eagles* (New York, 1961)

Yuri Suhl (ed.), *They Fought Back* (London, 1968)

Christopher Sykes, *Cross Roads to Israel* (London, 1965)

M. U. Schappes, *A Documentary History of the Jews in the United States 1654–1875* (New York, 1950)

Leonard Stein, *The Balfour Declaration* (London, 1966)

Arieh Tartakower and Kurt R. Grossman, *The Jewish Refugee* (New York, 1944)

Israel Zangwill, *Children of the Ghetto* (London, 1892)